A NEW KIND
OF
NORMAL

BACK TO THE BASICS

A COMPREHENSIVE SURVIVAL GUIDE FOR EATING

SUGAR -- GLUTEN -- DAIRY AND YEAST FREE

BY B. A. Smit

ISBN: 978-1-4269-7512-7 (sc)
ISBN: 978-1-4269-7513-4 (e)

Trafford rev. 01/04/2012

 www.trafford.com

North America & international
toll-free: 1 888 232 4444 (USA & Canada)
phone: 250 383 6864 ♦ fax: 812 355 4082

FOR MY PARENTS
ERNIE AND EVELYN

This book is for my Dad, who has waited patiently for over forty years for me to grow up. And especially for my Mom, the most gifted cook that I know. Her delicious recipes and her ability to throw a bunch of ingredients together and create a masterpiece, inspired me to be inventive and creative in the kitchen.

AND FOR LINDA

Once just a neighbour, who became a dear friend. Her words of wisdom gave me a better understanding of my illness. Her encouragement kept me experimenting with my limited food choices. And most of all, her honest opinions as my "official" taster. Her gentle guidance gave me the incentive to write this book.

And a special thanks to..........

Cousin June. Her experience as an author and constant help to understand computers made it possible for me to publish this book.

The information contained in this book is written by the author and is intended as an information guide with recipes to be enjoyed. It is not meant to be a medical guide and all medical issues should be addressed by a licensed physician or dietitian. The author hereby takes no responsibility for the use of information contained within this book.

Contents

Introduction

Several years ago my health decided to go on a long walk. It's destination is unknown, but it is still walking.

I noticed that after eating I did not feel well. When I changed the types of food I was eating, I felt better. I found it so frustrating as one by four, food was being eliminated from my diet. Removing all gluten, dairy, yeast, sugars and soy from my diet dramatically improved how I felt. As a true food lover, plain rice and carrots just wasn't going to cut it. Without access to a computer, finding information and recipes became an empty, exhaustive search. The few books I could find seemed incomplete or the recipes weren't adaptable to my diet. Thus began my long journey to **A New Kind of Normal.**

This is the reason I put this book together. I want to share basic information and recipes with others.

You should become familiar with all types of food that your diet will allow. Learning about the foods and understanding how they all work in harmony, both as nutrition for your body and in recipes, will open a whole new world for you. Once you learn about all the new foods, experimenting will become a fun new adventure. Soon you will be creating exciting, delicious foods and a whole new avenue of tastes will open up for you.

I hope that you will find this book informative and the recipes easy to create and fulfill your craving for real food. Enjoy your journey to **A New Kind of Normal.**

Safety in the Kitchen

Bacteria

Under ideal circumstances, bacteria is capable of reproducing itself every twenty minutes. Bacteria reproduces by fission, meaning one grows then splits into two. These divide into four, the four into eight. In less than 24 hours one single bacterium can multiply into sixty eight billion bacteria. Some bacteria can form endospores, a means of protection, which enables the bacteria to resume it's cycle (if the conditions are favorable), even after high heat, such as cooking.

A protein source, moisture and a moderate pH are the basic conditions for bacteria to grow. The acidity or alkalinity of food is measured on a scale known as pH. The scale ranges from 1 to 14. A moderate pH is between 4.5 and 10, which is ideal for bacteria growth. Most foods fall into this range.

Animal based foods are not the only foods containing protein. Meats, fish, poultry, tofu and dairy products are potentially hazardous. Vegetables and grains also contain protein. Cooked rice, pastas, beans, potatoes, melons, sprouts, as well as garlic and oil mixtures, are just a few examples.

Unsanitary handling can result in food-borne illness. Avoid cross contamination. Cross contamination occurs when harmful elements are transferred from a contaminated surface to a new one. Contamination most often occurs during food preparation. Separate cutting boards should be used for cooked and raw foods. You should always clean all surfaces after being used. For example, never cut chicken (raw or cooked) on a board that was just used to cut raw pork. Always wash thoroughly the board, the knife and your hands.

Bacteria doesn't need warmth to survive. It can grow in all temperatures. It is important to take care and develop good hygiene within the kitchen. Leaving any type of food out of it's safe storage temperature for up to four hours or longer is inviting bacteria to grow. These foods are considered unsafe and should not be eaten. Throw them out.

When shopping, always check for government inspection stamps and "expire by" dates. The following is a temperature guide for safe food storage.

Meat and Poultry - 32 to 36°F (0 to 2°C)
Fish and Shellfish - 30 to 34°F (-1 to 1°C)
Dairy Products - 36 to 40°F (2 to 4°C)
Produce - 40 to 45°F (4 to 7°C)

When serving food, especially picnics, barbecues or buffets, keep hot food hot and cold food cold. Steam trays, chafing dishes and slow cookers can keep foods hot, at or above 140°F/60°C. A bed of ice will keep cold food cold, at about 40°F/5°C.

One of the major causes of bacteria is improperly cooled foods. Leftovers that are going to be stored need to be cooled to 41°F/5°C as soon as possible. The cooling process should be completed within four hours. Food should be put in a shallow container in the fridge. The shallow container allows greater surface of food to be exposed to the cold air, thus speeding the cooling process. Meat and larger amounts of food, such as a pot of mashed potatoes, should be made into smaller portions, cooled to room temperature, then wrapped properly (well sealed) and placed in the fridge.

Food-borne illness can often occur when food is not properly reheated. Food should be reheated quickly to 165ºF/74ºC and remain at this temperature for at least 20 seconds. If the cooling and reheating procedures are done properly, food can be cooled and reheated more than once. Reheating in a steam tray or chafing dish does not bring the food hot enough quick enough to deter bacteria growth.

There are several safe ways to thaw food. Once thawed, use as soon as possible. Do not refreeze until the food has been cooked, cooled and wrapped properly. Proper wrapping is to seal the food in an airtight package. The best and safest way to thaw is to put the food, still packaged, in the fridge and let thaw. Placing the package in another container to catch the juices and leaks will save the food from contaminating other foods in the fridge. This method may take the longest time for the food to thaw, but it is the safest. Thawing food in a sink under cold water is also considered safe. Make sure the sink is empty and clean. Thaw food in it's package under cold, 70ºF/21ºC, water. Single servings or small portions can be thawed in the microwave, if reheating or cooking will be done right after thawing. Do not thaw at room temperature, it is an open invitation for bacteria.

Checklist for Kitchen Safety

- clean up spills when they occur
- a good habit to start is when cooking with someone, always warn them if you are behind them, especially when carrying hot items or knives
- do not attempt to put grease fires out with water, keep a working fire extinguisher close by or smother the fire with a wet towel
- remove pot lids away from the direction of your face to avoid steam burns
- use separate cutting boards for cooked and raw foods, wash thoroughly after each use, using hot soapy water
- wash hands thoroughly before and after handling raw foods
- use a taste spoon only once, do not use your finger (bacteria or burn from hot food can occur) or a knife, which may cut you
- store all cleaning supplies away from the kitchen and food
- use only a dry dish towel or pot holder when handling hot pans
- keep a phone near the kitchen for easy access in case of an emergency

Learning about bacteria in the kitchen is simple, if safe handling is practised daily. If you begin with safe habits, you will have a safe kitchen. Common sense in cooking goes side by side with a safe kitchen. Using care and common sense in the kitchen will enable you to enjoy many wonderful, tasty meals, by yourself or with friends and family.

B. A. Smit

Food Storage Guide

"It won't answer me, so how do I tell if it's still good, fresh and edible?" Foods can be stored, safely, if you store exactly as directed on the package. The food must be wrapped properly, in an airtight container such as jars, tins or in plastic. Note that natural foods contain no preservatives, therefore they can spoil easily, so take more care in their storage.

TIME   **FOOD**

FRIDGE

TIME	FOOD
2 weeks	Tofu
2 - 3 months	Products containing natural oil
2 weeks	Nut milks, soy milk
6 - 8 months	Pitted dates
6 months	Dried fruit
6 - 10 days	Cakes, muffins, breads (best frozen)

COOL DRY PLACE or FRIDGE

TIME	FOOD
6 months	Dried fruits
6 months	Coconut
3 - 5 months	Raw nuts and seeds

SHELF

TIME	FOOD
12 - 18 months	Carob powder
12 - 18 months	Honey (fridge after opening)
12 months	Dried herbs and spices
12 months	Corn, arrowroot, tapioca starches
12 months	Sea salt
3 months	Baking powder
6 months	Soy milk powder
6 - 12 months	Cream of tartar
6 - 12 months	Xanthan gum, guar gum
3 months	Boxed and puffed cereals
3 - 6 months	Corn and rice cakes

STORE ON SHELF and REFRIDGERATE AFTER OPENING

TIME	FOOD
3 months	Natural oils, mayonnaise, ketchup
3 months	Natural nut butters, tahini
3 months	Natural peanut butter
12 - 18 months	Real maple syrup

FREEZER

3 months	Ice cream products and ice
3 months	Breads
6 months	Soups, sauces, gravies and broth

BEST KEPT IN THE FREEZER

3 - 6 months	Rice bran
6 months	Cornmeal
6 months	Flours

FRUIT AND VEGETABLE TIPS

- produce should be kept in fridge for 3 - 4 days only to ensure freshness
- exceptions like potatoes, tomatoes, onions and bananas should be at room temperature, potatoes in a dry, dark place
- fruits and vegetables should be kept away from moisture, it can cause rot
- peel, wash and cut both fruit and vegetables just before using
- root vegetables like turnip, carrot, beet and radishes should have the tops removed before storing, these leafy tops absorb the nutrients from the root and can cause moisture loss
- when the fruit and vegetables need to be ripened, leave at room temperature until ripe, then refrigerate, peaches and avocado are good examples
- fruits such as melons, bananas and apples emit ethylene gas as they are stored; this can promote ripening in some fruits, but spoil others that are ripe, store these fruits alone
- odors from strong fruits and vegetables like onions, garlic and lemon can penetrate other foods, especially dairy, wrap these types securely in plastic wrap or containers

B. A. Smit

The Structure of Nutrition

Introduction

With a restricted diet, you often eat only because your hungry, not for the flavor, or more importantly, the nutrients in the food.

If you have restrictions for foods you can eat due to allergies, illness or sensitivities, you need to inform yourself. You need to understand the basics of nutrition and why your body needs specific foods. You need to have an understanding of what foods can be substituted and what is available for your diet.

In addition to flavor and taste, every food contains calories and a variety of nutrients that are vital to our bodies for energy, growth, repair and maintenance. Maintaining a balanced diet is vital for optimum health. If you can understand the structure of nutrition and how it works to keep your body at it's healthiest, then you can begin to restructure your diet within your limitations to keep at your best health. This will help you to feel much better, stronger, thus keeping you fit, healthy and much happier.

Knowing the types of food that keep each part of your body healthy will enable you to choose foods within your diet that will be the best for your healthy new kind of normal lifestyle.

B. A. Smit

Calories

Food provides our bodies with energy. This energy is important, as it keeps us moving during the day. The formal term is kilocalories. This is the amount of energy needed to increase the temperature of one kilogram of water by one degree celsius. Kilocalories are normally shortened to calories. Daily calorie intake will decide your body weight. You must equal the number of calories you consume with the number of calories you use as energy daily to maintain your weight. Consuming more calories than you use will increase your weight. Not having enough calories will result in weight loss.

Calories are found in only four sources. Carbohydrates, proteins, fats and alcohol. There are four calories per gram in both carbohydrates and protein. Alcohol has seven calories and fats have nine calories per gram. In doing the math, a food that contains ten grams of fat will contain ninety calories.

Nutrient-dense is a term used when a food contains a good supply of nutrients as well as calories. Examples of nutrient-dense foods include whole grains, fresh vegetables and fruit, low-fat dairy products, lean meats as well as poultry.

Foods and beverages that are not considered nutrient-dense include wine, alcohol, doughnuts, jams and candy.

To maintain weight and health, it is advised that daily calories should be divided into sections. Sixty percent from carbohydrates, fifteen percent from proteins and fats should be limited to about twenty-five percent.

There are many ways to determine the calories in your foods. Books are a quick and handy guide, most often small pocket sized, available at grocery, drug or book stores. Many packaged foods will also give the calorie count on their label.

Carbohydrates

Carbohydrates play a very important role to keep the body functioning. The brain and nervous system prefer carbohydrates as their source of energy. Muscle movements and red blood cells receive their energy from carbohydrates as well. Carbohydrates also have a part in the stabilization of fat metabolism. To maintain a healthy body, carbohydrates should make up about sixty percent of your daily calorie intake. That is about 1,200 calories of a 2,000 calories a day diet.

Units of carbon, hydrogen and oxygen create carbohydrates. Oxygen is also known as sugars, simple or complex. Table sugar (sucrose), fruit sugars (fructose) and the sugar found in milk (lactose) are considered simple carbohydrates. These break down quickly into glucose and are then absorbed by the body. Plant based foods such as vegetables, legumes and grains are known as complex carbohydrates, they break down at a slower rate.

Carbohydrates can be found in legumes such as beans - broad, kidney or butter, leeks, spinach and berry fruits. These are also high in fiber.

Other carbohydrates, high in starch, include rice, pasta, potatoes, breads and breakfast cereals.

Sweets, such as chocolate, cakes, puddings and jam are examples of carbohydrates high in sugar. Only about ten percent of your daily intake of carbohydrates should be from sweets.

B. A. Smit

Fiber

Fiber is a non digestible form of carbohydrates. Though it is not nutritive, it is another vital part of a healthy body. Fiber is a group of units found in complex carbohydrates. These units have cellulose, hemicellulose and lignin in them. Other units include pectin and gums. These units work together as builders of plant cell walls and metabolism. The number of units vary from food to food. Fiber is divided into two groups, soluble and insoluble.

Soluble fiber is able to be dissolved in water. The compounds break down in the digestive tract to form fatty acids. These are absorbed into the bloodstream. They help to reduce the cholesterol level within the bloodstream, therefore lowering the risk of heart disease or heart attacks. When it joins with cholesterol-rich bile in the tract, it can lower the risk of heart attack. The fiber and bile acids are excreted, taking cholesterol molecules with them, thus lowering the risk of heart attacks. Soluble fiber also slows the absorption of glucose into the blood, it helps to delay the feeling of hunger by slowing the digestion and release into the bloodstream of sugars. This can help to prevent low blood sugar and diabetes. Soluble fiber can be found in beans, fruit, oats, vegetables and barley.

Insoluble fiber does not dissolve in water. It actually absorbs water, and provides bulk in the diet, which leaves you feeling full. It also helps the body to eliminate waste. The added bulk stimulates the muscles to work within the lower digestive tract, moving waste through the system faster. Insoluble fiber is fermented by the large bowel's bacteria to produce fatty acids which nourish the intestinal wall, leaving this area healthier. When the diet lacks enough insoluble fiber, you may find health issues like constipation or hemorrhoids. An illness called diverticulosis can occur when protruding pockets within the intestinal wall fill with infection, resulting in major health issues. The illness is a direct result of lack of insoluble fiber in the diet. A major point to remember is that when waste is put through the system in proper speed, toxins do not have as much chance to build up and cause health problems.

Insoluble fiber can be found in most fruits and vegetables, wheat bran, nuts, whole grain flours and popcorn.

Gluten Free Sources of Dietary Fiber
The Best at a Glance

Food Item (before cooking) 1 cup	Dietary Fiber (in grams)
Flax Seeds	43.2
Amaranth Seeds	29.6
Crude Rice Bran	24.8
Chickpea (Garbanzo Flour)	20.9
Amaranth Flour	18.2
Millet Seeds	17.0
Dry Buckwheat Groats	16.9
Garfava (Garbanzo/Fava Bean)	12.0
Whole Groats Buckwheat Flour	12.0
Enriched Cornmeal	10.2
Quinoa Seeds	10.0
Wild Rice	9.9
Romano (Cranberry) Beans	17.7
Split Peas	16.3
Lentils	15.6
Pinto Beans	14.7
Kidney Beans	13.1
Garbanzo (Chickpea) Beans	12.5
Sesame Seeds	17.4
Almonds (Whole)	15.1
Sunflower Seeds	14.2
Peanuts	12.2

Fruits that are good sources of dietary fiber include apples, apricots (dried), blackberries, boysenberries, whole cranberries, dried figs, pears, raisins, raspberries and rhubarb.

Vegetables that are good sources of dietary fiber include green beans, broccoli, brussel sprouts, carrots, corn, okra, parsnips, peas, potato (with skin), pumpkin, snow peas, spinach, acorn squash and turnip.

B. A. Smit

Fats

Fat is the focus of so many. Diet plans, books, advertising and numerous articles always try to make fat the bad guy. Too much can be harmful is true. Excess fat in your diet can be unhealthy, leading to coronary artery disease, certain cancers and the most obvious risk is unwanted weight gain. It is however, necessary for energy and body functions. Fat is needed to make fat soluble vitamins A, D, E and K available to our system. Satiety, the feeling of fullness, occurs because fat digests slowly. Fat also slows the digestion of carbohydrates and protein, enabling the body to absorb the nutrients found in foods. Fats are also used in cooking, adding flavor to foods.

The molecular structure of fat is referred to as saturation. The three main groups are based on their amount of saturation. A single fat is really a number of chains known as fatty acids. These are carbon, hydrogen and oxygen, which link together. Fatty acids can be saturated, monounsaturated or polyunsaturated. How many open sites for hydrogen atoms to bond with a carbon atom will determine the type. Saturated fatty acids cannot handle anymore hydrogen, monounsaturated have one spot open and polyunsaturated have more than one opening available.

Fat should be only twenty five percent of your daily calories, thirty percent at the highest. Most of these fats should be monounsaturated and polyunsaturated. The saturated fats should not exceed ten percent of your daily calorie intake. It has been realized that these fats have a negative effection on serum cholesterol levels. To do the math, at 2,000 calories a day, about 600 calories, at the most, should come from fats. Less than 200 of these calories should be saturated fats.

Fat alone does not make you fat. Calories in excess can make you fat. One gram of fat contains about nine calories, there are only four calories in one gram of carbohydrates or protein. This is why it is so easy to consume so many calories in just a small amount of food that is high in fat.

Recently, trans fat has been the focus of many media topics. Trans fat occurs when liquid oils are made into margarines and shortenings. In order for the oil to become solid and remain solid at room temperature, a process known as hydrogenation occurs. This is additional hydrogen atoms forced to bond with liquid unsaturated fats, increasing their saturation levels, resulting in the margarine to remain solid at room temperature. The hydrogenation process creates what is known as trans fats. Trace amounts of trans fats do occur naturally in some foods.

Compared with saturated fats, it was thought that trans fats were not as harmful to the serum cholesterol levels. Research has since changed this fact. It is believed that trans fats will raise blood cholesterol levels and may cause some cancers. Daily we consume less trans fats than saturated fats so we should work at reducing saturated fats from our diets.

Foods made from shortening that is solid at room temperature include baked goods, fried foods and margarine. Though trans fats are not listed on ingredient labels, products that contain hydrogenated fat usually contains trans fats. If the hydrogenated fat is listed near the beginning of the ingredients, you should use the product sparingly because ingredients are listed from the most to the least. Hydrogenated fat near the beginning means a greater amount was used in the product.

Omega-3 fatty acids have also gotten a lot of attention recently. These polyunsaturated fatty acids are found in some fish, spinach, broccoli, walnuts and canola oil. Omega-3 fatty acids help to lower the amount of cholesterol the liver produces. It also reduces the occurrence of blood clots around deposits of arterial plaque. It stimulates the immune system, lowers blood pressure and helps to prevent the growth of tumors. Once you realize the importance of fat in your diet, you will be able to understand the ingredient labels and make a healthy, wise choice for your diet. You will now be able to choose the best balance of healthy fats for your diet.

Samples of foods containing saturated fats include dairy: milk, cream, butter and cheese, as well as hydrogenated margarine. Olive oil, margarines that contain olive oil and peanuts contain monounsaturated fat. Soy, corn, safflower oils, salmon, tuna, mackerel and sardines contain polyunsaturated fat.

B. A. Smit

Cholesterol

Cholesterol is a fat related compound, but is not the same as cooking fats or fats located in the body. All substances known as fats are scientifically named Lipids. Cholesterol is a subcategory known as sterol. There are two kinds of cholesterol, dietary and serum. The dietary type is only found in animal foods, never in plant foods. Serum, also known as blood cholesterol, is found in the bloodstream and is needed to sustain life.

The liver is capable of manufacturing about 1,000 milligrams of serum cholesterol daily. It then provides a protective lining around nerve fibers. For the skin, cholesterol is made into vitamin D, with a little help from the sun. Cholesterol acts as a building block for some hormones and works with the outer membranes of cells. Our body is capable of producing cholesterol using dietary components, so it is not necessary to consume cholesterol. Foods that are high in cholesterol often are also high in fat, so daily consumption should not be higher than 300 milligrams, no matter what the calorie count is.

Two types of proteins in the blood moves the cholesterol, high density lipoproteins (HDL) and low density lipoproteins (LDL). The LDL moves cholesterol into the circulatory system and the HDL moves it out of the system. A high level of HDL is considered good, as it can reduce the risk of heart disease. LDL is a sticky substance that places cholesterol in high blood flow areas such as arterial walls. Eventually it will build up and block the arteries, restricting blood flow. This is known as atherosclerosis, which can lead to aneurysm, embolism, stroke or heart attacks. A high LDL reading is not healthy. Consuming saturated fat can raise the level of LDL in the blood more than dietary cholesterol. It is recommended that you should limit your daily intake of saturated fat to less than ten percent of your calories. When you limit your total fat intake to thirty percent or less of your total daily calories, with most of that fat being monounsaturated fats, you lower the serum cholesterol level and lower your chance of heart disease. This also provides a healthier HDL reading. Polyunsaturated fats can also lower the serum cholesterol level, but large amounts of these fatty acids may lower the HDL as well.

There has been an increased use of monounsaturated fats, such as olive oil, in cooking. The balance needed is to try using more unsaturated fats than saturated fats in your diet.

Protein

Protein works with carbohydrates and fats. It is vital for the body, providing calories that are used as energy. Protein is a valuable asset used in the growth of hormones, enzymes and antibodies. It can also regulate body fluids and helps with the growth and maintenance of body tissues.

In a daily 2,000 calorie intake, protein should account for about 300 calories or about fifteen percent of the total. Though it is needed more in children and expectant or nursing women, too much protein can lead to osteoporosis and gout. Damage can occur to the kidneys and liver from too much protein as well. Attacks on the immune system, infection, illness and malnutrition can affect how efficiently your body uses the protein it is provided.

Amino acids are the units found in protein. The proteins in a human cell are comprised of about twenty amino acids. Most of these are produced by the body, but there are eight essential amino acids the body cannot produce and must be supplied by diet. Foods that are abundant in protein contain some or all of these acids. Other amino acids are known as conditionally essential. Using the eight essential acids, the body usually can produce the conditionally essential acids, but, for whatever reason, when the body is unable to produce these, then they must come from the diet.

Food is divided into two groups, complete protein and incomplete protein. The complete protein group contains all of the eight essential amino acids, the incomplete does not. Though meats, poultry, fish and other animal products are an excellent source for complete protein, remember that they may not be the healthiest source. Many of these foods are high in cholesterol and saturated fats. Incomplete protein is comprised of vegetables, grains, legumes and nuts. Alone, you may miss some of the important eight, but combinations of these foods can provide the eight essential amino acids that your body needs. This combining is called mutual supplementation. Traditional meals that use plant foods as their major source of protein are an example of this. Pasta and beans, lentils and rice, tortillas and beans, tofu and rice or hummus and pita bread are just a few of the more popular combinations. You do not need to find your daily quota in one meal, you can balance your daily meals so you have received the necessary amino acids needed during the whole day.

B. A. Smit

Water

The human body is about sixty percent water. It is in our blood, bones, tissues, hair, teeth and skin. It is vital to our existance. The water can dissolve minerals, transport nutrients to cells, remove impurities from the blood and body, as well as forming a part of the cells. Not easily compressed, water is used to cushion joints, organs and sensitive tissues, like the spinal cord. Water works in the eyes also. It stabilizes pressure on the optic nerves to ensure correct vision. Water also balances blood pressure and helps maintain the body temperature. When the body experiences excess heat, by exercise, illness or climate, water is turned to vapor thru sweating. This cools the body by releasing heat away from the body. We are capable of losing up to one quart of water daily. It is very important to replace lost water through drinking fluids or by eating foods that contain water. There are no calories in water, so drink as many glasses of water daily, eight glasses is recommended, as you can.

Vitamins and Minerals

As with water, vitamins and minerals have no calories. They are needed daily to keep the body healthy. You do not need as much as energy nutrients, but a daily balance will keep you healthy. Daily values (DV'S) have been established to provide recommended daily amounts of vitamins and minerals needed by your body.

Vitamins have two categories, water soluble and fat soluble. Water soluble, as the name implies, dissolves in water and is transported through the body in the bloodstream. Though rare, it is possible to develop toxic levels when large quantities are consumed. The excess is released with waste water so a build up is not common. Small amounts may be stored in the muscles and organs, but the vitamins should be replaced daily.

Vitamin C and the B complex vitamins are water soluble. B complex consists of thiamine, riboflavin, niacin, folate, biotin, pantothenic, B6 and B12. They are found in legumes, grains, meats and vegetables. The B complex vitamins are important because they release energy within the body. A lack of these vitamins may lead to beriberi, anemia or pellagra. Vegetarians need to include B12 supplements, or eat foods with it added, because B12 is only found naturally in animal foods.

Fruits and vegetables contain vitamin C. This vitamin increases the body's absorption of iron, and is important for the growth and maintenance of body tissues. It encourages the production of collegen, which is a protein substance that holds together tissues. Vitamin C can also improve the immune system and help to lower serum cholesterol levels. It has been established that vitamin C has antioxidant properties capable of protecting cells from damage by oxygen, and help fight against cancer or heart disease.

Fat soluble vitamins are stored in fat tissues and once there, are not easily removed from the body. The fat soluble vitamins are known as A, D, E and K. They are found in a number of foods, and often more than one can be found in plant foods and fish oils. These vitamins are vital, in the appropriate doses, but can be harmful if the daily amounts are continually exceeded. The body can store these vitamins in limitless amounts, causing toxic levels to develop. When the toxic levels are formed, a number of life threatening conditions may occur, some being fatal.

Retinol is the type of vitamin A that is found in animal foods. Plant foods do not provide vitamin A, but a pigment known as beta carotene. The body uses this to produce vitamin A. Deep yellow, orange and dark green leafy vegetables are high in beta carotene. The body does not convert beta carotene to vitamin A fast enough for toxic levels to develop. Beta carotene is stored in the fat layers just below the skin, so too much of it may cause a person's skin to appear yellowish.

Vitamin D is important for the growth of bones. A shortage of vitamin D can cause rickets. This disease causes bones to grow abnormally. Sunlight is needed for the body to be able to produce vitamin D. Foods can be fortified with vitamin D, milk and cereal being the most common. If your exposure to sunlight is limited, try to eat foods with vitamin D added to ensure a healthy body and bones.

Like vitamin C, vitamin E is an antioxidant which protects the body from free radicals. These are the reactive forms of oxygen produced by the body's metabolic process. These may also help to prevent cancer. Vitamin E is found in a variety of foods and it is easy to get your daily needs from a well balanced diet.

B. A. Smit

Vitamin K is necessary for proper blood clotting. It is produced by bacteria in the intestines, but you can obtain at least half of your daily needs by following a well balanced diet that includes dark green leafy vegetables.

The amounts may vary, but the body needs minerals daily to keep balanced and healthy. Macrominerals are named this because they are needed in large amounts. Calcium, phosphorus, sodium, potassium and magnesium are macrominerals. Fluoride, iodine and iron are microminerals. Though equally important, smaller amounts are needed daily of these minerals.

Calcium is the body's most plentiful mineral. Ninety-nine percent of the body's calcium is used in the growth and maintenance of bones and teeth. One percent is needed to balance blood pressure, clotting of the blood, muscle contractions and help transmit nerve impulses. A shortage of calcium, especially in children, can impair growth and cause a loss in bone density. Dairy products, especially milk and yogurt, broccoli and leafy vegetables are excellent calcium sources.

Phosphorus is a major contributor to all energy-releasing reactions. It works with calcium to maintain healthy bones and teeth. It is rare to find a shortage within the body, but when it occurs, it may cause weakness, impaired heart function, or neurological problems. Animal protein, cereal, legumes and nuts are excellent sources for phosphorus.

Sodium and potassium are known as electrolytes. They are vital for the regulation of body functions by balancing the body's fluids and aiding in the performance of nerves and muscles. Muscle cramps, loss of appetite, confusion and forgetfulness may occur when there is a sodium shortage in the body. Sodium is found in many foods, so a deficiency is rare. Too much sodium in a diet can cause problems for people who suffer from high blood pressure. Good sources of potassium include almost all fruits and vegetables. A shortage of potassium may result in weakness, low blood pressure and confusion.

Magnesium is needed to support healthy bones and teeth, nerve transmission, bowel function and muscle contraction. We seem to miss our daily quota, which can lead to stunted growth, behavior problems, weakness, tremors and seizures. Magnesium is found in nuts, legumes, whole grains and green vegetables.

Fluoride is a part of teeth and bones. It helps in the prevention of tooth decay and aids in the prevention of osteoporosis. Many cities include fluoride in their water supply. You can also find it in certain teas, saltwater fish and shellfish.

Iodine is required for a normal thyroid gland, to regulate energy metabolism, growth and cellular oxidation. Not enough iodine can effect the thyroid gland, causing enlargement known as goiter. It was common in the Midwestern United States in the early 1900's, resulting in iodine to be added to table salt (iodized salt) to lessen the shortage in our body.

Iron's work is found mostly in the blood. About seventy five percent of our total iron is in the bloodstream. It is a vital part of hemoglobin, a pigment in red blood cells, which carries oxygen from the lungs to the cells. The other twenty five percent of iron has several jobs. One is part of myoglobin, the molecule that supplies oxygen to muscles and another is part of certain enzymes that work in cellular energy metabolism. A shortage of iron is prominent throughout the world. Anemia occurs when blood cells are deprived of enough hemoglobin needed to properly function. Weakness, an impaired immune system or looking pale are all signs of iron deficiency. Red meat, liver, legumes, whole grains, green leafy vegetables and dried fruit are excellent sources of iron.

Gluten Free Sources of Iron
The Best at a Glance

There are two types of iron in foods. Those with celiac disease often lack iron in their system. Heme iron is best absorbed, with other foods not interfering, by the body. This iron is only found in fish, poultry and red meat. Non-heme iron is not easily absorbed, only about three percent is taken by the body. Other foods can affect how much non-heme iron is absorbed. This iron is only found in eggs, fruits, grains and vegetables. To maximize your balance of iron absorption, try to eat foods containing both types of iron at each meal. Combining foods that are rich in vitamin C with foods rich in non-heme iron will also help to maximize the absorption. Tea and coffee contain tannins which will interfere with the work of iron, so try to avoid these beverages when eating an iron rich meal.

Food Item (1 cup)	Iron (mg)
Grains	
Rice Bran	21.9
Quinoa, raw	15.7
Amaranth	14.8
Quinoa Flour	9.4
Garfava Flour	7.9
Flax, ground seeds	7.5
Buckwheat Bran	6.8
Raw Millet	6.0
Cornmeal	5.7
Soy Flour (full fat)	5.4
Whole Groat Buckwheat Flour	4.9
Sorghum Flour	4.7
Seeds and Nuts	
Pumpkin Seeds	20.7
Sesame Seeds	11.7
Peanuts	6.7
Whole Almonds	5.4
Sunflower Seeds	4.9
Brazil Nuts	4.8
Lentils, Beans, Peas (cooked)	
White Beans	6.6
Lentils	6.6
Kidney Beans	5.2
Chickpeas (Garbanzo)	4.7
Navy Beans	4.5
Pinto Beans	4.5

B. A. Smit

Meats and Alternatives (cooked)

Beef Liver 100 gr	5.8
Clams 9 small or 4 large	3.4
Beef Steak 100 gr	3.1
Fresh Shrimp 100 gr	3.1
Canned Shrimp 100 gr	2.7
Beef, Ground 100 gr	2.1
Chicken Breast Meat 100 gr	1.0
Turkey Dark Meat	2.3
Canned Tuna 100 gr	1.0
Canned Salmon 100 gr	1.1
Pork Chop 100 gr	1.0
Egg 1 large	.7

Fruits (1 cup)

Dried Apricots	6.1
Dried Prunes	4.2
Seedless Raisins	3.4
Prune Juice	3.0

Vegetables (cooked, 1 cup)

Spinach	6.4
Baked Potato, skin on	2.7
Green Peas	2.5
Acorn Squash	1.9
Brussel Sprouts	1.8
Broccoli	1.3

Phytochemicals and Antioxidants

For a long time we have heard so much about foods that should be avoided because they could be harmful to us. It has made it difficult, and at times confusing, to make sensible choices for a healthy diet. The research on phytochemicals and antioxidants is providing us with a list of foods that are healthy and should be eaten.

Phytochemicals are like vitamins, they can be present naturally in fruits, legumes, grains and vegetables. Vitamins are recognized as essential to life, and the amount needed to remain healthy has been calculated. The benefits of phytochemicals are so recent, the actual amounts needed are still being calculated. Research has found that these compounds are capable of reducing the risk of heart disease, cancer, as well as other chronic ailments.

Phytochemicals appear to function in variants of three distinct ways. One has antioxidant properties, another has an effect on hormone levels and the other prominent way is to work with enzymes that help to eliminate carcinogens which create cancer. For centuries, phytochemicals, like digitalis and quinine, have been applied to medical uses. Plant-based substances are also being researched for their anticancer effects.

One subcategory of phytochemicals are antioxidants. They are important in combating cellular damage created by free radicals, which are present in abundance during times of stress, exposure to toxins or illness. Vitamins A, C, E and the mineral selenium are antioxidants. Pigments called carotenoids are also antioxidants, which are found in yellow, red and orange vegetables, along with leafy green vegetables.

Over six hundred different carotenoids are found in nature. Only about fifty of these are used by the body. Lycopene is one type found in large amounts in tomatoes. It appears to hinder the growth of cancer cells, therefore reducing the risk of several types of cancer, including prostate cancer. There are about one hundred types of phytochemicals in a single tomato. Every plant food appears to have it's own blend of phytochemicals which work in harmony for a healthier body. To ensure continued good health, eating a good variety of grains, legumes, fruits and vegetables will give you the assortment of phytochemicals needed daily, and this will include antioxidants as well.

Illness, Allergy and Gluten Free Diets

Allergy and Intolerance
Illness and Allergy Related to Foods
The Starting Point
Celiac Disease
Drugs and Food
Ingredients to Avoid
Why Some Foods Are Not Allowed
Gluten Free Diet - What to Avoid
Some Famous, Some Not So Famous Dishes to Avoid
Gluten Free Additives and Ingredients

Allergy and Intolerance

The immune system is designed to protect the body from bacteria or viruses. It can identify proteins on the bacteria. B-lymphocytes of the immune system produce proteins called antibodies which can attach to the proteins on the bacteria, thus destroying the organism.

In allergies, the immune system reacts to harmless substances. The antibodies or immunglobulins can be found in your blood and a test can show it, defining an allergy. Though skin tests are often used for testing, other variants can cause the inflammation, leaving this form of test questionable. Food elimination is recommended. Certain foods are eliminated for three to five days, then reintroduced one at a time. When a reaction occurs, the food that triggered the reaction is considered the allergy food.

The elimination diet is also used for food intolerance. Often a deficiency of an enzyme within the body can be the cause. Two main enzymes are within the digestive system. Lactase and pancreatic lipase. With the lactase enzyme, an intolerance to milk sugars called lactose is the result. Avoiding dairy products is the way to control this intolerance. An intolerance to dietary fats is caused by a lack of pancreatic lipase. Migraines can be caused by the enzyme that breaks down active substances called amines. This enzyme is called monoamine oxidases.

Illness and Allergy Related to Foods

To maintain a healthy body, you must eat healthy foods. Migraines, eczema, Crohn's disease, irritable bowel syndrome and even rheumatoid arthritis are some ailments that proper nutrition for your body can help to improve, or ease the discomfort.

The body has free radicals which are unstable molecules created by the body, a by-product of normal metabolism. These are also in our environment. Exhaust fumes, factory emissions and chemical pollution are also free radicals. Within the body, free radicals are very destructive and if combined with oxygen, can cause severe cell damage. Antioxidants, found in carotenoids, especially beta carotene and vitamins C and E, seek out free radicals and destroys them.

Processed foods and "fast food" burgers and hot dogs, along with sausages and even meat pies, may contain chemicals and hidden fats. Natural butter is best instead of margarines which may contain chemicals and possibly trans fats. For those who are lactose intolerant, lactose-free margarines should be used.

At least one third of your daily food should be raw. Fruits, vegetables and salads contain the needed vitamins, protective phytochemicals, fiber and minerals. Gluten free pasta, brown rice, lentils, beans and gluten free cereals provide calcium, protein, fiber, minerals and vitamins. Protein can be found in poultry, seafood and fish, leaving red meat as an occasional food, not a necessary food. Eggs and dairy substitutes are also vital for a well balanced diet. Low fat options are available for those who are concerned about calories.

Unfavorable reactions to foods can simply be put into two sections. When the immune system is involved, it is usually considered a food allergy. Allergy is often immediate or soon after consumption. The most common food allergies include shellfish, cow's milk and products from cow's milk, eggs, yeast, soy and soy products, alcohol and some fruits and nuts. For most other reactions that occur, food intolerance is often the cause. When a reaction occurs between one hour up to several days later, intolerance, not allergy, is usually the cause.

The best way to determine intolerance is by testing. With your doctor or a dietitian's guidance, you can test yourself. Symptoms vary from one person to another, from minor discomfort to crippling, painful ailments. Some food intolerance is quite obvious, like nausea, diarrhea, cramps, or skin outbreaks like cold sores and hives. When it is that apparent, avoiding the problem food is the logical answer. It can be difficult to adjust to food restrictions. It can be even harder trying to discover what foods to remove from your diet.

It is best to keep a food and feeling journal. It may be time consuming and daunting at first, but you will soon see the benefits. If you are not sure what makes you react, listing daily everything you eat, and how you feel, a pattern may begin to emerge. If you react to soy, for example, after drinking a soy beverage you won't feel well, or if you notice days of extreme fatigue, you may be able to backtrack and notice a specific food that you ate before feeling so tired or unwell. Experiment by eliminating the suspect food and see if there is improvement. As I said, it can be daunting, but a journal is the best way to get an overall view of the correlation of food to symptoms. Remember to work this journal with the guidance of your doctor or dietitian.

Every person who experiences food sensitivities or allergies can experience completely different symptoms. This makes it vital that you learn to treat yourself. Learn what foods you react to and learn how to substitute other foods to replace problem foods to maintain a healthy balance of nutrition. Always work with a doctor or dietitian, keeping a journal and showing it to your professional will help to speed up your road to a new kind of normal.

This is why a food and feeling journal is so vital. Once you can recognize what food is provoking what reaction, it becomes easier to stabilize your health. Remember that lifestyle is a major factor in your health as well. Adopting a new, healthy attitude with a good diet and exercise is key to an overall health improvement. Once you eliminate problem foods, you will not have the reactions, which will result in your health improving.

Food is only one aspect of reactions, health and beauty products may contain ingredients you cannot tolerate. This is why the journal can help, writing everything down, what you eat, where you go, change in medication, toothpaste, shampoo, everything. Yes, as I said, it can be daunting. Once in the habit, you may be able to see a pattern. This food was eaten before I got tired, or this medication was o.k. until I changed brands. It will make life easier and once you stabilize, you may not have to write daily into your journal, but will be able to avoid problem foods and mentally track reactions related to foods and other products.

Nutrition is key to a healthy body. When you eliminate foods you should replace them with ones you can tolerate that will give you the same nutrient value. Try to develop a schedule of eating. Don't skip meals, regardless of how you feel. When you are sick, eating prepackaged food or frozen food may be easier, but they may also prolong your reaction and you may feel sicker, longer. Try to develop a healthy meal plan and stick to it. Your doctor or dietitian will be able to help you with this.

When you go shopping, try to stick to fresh ingredients, even canned food may not always list every single ingredient. Read labels, products can change their ingredients without any notice. When creating meals, try to ensure a variety in color and texture. Baked chicken with potato and cauliflower looks very bland, but changing to peas and carrots instead of cauliflower visually changes the plate to look more appealing. Even if you are only cooking for yourself, try to create visually pleasing meals with the nutrition value needed.

Depression can creep into your life, especially as you struggle to regain the control of your health. It is vital to remain positive and take it one day at a time. The information in this book may help you to reclaim stability in your health.

Remember the importance of reading labels. Some companies will change some of the ingredients without any warning. This means that what was once safe, may no longer be a compatible food or product for you.

When it is not clear what food you react to, an elimination diet is a starting point. I recommend following a guide like the one I am including for ten to fourteen days. Keep to basic, simple foods. Add one food every two to three days. Watch for signs of intolerance. If there is a reaction, stop eating that food. When the reaction clears, introduce one more food.

Any diet that is restricted can leave your health at risk. You can experiment yourself, but it is advisable to consult your doctor or dietitian. Any long term removal of any part of a food group should be done under guidance of a professional. Remember that drinking lots of water is important to help flush your system as well.

The Starting Point

Beverages - It is best to avoid all juices and drinks that contain added sugars, colors and additives. Pure juices, herbal teas, mineral or distilled waters are best. Orange, grape and grapefruit juices are best avoided. When you have stabilized your diet, then introduce these juices. It is also best to refrain from regular tea and coffee until you have your diet set.

Cereals - Avoid all cereals containing gluten. Try rice, corn or other gluten free cereals and grains. Read labels.

Fish - Stay away from smoked fish and shellfish. Try tuna, halibut, sole or cod. Bake the fish when possible and avoid breading or sauces.

Fruit - Try avoiding citrus and tropical fruits. Eat basic, fresh fruit such as apples, pears and peaches. Introduce berries next. Strawberries, blueberries and raspberries are the best choices.

Meats - Refrain from processed meats like bacon, ham, pork, sausage, cold cuts and red meats. Try to limit yourself to turkey and chicken.

Vegetables - Avoid "strong" vegetables like potatoes, beets, rutabaga, corn, onion, eggplant, broccoli and cauliflower. It is best to start with "mild" vegetables, carrots, peas, beans, salad type vegetables, except tomatoes and legumes.

When you have been able to compile a list of foods you need to avoid, then begin to explore recipes. Finding recipes that have ingredients you can tolerate, or ingredients you can substitute to your needs will be easier to find once you know your limits. My recipes are designed to tailor to your needs, don't be afraid to experiment, it is the fastest way to learn. Again, each person is different. Reactions, foods and tolerance is individual. You need to find what to avoid and what works for you.

Celiac Disease

This is the most common illness that requires a gluten free diet. It is a gastrointestinal disorder. The absorptive surface of the small intestine is damaged by gluten, which is protein found in rye, wheat, triticale, barley and oats, to name the most common sources. The result is that the body cannot absorb protein, fat, vitamins, minerals and carbohydrates. Many with celiac disease cannot digest lactose, the sugar found in milk, so they must also be on a dairy free diet as well. Legumes are vital for a gluten free diet. They add variety, but are also a good source of B vitamins, niacin and calcium. The calcium is vital for healthy bones. Celiac disease is a lifelong illness that avoidance of certain foods is the most effective way to control the symptoms. Because the body has difficulty absorbing the nutrients in foods, maintaining a healthy and balanced diet is important.

The most common symptoms include:
Diarrhea, constipation, or both
Bloating, gas, abdominal pain
Nausea and vomiting
Weight loss
Chronic fatigue and weakness
Anemia and/or iron deficiency
Vitamin deficiency
Mouth ulcers
Joint/bone pain
Depression
Lactose intolerant (may change once you are on a gluten free diet)

If you suspect celiac disease:
With guidance from your doctor, you may want to try a gluten free diet for 10 - 14 days. If your symptoms decrease, return to a diet including gluten for 7 - 10 days before being tested to confirm celiac disease. If you remain on a gluten free diet before being tested, the results may not be accurate. Starting a gluten free diet before testing may interfere with the results of the tests.

Drugs and Food

Oral medication travels through the same system as foods. When certain foods and drugs are mixed within the system, it may cause a reaction, delay, decrease or increase of absorption of the drug.

Alcohol may react with antidepressants that can result in impairment of both the nervous system and the brain. Continued long term, it may also result in liver damage. It is best to refrain from all alcohol while on medication.

Chocolate and antidepressants can result in a sudden rise in blood pressure. The caffine in chocolate can also react to sedatives and stimulants.

Grapefruit can react to some medications. Some medication levels may be increased within the bloodstream that may have a toxic effect. Also, with some medication, when grapefruit is eaten, the medication's level of absorption may be significantly decreased.

Licorice may lower the effects of some diuretic or blood pressure medications.

Potassium levels may change when some antibiotics, ACE inhibitors or diuretics are taken with potassium rich foods. It may cause a dangerous increase of potassium levels within the body.

When taking antibiotics, especially tetracycline, remember that cheese, milk and even ice cream, along with vitamins and antacids that contain iron, can decrease the effectiveness of the antibiotic.

Talk to your doctor or pharmacist to ensure that your diet and medication can work in harmony.

Ingredients to Avoid

Barley	Kamut	Rye
Bran	Malt	Semolina
Bulgar	Malt Extract	Spelt
Cereal Binding	Malt Flavoring	Triticale
Couscous	Malt Syrup	Wheat
Durum	Oat Bran	Wheat Germ
Filler	Oats	Wheat Starch
Graham Flour	Oat Syrup	

Less Common Names for Wheat

Einkorn
Emmer
Farro

Questionable Ingredients

Hydrolyzed plant or vegetable protein (HPP/HVP)
Dextrin
Flavorings
Seasonings
Starch
Modified food starch

Seitan: This is a very dense wheat gluten that is used by vegetarians to make a meat like product.

These are some of the most common ingredients that include gluten. Remember to read labels, many products have "hidden" gluten.

B. A. Smit

Why Some Foods Are Not Allowed

Some food is obvious that it contains gluten. Regulations allow for some ingredients to not be fully identified. These hidden glutens are what you should learn to recognize. Some samples are listed for you.

Hydrolyzed Plant or Vegetable Protein (HPP or HPV)

Hydrolysis is when protein is broken down by enzymes or acids. Hydrolyzed plant proteins are most commonly made from wheat, soy, corn or peanuts. Hydrolyzed plant proteins are included in a wide variety of foods, such as spice mixtures, sauces, soups and gravies. In Canada, the source of the hydrolyzed plant protein does not have to be identified.

Dextrin

Dextrin is a starch that is partially hydrolyzed by heat, or heating with suitable food-grade buffers and acids from grains or root-based unmodified native starches. The most common are wheat, tapioca, arrowroot, corn, waxy maize, potato milo or waxy milo. Dextrin is used as a binder, colloidal stabilizer, thickener or surface-finishing agent. In Canada, corn or tapioca are usually used to make dextrin. Read labels, or contact the manufacturer for more information.

Flavorings

The actual term for flavorings is varied. Flavorings used in meat or products containing meat can often include gluten. In Canada, grains that contain gluten are rarely used in flavorings, except for barley malt.

Seasonings, Herbs and Spices

There are various regulations, depending on the country, for defining seasonings, herbs and spices. Pure spices, seeds and herbs are safe, as they do not contain gluten. Some products, like imitation seasonings, spices and spice blends, can use fillers. Read labels. In seasonings, there are a blend of flavorings like protein hydrolysates, herbs and spices, that are then mixed with a carrier, like lactose, whey powder, milk powder, sugar, salt, cereal flours or starches. Snack foods, sauces and gravies often contain wheat. Manufacturers are not compelled to declare all components, so it is best to avoid questionable foods.

Starches

The word starch on a food label most often refers to corn starch. It is required by manufacturers to identify the starch source on labels, such as potato starch, wheat starch or tapioca starch, if it is not corn.

Modified Food Starch

These are most commonly made from corn, tapioca, wheat or potato. In Canada, it is rare for these starches to be made from gluten sources.

Gluten Free Diet - What To Avoid

Beverages - Avoid malt beverages, beers and ales. Coffee, tea and herbal teas should, if pure, be safe. Sodas and pure juices, should be safe.

Breads - All breads, buns, pancakes etc. that contain wheat, rye, barley, oats or other gluten flours, should be avoided. This includes crackers and prepared mixes.

Cereals - All cereals, hot, cold, or for baking, that include wheat, oats, rye, barley, bran, malt flavorings or other gluten grains should be avoided.

Cheese, Dairy, Eggs - Again read labels. Cheese spreads may contain gluten. Cheese sauces and spreads use wheat as a stabilizer and/or as a thickener. The flavorings in the sauces may originate from a wheat source. Be aware of the dairy products made from cow's milk, including butter, yogurt and sour cream. Some sour creams use oat gum in their product and yogurts may include gluten as a thickener or stabilizer. Chocolate milk may contain barley malt or wheat starch. Try using either soy, goat or sheep's milk products, one source at a time, to see if you react. Soy could be a problem for some people, so I suggest trying it first. If you have no reaction, try goat or sheep products for variety. Eggs may also be a source for intolerance, so try eggs separately.

Cooking Oils - Cooking oils may also be a source of intolerance. Try using only one type, preferably soy, olive, canola or safflower, for both cooking and salad dressings. If you react to a "safe" food cooked in the oil, or the oil is used in a salad dressing on "safe" food, and you react, try using a different oil on the same foods to see if you react before removing the food from your safe list.

Desserts and Sweets - Stay away from baked goodies made with gluten flours. Remember that even chocolate bars and candy are often made in a gluten environment and can contain hidden gluten, unless the product states that it is made in a gluten free environment. It is not always just what goes into a product, but also cross contamination from gluten products made in the same plant as gluten free products, that can produce hidden gluten in the gluten free products. Read labels. Puddings can use gluten products as thickeners. Cakes, cookies, pies and pastries all contain gluten, unless they are gluten free products. Read labels. Most desserts, unless gluten free, have either gluten and/or lactose. Read labels, and be aware of hidden gluten.

Drugs - Read labels, and ask your pharmacist. Some over the counter as well as prescription medicines can include gluten, often as a filler.

Fruit - Dried fruit, like dates, apricots and pineapple, are often dusted with wheat or oat flour to prevent the fruit from sticking together. Pie fillings often use wheat flour as a thickener. Some fruit dishes, like apple crisp, include oat flakes. Like vegetables, avoid fruit if it is battered or breaded, unless you are sure it is gluten free. Gluten can be hidden in some fruit products, so again, read labels.

B. A. Smit

Grains - Some of the corn and rice cereals contain oat syrup or barley malt extract. Corn or rice cakes may contain barley or oats, especially the multigrain varieties. Rice crackers may include soy sauce, which can contain gluten. Pastas, like buckwheat, corn or rice may be mixed with semolina, a type of wheat. Some flours, like buckwheat, may also contain wheat. Always read the ingredient label to ensure that the product is gluten free.

Meats, Fish and Alternative Protein Sources - As with fruits and vegetables, try to avoid products coated in bread crumbs or batter. Canned meats, processed meats, bread stuffings, butter basted turkey and gravies should be avoided unless you know it is gluten free. Many of the processed meats use fillers containing wheat. They may also include HPP or HVP, which may be derived from a wheat source. The added flavorings may also contain gluten. Imitation meats and seafood often contain wheat. Baked beans can use wheat flour as a thickener. Dry roasted peanuts may have wheat added, and peanut butter sometimes includes icing sugar, which could have wheat as a filler. Read labels to know what should be avoided.

Oils and Fats - Read labels. Most are gluten free. Some oils, like wheat germ, are not gluten free.

Soups - Hidden gluten can be found in canned soup and soup mixes. Read labels. Soups that are canned or the dry mixtures may contain noodles or pasta made from wheat or other flours that contain gluten. Barley is another common ingredient used in soups. The seasonings may also contain a gluten flour. Whether a dry mix or canned, HPP or HVP from wheat could be included in the ingredients. Cream soups are almost always thickened with flour containing gluten, and for those who are lactose intolerant, cream soups contain milk products.

Vegetables - Like fruits, there are no restrictions unless the vegetables are battered or breaded with a product containing gluten. Vegetables that are in sauces should be avoided also, as most may include gluten. For those who are lactose intolerant, milk products are often used in sauces as well. Frozen french fries may use wheat as an additive for browning and crisping. Read labels.

Miscellaneous - Many food items also include gluten, often hidden. Avoid gravies, sauces and bottled dressings that may contain gluten. Salad dressings can include wheat flour in the seasonings. Icing sugar may contain up to five percent starch, often wheat. Baking powder is the same, using wheat starch as a filler. Beverages may have grain additives. Read labels on teas, both regular and herbal, instant coffee and non-dairy substitutes. The dairy substitutes may include barley malt extracts, though a small amount, it may be enough to bother some people. Lemon curd, mainly used in desserts, may be thickened with a wheat flour. Imitation pepper and seasonings may contain gluten. Potato chips, tortilla chips, snack foods and soy nuts all may contain gluten in their seasonings. Malt vinegar, soy sauce and barbeque sauce can also include gluten. Every condiment, sauce or flavoring that you see may contain gluten.

Read labels. Gluten can be found in many foods. Vinegar may be safe for some, while others may not be able to use it. Test foods with this in mind. Cooking sprays may contain grain alcohol. Ketchup, mustard and horseradish contain vinegar, which could contain enough gluten for you to react. Read labels, wheat free does not always mean gluten free. Even refined sugar, honey, chocolate, yeast, MSG, artificial colorings and flavorings may be a problem for you. Cane sugar, maple syrup, pure cocoa and carob could be a better choice.

B. A. Smit

Some Famous, Some Not So Famous Dishes To Avoid

Albondigas - Mexican meat cakes, usually with flour added, then fried.

Au Gratin - Cheese sauce and bread crumbs. A mixture used in meat, seafood and vegetable dishes.

Beef Wellington - A beef dish that has a flour pastry around the beef, then baked. The pastry has gluten in it.

Beignet - Cajun cuisine, it is a dessert fritter. The fritter batter contains gluten.

Bisque - A type of soup that is often thickened with flour.

Blanquette - Veal or chicken stew based on a white roux. The roux is made with butter and flour.

Couscous - This dish originated in North Africa, it is often made with crushed durum wheat.

Crouton - A small cube of buttered, flavored, then toasted bread. They are usually about one half to one inch square. Croutons are often added to salads, usually a handful tossed on top of the salad. Caesar salad is the most common salad with croutons. The bread contains gluten.

Fricassée - A type of stew, often made with poultry, that is thickened with flour.

Fritomisto - This is an Italian dish. Food is coated in a flour and egg batter, then fried.

Gnocchi - An Italian potato dumpling which almost always contains some flour.

Goulash - A Hungarian stew flavored with paprika, with a roux base, which is flour and butter.

Matelote - This is a fish stew made with wine and thickened with flour.

Moussaka - Greek eggplant casserole, thickened with a bechamel sauce containing flour.

Pasticcio - This is a casserole type dish made with a mixture of meat, vegetables or pasta, with eggs, bechamel sauce and bread crumbs, which contain gluten.

Soufflé - Most contain flour, whether a main course or dessert.

Stroganoff - A beef stew that includes sour cream. It is thickened with a roux, made with flour and butter.

Gluten Free Additives and Ingredients

Some of the better known, or most common additives, sweeteners, flavorings, including vegetable gums and miscellaneous, are listed here for your convenience.

Additives

Acetic Acid	Fumaric Acid	Sodium Metabisulphite
Adipic Acid	Lactic Acid	Sodium Nitrate
Benzoic Acid	Malic Acid	Sodium Sulphite
BHA and BHT	Polysorbate 60;80	Stearic Acid
Calcium Disodium EDTA	Propylene Glycol	Tartaric Acid
Carboxymethyl Cellulose	Sodium Benzoate	Tartrazine
		Titanium Dioxide

Sweeteners

Aspartame	Lactose	Xylitol
Brown Sugar	Mannitol	
Corn Syrup/Solids	Molasses	
Dextrose	Sorbitol	
Fructose	Sucralose	
Glucose	Sucrose	
Invert Sugar	White Sugar	

Flavorings

Acacia Gum (Gum Arabic)	Ethyl Maltol	MSG
Algin (Alginic Acid)	Guar Gum	Tragacanth
Carageenan	Karaya Gum	Vanilla Extract
Carob Bean (Locust Bean)	Maltol	Vanillan
Cellulose	Methylcellulose	Vegetable Gums
		Xanthan Gum

Miscellaneous

Annatto	Caramel Color	Maltodextrin
Baking Yeast	Cream of Tartar	Papain
Beta Carotene	Gelatin	Pectin
Brewer's Yeast	Lecithin	Psyllium

Now that you have a list of gluten free additives and flavorings, you will be able to better understand the ingredient labels on foods. Again, this list is only the most common, there are many more gluten free additives. This list will help you to make the right choices in foods, based on your restrictions.

Plant Foods and Families

When you develop allergies and/or sensitivities to foods, often you are overwhelmed or "lost" as to how to isolate the problem food. One way to begin is to understand that foods belong in families. Most times, when you find the family, avoiding all foods in that family will ease or solve the problem. The list that I have put together is only a guide. There might be foods that you can tolerate from one family, but not other foods within the same family. It will give you somewhere to begin.

Apple
Apple
Pear
Quince

Banana
Banana
Plantain

Beet
Beet
Chard
Lamb's Quarters
Spinach

Buckwheat
Buckwheat
Rhubarb
Sorrel

Cashew
Cashew
Mango
Pistachio

Cereal
Bamboo
Barley
Corn
Malt
Millet
Molasses
Oats
Rice
Rye
Sorghum

Cereal - cont.
Sugar Cane
Triticale
Wheat
Wild Rice

Citrus
Citron
Grapefruit
Kumquat
Lemon
Lime
Orange
Tangerine

Composite
Artichoke
Chicory
Dandelion
Endive
Escarole
Jerusalem Artichoke
Lettuce
Safflower
Salsify
Sunchoke
Sunflower

Fungus
Mushroom
Yeast

Ginger
Cardamom
Ginger
Turmeric

Gooseberry
Currant
Gooseberry

Gourd
Cantaloupe
Cucumber
Melons
Muskmelon
Pumpkin
Squash
Watermelon

Grape
Cream of Tartar
Grape
Raisin

Heather
Blueberry
Cranberry
Huckleberry
Wintergreen

Laurel
Avocado
Bayleaf
Cinnamon
Sassafras

Legumes
Alfalfa
Beans
Carob
Cowpea
Lecithin
Lentil
Licorice
Peas
Peanuts
Soybeans
Tragacanth

Lily
Aloe
Asparagus
Chives
Garlic
Leek
Onion

Mallow
Cottonseed
Okra

Mint
Basil
Horehound
Marjoram
Mint
Oregano
Peppermint
Sage
Savoury
Spearmint
Thyme

Mulberry
Fig
Hop
Mulberry

Mustard
Broccoli
Brussel Sprouts
Cabbage
Cauliflower
Collard
Horseradish
Kale
Kohlrabi
Mustard
Mustard Seeds
Radish
Rutabaga
Turnip
Watercress

Myrtle
Allspice
Clove
Guava
Pimento

Nutmeg
Mace
Nutmeg

Palm
Coconut
Date
Sago

Parsley
Anise
Caraway
Carrot
Celery
Coriander
Cumin
Dill
Fennel
Parsley
Parsnip

Plum
Almond
Apricot
Cherry
Nectarine
Peach
Plum (Prune)

Potato
Cayenne
Chili
Eggplant
Green Pepper
Paprika
Potato
Red Pepper
Tobacco
Tomato

Purslane
New Zealand (Velvet-Leafed)
        Spinach
Purslane

Rose
Blackberry
Boysenberry
Dewberry
Loganberry
Raspberry
Strawberry

Stercula
Chocolate
Cocoa
Cola

Walnut
Butternut
Hickory Nut
Pecan
Walnut

Single Food Families

Arrowroot
Brazil Nut
Caper
Chestnut
Coffee
Elderberry
Filbert (Hazelnut)
Ginseng
Honey
Lichi Nut
Macadamia Nut
Maple
Olive
Papaya

Pepper (Black)
Pepper (White)
Persimmon
Pineapple
Pine Nut
Pomegranate
Saffron
Sesame
Sweet Potato
Tapioca
Taro
Tea
Vanilla
Water Chestnut
Yam

B. A. Smit

The Canadian Food Guide

Food Guide for a Balanced Diet

The food guide was established to show people the importance of maintaining a healthy, balanced diet. I have included the basic guide for both general and vegetarian diets. They were developed to be used as a guide to help you choose foods from all food groups on a daily basis. To keep your body at it's optimum health you should try to eat a well balanced diet. Too much of one food group or not enough of another may change how healthy you are.

The old saying "you are what you eat" really does apply. Be careful to avoid too much sugar and salt in your diet. Try to be physically active each day. Choose variety in the foods you can eat. Don't be afraid to try new foods, if your body can tolerate change. Use the charts as a guide, be adventurous, and enjoy creating new, tasty, balanced meals.

Milk, cheese and yogurt are excellent sources of calcium. Your body needs calcium daily, so try to find substitutes for dairy if you are lactose intolerant, and remember that cheese can also provide protein into your diet. Besides goat and sheep, there are many products now made from soy, rice and even potato that replace cow's dairy products.

Fruit provides us with vitamin C. It is available fresh all year. You can replace fresh fruit with frozen or canned and still get the same nutrients as fresh. Juice is also a good replacement for fresh fruit.

Vegetables, like fruit, are available year round. There are so many varieties that contain nutrients like vitamins A and C, plus iron, which keep you healthy. Like fruit, you can choose fresh, frozen or canned vegetables to obtain your daily requirements.

Enriched breads, whole grain breads and cereal provide B vitamins and small amounts of iron and protein. Reading the ingredient label will help you to decide what product is most nutritious for your needs.

Meat, fish and poultry are good sources of protein. Fish also provides iodine. Vitamin B and iron are also found in meat, fish and poultry. Eggs contain vitamins A, B2 and D, which is used with calcium to keep bones strong and healthy.

** Many gluten free foods are not good sources for dietary fiber. To ensure a good balance, try to pick a variety of high fiber foods more often. Start off slowly and gradually increase the amount of fiber in your daily foods. With this increase of fiber, you should increase your fluid intake as well. Water is the best fluid to use as the body needs it to digest and maintain a healthy system. Try to consume at least six to eight glasses per day.

Canada Food Guide

Daily Guide

Grain Products - 6 - 7 servings

    1 serving -   1 slice bread
                      1 muffin
                      30 g cold cereal (2 TBSP)
                      3/4 cup hot cereal, rice, corn, buckwheat etc.

    2 servings -   1 bagel, pita or bun
                      1 cup cooked rice or pasta

Vegetables and Fruits - 7 - 8 servings

    1 serving -   1 medium sized fruit or vegetable, pear, apple, carrot or potato etc.
                      1/2 cup fresh, frozen or canned fruit or vegetable
                      1 cup salad
                      1/2 cup fruit or vegetable juice

Milk Products - Adults - 2 - 4 servings
                    Youth   - 3 - 4 servings
                    Child   - 2 - 3 servings

    1 serving -   1 cup milk or milk substitute
                      50 g (3" x 1") cheese or substitute 2 slices cheese from package
                      3/4 cup yogurt or custard

Meat and Alternatives - 2 - 3 servings

    1 serving -   75/125 g (2 1/2 oz - 1/2 cup) meat, fish or poultry
                      1 - 2 eggs (2 small, 1 large)
                      3/4 cup legumes
                      3/4 cup tofu
                      30 ml (2 TBSP) peanut or other nut butter.

Try to include legumes, lentils and tofu more often as an alternative to meat, fish and poultry.

Oils and Fats - Include about 2 - 3 TBSP per day. It can be added into any meal as mayonnaise, salad dressing, margarine or what you use in cooking.

Meal and Snack Suggestions

Breakfasts
- Gluten free cold cereal with milk and fruit; pear, peach, apple, berries or banana
- Gluten free hot cereal cooked with dried fruit; dates, cranberries, raisins or apricots, with milk
- Gluten free pancakes or french toast with bacon or fruit
- Gluten free muffin or toast with jam
- Egg with pan fried potato and fresh fruit

Lunches
- Homemade gluten free soups with toasted sandwiches and fruit
- Gluten free pasta and tomato or cheese sauce
- Salads with chicken, shrimp or meat
- Dinner leftovers
- Pancakes or waffles with fruit
- Scrambled eggs and cheese with fruit
- Corn tortillas made into wraps using cheese, vegetables, seafood or meat
- Gluten free pasta and vegetable salad with seafood or meat

Dinners
- Baked meat and vegetables
- Rice, vegetables and fried ground meat
- Lentil soup and salad
- Stir fry with meat and vegetables
- Turkey meatballs in tomato sauce with pasta
- Meatloaf with mashed potatoes and vegetables

There are many corn and rice pasta varieties to experiment with. Add your own sauce, meat and vegetables. Baked fish with sweet potato can be a nice change. Pizza using a rice or gluten free crust with your favorite sauce and toppings. Roast pork with applesauce, potato and vegetables. There are many foods to be adventurous with to create meals.

Snacks
- fresh fruit
- fresh vegetables and dip
- dried fruit
- rice cakes or corn thins with nut butter
- mixed dried fruit with nuts
- popcorn
- muffin
- celery and cheese
- cheese and crackers

Remember that food does not have to be bland and boring. With very little effort you can create variety and flavor with food. Read labels and don't be afraid to try new foods that are gluten free.

B. A. Smit

Tips for Gluten Free Sandwiches
- Always slice, if unsliced, and freeze gluten free breads. The breads often spoil easily and become dry. Freezing keeps the bread fresh tasting.
- Toasting improves flavor and texture. Toast bread straight from the freezer, before making a sandwich, or grill sandwich before eating.
- I often slice each slice to half the thickness. I lightly toast the bread before slicing, then I cut around the outer edge which also cuts the center of the slice. I toast the slices again before making the sandwich.
- Open faced sandwiches like tuna, egg or chicken toast nicely, especially with cheese. Goat, soy and lactose free cheese products can melt nicely when toasted.

Portion Sizes
To better understand portions, there are some tricks to help you. Meat is often thought of as three to six ounces per serving, or about the size of a deck of cards. Three ounces is about 85 grams. Cheese is another food that can be confusing. One ounce of cheese is the size of four dice or 28 grams. A clenched fist is used to show the size of one serving of fruit or vegetables. When you see one serving of oil or salad dressing, one teaspoon is the size.

Product Label Abbreviations
cm - centimeter
DFE - dietary folate equivalent
DHA - docosahexaenoic fatty acid (22:6n-3)
diam - diameter
EPA - eicosapentaenoic fatty acid (20:5n-3)
g - gram
kcal - kilocalories
kj - kilojoules
mcg - microgram

M.F. - milk fat
mg - milligrams
mL - milliliter
N/A - no suitable value available
NE - niacin equivalent
RAE - retinol activity equivalent
tr - trace
TM - trademark (brand name)
% - percent

The labels on products are to give you facts about the product. The ingredients are listed in the order of most to least. This means that the first ingredient listed is the most, to the last ingredient being the least in the product. This also gives you a list of exactly what is in the product to help you to decide if the product will be suitable for your diet. The nutrition guide gives you a list of the nutritional value of the product. When you are reading product labels, be aware of these words; high source of, good source of, less, more, reduced and low. These will give you an idea of the true nutritional value of the product. Some products can be misleading, for example, organic or wheat free does not mean gluten free. The organic label can sometimes be confusing, at a glance, you may think gluten free. Read labels. The nutritional value label is based on a specific amount of food per serving. This will enable you to decide if the food is nutritionally right for you, but you must realize the portion size and base your own calculations on the size of your serving. For example, if the label serving is one cup and you have two cups per serving, you must double the totals on the label. Using the nutrition facts label, you can easily compare products, nutritional values and manage your dietary needs much easier. Reading labels becomes a vital part of your shopping routine. The labels allow you to compare ingredients, nutritional value and help you to make informed decisions on your special dietary needs. Read labels.

Definition of Vegetarians

Vegan - A very strict diet, contains absolutely no foods of animal origin, including eggs and dairy.

Lacto Vegetarians - This diet includes dairy products, but no other animal originated foods, including eggs.

Ovo-Lacto Vegetarians - This diet includes eggs with dairy products, but no other foods of animal origin.

Semi-Vegetarians - This diet includes eggs, dairy and the occasional meat product.

Fruitarians - They eat no foods of animal origin, no legumes or cereals. The diet consists of only fruit, nuts and honey.

Macrobiotic - Extreme level of vegetarian. Working through ten levels of elimination, beginning with no animal product to no fruit to no vegetables, until after ten levels, will only eat brown rice, the purist level.

B. A. Smit

Vegetarian Food Guide

Daily Guide

Grain Products - 6 - 10 servings

1 serving - 1 slice bread or 1/2 bagel
1/2 cup cooked cereal
1/2 cup cooked pasta, rice or other grain

Vegetables and Fruit - 5 - 9 servings

1 serving - 1/2 cup cooked or raw vegetables
1 cup leafy vegetables (kale, spinach or collard greens)
1/2 cup fruit or vegetable juice
1/2 cup canned or fresh fruit
1/2 cup dried fruit
1 medium sized fresh fruit, apple, pear, banana

Milk Products - 4 - 5 servings

1 serving - 1 cup milk, milk substitute or yogurt
1 ounce cheese or substitute product

Beans, Nuts, Eggs, Meat Substitutes - 2 - 3 servings

1 serving - 1/2 cup cooked beans or peas
1/4 cup tofu
1/4 cup nuts
2 TBSP peanut or other nut butter
1 egg or 2 egg whites

Oils and Fats - Include about 2 - 3 TBSP in cooking, salad dressings, mayonnaise or margarine.

Measurements, Temperatures and Abbreviations

There are three ways to measure; count, volume and weight.
You may purchase by weight, and measure the same food by volume.
Bunch and dozen are examples of count, one example of count would be garlic cloves, your dish will call for two cloves of garlic, but the flavor will vary depending on the size of garlic cloves used.

Volume is the measurement of space occupied by solid or liquid. The terms teaspoon, tablespoon, fluid ounce, cup, pint, quart, gallon, milliliter and liter are all units of volume measurement. Volume measurement works best for liquids, but is useful for some solids. Spices are one example.

Weight is the mass of a solid or liquid. The terms ounce, pound, gram and kilogram are all used for weights. Scales are used to measure weights. Volume and count are the most popular measures for home kitchen use.

Converting Measures

Ounces and Pounds to Grams
Multiply ounces by 28.35 to find grams
Multiply pounds by 453.5 to find grams
Divide pounds by 2.2 to find kilograms

Grams to Ounces or Pounds
Divide grams by 28.35 to find ounces
Divide grams by 453.59 to find pounds

Fluid Ounces to Milliliters
Multiply fluid ounces by 29.58 to find milliliters

Milliliters to Fluid Ounces
Divide milliliters by 29.58 to find fluid ounces

Cups to Liters
Multiply cups by .24 to find liters

Fahrenheit to Centigrade
Subtract 32 from fahrenheit, multiply by 5, then divide by 9

Converting to Common Measure

1 pound	n/a	16 fluid ounces
1 gallon	4 quarts	128 fluid ounces
1 quart	2 pints	32 fluid ounces
1 cup	16 tablespoons	8 fluid ounces
1 tbsp	3 teaspoons	1 fluid ounce

Metric Prefixes

kilo - 1,000	hecto - 100	deka - 10
centi - 1/100	milli - 1/1,000	deci - 1/10

Abbreviations

tsp - teaspoon	pt - pint
tbsp - tablespoon	qt - quart
c - cup	ml - milliliter
oz - ounce (or fl oz)	ltr - liter
fl oz - fluid ounce	k - kilogram
lb - pound	gr - gram (or g)
in - inch	cm - centimeter
ft - foot	

Measurements

3 tsp - 1 tbsp	1/2 tsp - 2.5 ml	1 tbsp - 15 ml
4 tbsp - 1/4 cup	1 tsp - 5 ml	2 tbsp - 1 fl oz / 30 ml
8 tbsp - 1/2 cup	2 tsp - 10 ml	3 tbsp - 44 ml
1 fl oz - 2 tbsp	3 tsp - 15 ml	4 tbsp - 1/4 cup / 2 fl oz / 59 ml
4 fl oz - 1/2 cup	4 tsp - 20 ml	8 tbsp - 1/2 cup / 4 fl oz / 120 ml

3/4 cup - 6 fl oz / 178 ml	2 cup - 1 pint / 16 fl oz / 473 ml
1 cup - 8 fl oz / 237 ml	4 cup - 1 quart / 32 fl oz / .95 liters
1 1/2 cup - 354 ml	5 cup - 1185.0 ml / 1.183 liters
16 cup - 1 gallon / 128 fl oz / 3.8 liters	

Butter

2 tsp - 10 g	1 1/2 tbsp - 22.5 g	3 tbsp - 70 g
1 tbsp - 15g	2 tbsp - 1 oz / 55 g	1/4 lb - 1 stick / 110 g

Weights

U.S.	Metric	U.S.	Metric
1 oz	28 g	7 oz	199 g
2 oz	58 g	8 oz / 1/2 lb	227 g
3 oz	85 g	10 oz	284 g
4 oz / 1/4 lb	113 g	12 oz / 3/4 lb	340 g
5 oz	142 g	14 oz	397 g
6 oz	170 g	16 oz / 1 lb	457 g

B. A. Smit

Length

1/2 inch - 1.25 cm	6 inch - 15.00 cm
1 inch - 2.50 cm	8 inch - 20.00 cm
3 inch - 6.00 cm	12 inch - 30.50 cm / 1 ft
4 inch - 8.00 cm	15 inch - 38.00 cm

Degrees Fahrenheit	Degrees Centigrade	British Gas Mark
200º	93º	/
250º	120º	/
275º	140º	1
300º	150º	2
325º	165º	3
350º	175º	4
375º	190º	5
400º	200º	6
450º	230º	8

Oven Temperatures and Terms

Term	Degree / Fahrenheit	Degree / Centigrade(Celsius)
very slow	200º	93º
	225º	110º
	250º	120º
slow	275º	140º
	300º	150º
moderately slow	325º	165º
moderate	350º	175º
	375º	190º
hot	400º	200º
	425º	215º
	450º	230º
very hot	475º	245º
	500º	260º
broil	525º	275º
	550º	290º

Cooking Terms

There is a universal language for cooking and baking. Most people are familiar with most terms, but for some who are just beginning to enter the world of cooking, the words can be a little confusing. I have tried to put together a blend of both known and not so well known terms to help you. The list is first with the definitions on the next page.

Al Dente	Dough	Pour
Au Gratin	Dredge	Preheat
Au Jus	Drippings	Pressure Cook
Bake	Dust	Purée
Barbecue	Fillet	Render
Baste	Flake	Roll
Batter	Flame	Roux
Beat	Fold	Sauté
Bechamel	Forcemeat	Scald
Blanch	Fricassée	Scallop
Blend	Frost	Score
Boil	Fry	Sear
Bouquet Garni	Garnish	Shred
Braise	Glaze	Sift
Bread	Grate	Simmer
Broil	Grease	Slice
Brown	Grind	Sliver
Caramelize	Infuse	Soak
Chop	Julienne	Steam
Chutney	Knead	Steep
Clarify	Marinate	Sterilize
Coat	Mince	Stir
Coddled	Mix	Stirfry
Combine	Oven Poached	Stock
Cool	Pan Broil	Strain
Cream	Parboil	Toast
Cube	Pare	Toss
Cut In	Peel	Truss
Dice	Poach	Whip
Dot	Pot Roast	

Definitions

Al Dente - Italian for barely tender, this term is used to describe how pasta, rice or vegetables should be cooked.

Au Gratin - Food that is topped with bread crumbs and/or grated cheese then broiled or baked until cooked and the topping browned.

Au Jus - This is the French term for the natural, unthickened juices that are released from the meat during the cooking process. Au jus is then served with the meat after it is cooked.

Bake - To cook using dry heat in the oven.

Barbecue - To roast meat or vegetables on a rack, often over open coals. Usually the food is basted during the cooking process, often with a spicy, seasoned sauce.

Baste - To moisten food while it is cooking. Liquid or fat is used. This will prevent the food from drying out, plus add more flavor to the food, often meats.

Batter - Flour, liquids, and usually other ingredients, that are combined to make a liquid that is pourable, thinner than dough, then cooked. Pancakes, muffins and cakes are made from batters.

Beat - The manner in which air is incorporated into a mixture by using an electric mixer or spoon. Beating brings the mixture from the bottom to the top of the bowl quickly, thus adding air to the mixture.

Bechamel - The French term for a basic white sauce.

Blanch - This is another French word meaning white. Blanching is done by dipping fruits, nuts or vegetables first into boiling water for a few seconds to a few minutes, then into ice cold water. This removes the skin or if freezing the food, prepares the food for better flavor and texture after freezing.

Blend - To completely mix two or more ingredients.

Boil - To cook in a liquid that has reached the temperature that results in bubbles breaking the surface of the liquid.

Bouquet Garni - A combination of herbs and/or seasonings tied in a cheesecloth, which are added to soups or stews, then left to simmer. The bouquet garni is usually left to simmer about thirty minutes before the end of cooking. It is removed and discarded before serving.

Braise - To cook meat using moisture.

B. A. Smit

Bread - Foods that are coated with fine bread crumbs, often after being dipped in milk and/or beaten egg. The food is then often deep fried, sometimes baked. Fish, meats and vegetables are all examples of food that can be breaded.

Broil - To cook food directly below a heat source, often in the oven.

Brown - Food that is cooked in a small amount of fat, over medium heat to darken the food.

Caramelize - To melt sugar over a low heat. The sugar will become brown in color; the darker the color, the stronger the flavor.

Chop - To cut food into small pieces.

Chutney - A very spicy relish made with fruits and vegetables. It is often served with curry dishes. Chutney originated in India.

Clarify - Remove small particles from liquid, resulting in a clear liquid. It is used in making some soups, stocks, coffees and fat for frying.

Coat - To cover food with a fine film, often of flour, fine crumbs or nuts.

Coddled - The term used when you gently cook eggs, often in water, until just set.

Combine - To mix two or more ingredients together to form a mixture that the original ingredients are completely blended.

Cool - To allow food or a mixture to reach room temperature from a hot temperature.

Cream - Beating, either by a spoon or an electric mixer, a mixture until it is soft and smooth. Butter and sugar are often creamed together in recipes.

Cube - Cutting food into uniform squares, often one half inch in size.

Cut In - Combine solid fat with dry ingredients using a pastry blender, coarse grater or two knives.

Dice - To cut food into very small cubes, often only one quarter of an inch in size. First cut the food into thin strips, then turn the food and cut the strips into cubes.

Dot - Scatter small bits of food, often fat (butter or margarine), over the surface of a food, usually before baking.

Dough - A mixture of liquid and flour that can be handled or kneaded. Cookie dough and bread dough are two examples.

Dredge - To coat food, meat or vegetables, with flour before cooking.

Drippings - This is the fat and juices released from meat during cooking, often roasting.

Dust - Sprinkle a light coating, often flour or sugar, over food or baking pans, before the batter is added.

Fillet - A boneless piece of meat or fish. The French spelling is filet.

Flake - To break food into smaller pieces, usually with a fork.

Flame - Also flambe', it is to ignite warmed alcohol, often brandy, over food. This is done either during cooking or when the food is served.

Fold - To combine one ingredient gently into another. Cut vertically thru the mixture with a spatula, slide across the bottom of the bowl, then gently up the side which turns the mixture without loosing air volume. Often egg whites that are beaten are then folded into a batter.

Forcemeat - Meat that is finely minced and seasoned then used in stuffing recipes.

Fricassée - To cook food by stewing or braising.

Frost - To spread over the top and sides of a food, often sweets like cake, which would be frosted with icing.

Fry - To cook food in very hot fat or oils. Deep or french frying is when the food is completely covered by the oil. Pan frying is to sauté or fry in a small amount of fat or oil, often just enough to cover the bottom of the fry pan.

Garnish - Small pieces of food, usually artfully cut, that are arranged as decoration to enhance the look of plates or platters of food.

Glaze - This is a shiny coating on food that is often made with egg, fruit syrup or sugar.

Grate - To shred food, often using a sharp metal kitchen gadget called a grater. Cheese is an example of food that is grated.

Grease - Rub surface of pan or dish with shortening, oil or butter, or spray with a vegetable oil from a can, to keep food from sticking while baking.

Grind - To mash or mince food using a food grinder or grater.

Infuse - To extract flavor from foods using a boiling liquid. Tea is made by infusing the tea with boiling water, called steeping.

Julienne - To chop food, often vegetables, into matchstick sized strips.

Knead - This is when you fold, press and push dough with the palms of your hands to prepare the dough to rise before or during baking. This is often used for bread doughs.

Marinate - A mixture of oil, acid and seasonings that are used to flavor foods. The food, mainly meat, will stand covered in the liquid for one up to ten or more hours to allow the flavors to blend before cooking.

Mince - The combination of chopping and grinding of food until it is in very tiny pieces.

Mix - Stirring two or more ingredients to form a mixture.

Oven Poached - Baking one dish of food in another slightly larger dish with water in a medium temperature oven. Cheese and egg dishes are often baked in this manner to prevent curdling.

Pan Broil - To cook, uncovered, in a hot, lightly greased fry pan.

Parboil - To partially cook food, often vegetables, in boiling water.

Pare - To cut off the outer shell, skin or peel of a food.

Peel - To pull off, trim with a knife or vegetable peeler, the outer covering of food.

Poach - This is when you cook food in a liquid that is kept below the boiling point.

Pot Roast - A combination of stewing and roasting meat and vegetables in the oven.

Pour - Transferring batter or liquid that flows easily, from one bowl or pot to another. You pour the batter from the mixing bowl to the baking pan.

Preheat - To heat the oven or pan to the desired temperature before cooking the food.

Pressure Cook - Cooking foods in steam under high pressure, using a pot specifically designed for this called a pressure cooker.

Purée - Food that is pushed thru a sieve to make a pulp. A blender or food processer can often be used. Soup that is made with this method is called a purée.

Render - Using low heat, you remove the clear fat from the fatty parts of meat.

Roll - To place dough on a floured surface and with a rolling pin, roll back and forth to flatten the dough. Some cookies are made this way.

Roux - A mixture of flour and melted butter that is mixed into a paste then added to stews, soups and sauces to thicken them.

Sauté - This is using a small amount of fat in a fry pan to brown or cook slowly meat or vegetables.

Scald - To pour boiling water over food. You can drain immediately or let stand a few minutes before draining. Vegetables are an example of foods that can be cooked this way.

Scallop - A casserole usually made of alternate layers of sauce or liquid and food with crumbs on top then baked in the oven.

Score - To cut gashes part way through the surface or skin of food, often meat, before cooking. Ham and fish are often done this way.

Sear - To quickly brown the surface of a food over very high heat.

Shred - To cut food into very thin, long strips. Cabbage is often shredded.

Sift - This is done to mix and add air to dry ingredients. You use a sieve to sift the ingredients, most common is flour and baking powder, sifting at least two to three times to ensure even mixing.

Simmer - To cook food for a long period of time, often one or more hours, at a lower heat. The food is kept below the boiling point, with bubbles slowly appearing on the surface.

Slice - To cut a thin, flat piece off the food, as a slice of bread off the loaf.

Sliver - To cut or shred paper thin slices of food.

Soak - To completely immerse in liquid.

Steam - To cook foods, often vegetables, in steam that rises above boiling liquid.

Steep - As with infuse, to steep is to infuse flavor. To leave food in a liquid that is just below the boiling point, to extract flavor, as in tea.

Sterilize - Destroying micro-organisms using boiling water, dry heat or steam.

Stir - To mix ingredients using a spoon in a repetitive circular motion.

Stirfry - Cooking sliced foods quickly over high heat, often using a wok or fry pan.

Stock - This is the liquid that remains after cooking meat or vegetables in a pot of liquid to infuse flavors. Stock is often the base for soups and sauces.

Strain - To remove liquid from a food. You can strain the juice from canned fruit.

Toast - To use direct heat to brown food. Bread is often toasted.

Toss - Mainly related to salads, it is when you lightly mix ingredients together.

Truss - To tie a fowl or meat with twine so it will hold together during cooking.

Whip - Using a wire whisk, electric mixer or spoon, you incorporate air into a mixture by beating rapidly.

Cookware, Bakeware and Utensils

Before you can efficiently create in your kitchen, you should invest in the basic tools and equipment needed to prepare and cook food. A kitchen runs smoothly when you have the necessary bowls, pots and pans. This makes creating in the kitchen an enjoyable experience. I have put together a guide of the basics needed to create in your kitchen.

Cookware -

> nonstick pots with lids - 1 and 2 liter sizes
> dutch oven with lid
> roaster with lid - up to ten pound capacity
> broiler pan
> wok - stove top or electric
> nonstick fry pan - 8" or 12" in size
> egg cooker - electric takes the guess work away
> electric fry pan
> microwave oven
> toaster oven
> deep fryer
> electric grill
> electric sandwich maker

Bakeware -

> 2 - 8" square cake pans
> 2 - 8" round cake pans
> set of glass or stainless steel mixing bowls
> 2 - 8" pie plates
> cutting board - I prefer wood - ideally one for meats, one for other foods
> blender or food processor
> electric hand mixer
> coffee grinder
> 1 set of measuring cups - dry
> 1 - glass measuring cup (2 cup size) - liquid
> 1 set of measuring spoons
> rolling pin - I prefer wood
> 2 cookie sheets
> 1 pizza pan
> 1 nonstick small - 6 cup - muffin pan
> 1 nonstick mini loaf pan
> 1 nonstick tart pan
> 1 casserole dish - 2 liter - with lid
> 2 cooling racks

Utensils -

        wooden spoons - various sizes, at least three
        spatulas - various sizes, at least three
        mixing spoons
        pastry cutter
        6" stay sharp paring knife
        large chef's knife
        grater - best to get the four sided type with various grate sizes
        set of cook utensils - flipper, masher, slotted spoon
        1 set of cookie cutters
        1 vegetable peeler
        pastry brush
        meat baster

    You will also need to have at least six tea towels and dish cloths plus a set of good pot holders. There are many varieties of scrubbers available and it is good to have at least one type in your kitchen, preferably the non abrasive type for nonstick items. Remember that this is only a guide, there are many gadgets and tools available for the kitchen. Though a kitchen store will have a multitude of products at a price, many big box stores also carry the items at an affordable price. Staff will be able to help you.

    I use a coffee grinder to grind my spices. For some people, a mortar and pestle works best. It is simply a bowl, usually made of stone, with a heavy stick to pulverize or crush spices and herbs. They can vary in size, but the most common has a bowl that is about six inches across with the pestle about four to six inches in length.

B. A. Smit

Pots and Pans

The best type of pot, or saucepan, is one that distributes heat both quickly and evenly. There are numerous types of material used to make pots, with a range in price from economical to very expensive. What materials are used to make pots will determine how effective they are for cooking. Here is a description of the most common to help you decide which is best for you. To ensure a longer life for your cookware, remember that if you learn to cook on medium high heat, not using direct high heat, the life of your pots will be much longer.

Aluminum - A common metal for pots and pans. Heat is distributed evenly. These pots can react to acid elements, lemon, tomato or vinegar, which can cause the food to become poisonous. To ensure food safety, do not leave these types of food in the pot after cooking.

Calphalon - This is a safer choice than aluminum, with the same quality for heat distribution and cooking results.

Cast Iron - This type has been used for many years and though heavy in weight, it is excellent for cooking. The drawbacks are that if dropped, it can crack, or if scratched, can cause iron to leak out. You will notice a black mark on your cloth as you wipe the pan, this is the iron. This is not healthy, therefore, those with health issues, cast iron should not be used without caution.

Copper - The best for conducting heat, but can react to certain foods, which is why they are often lined with another metal, such as stainless steel. Copper pots can be very expensive, and not vital for quality, everyday cooking.

Glass - Visionware is a good example of glass cookware. Glass pots may break, but unlike aluminum, you have no reactions to acidic foods. This type is ideal for baking in the oven, like casseroles.

Stainless Steel - This is popular, but is not a good conductor of even heat.

Teflon - This is also very popular, as food does not stick to the surface. This makes them a poor choice if you are browning meat to make gravy, it won't give you the "bits" for good flavor. These pots are ideal for low fat cooking, as little fat is needed for cooking. Once these pots are scratched, they should be discarded, they are a health hazard for what can be leaked from the scratch.

Baking and Cooking Gluten Free

Gluten Free Flours
Five Cup Blend
Gluten Free Flours and Companies That Supply
Cross Contamination - In the Home
Cross Contamination - Outside the Home - Restaurants

Gluten Free Flours

The gluten in wheat flour provides the structure and texture in baked goods. Gluten free products are often dense and dry. Finding the right balance is key in gluten free baking. Smaller items bake better, muffins much more successful than a normal sized loaf. Try different mixtures for added taste and texture.

Arrowroot Flour - This flour is ground from the root of a plant which originated in the West Indies. Arrowroot flour, when blended with other flours, is used in baking. Alone, it is excellent as a thickener, from sweet to savory sauces. It is easily interchangeable with cornstarch.

Buckwheat Flour - This flour is available in dark or light varieties. It is the ground unroasted buckwheat groats that are used to make the flours. The dark flour is made from the whole groat, including the hulls. It has a strong, nutty flavor, with more nutrients and fiber than the light buckwheat flour. The light flour has a milder flavor and has fewer buckwheat hulls, if any at all. Buckwheat flour is best if combined with other flours for baking.

Corn Flour - Made from maize, corn flour has a light texture. It is often combined with cornmeal and other flours for baking, especially for corn bread.

Garfava Flour - This is a combination of garbanzo beans (chickpea) and fava beans (broad) and is rich in nutrients, like protein and fiber. It can create baked goods with moist texture and a mild, earthy flavor. This flour is best blended with other flours.

Garbanzo Flour - Ground garbanzo (chickpea) beans are used to create this flour that is high in protein and fiber. It is also best when used in combination with other flours.

Potato Flour - Often people assume that potato starch and potato flour are the same. Actually, potato flour is more coarse than the starch. It is heavy in texture and absorbs more liquid than the starch. When baking, it is best to use small amounts blended with other flours or a dry, crumbly texture could result.

Rice Flour - There are several varieties of rice flour, brown, white and sweet. When baking, sweet rice flour is a sticky flour that works well, it acts as a binder. Brown rice flour should be stored in the fridge or freezer. The oils in the bran could turn rancid. This variety of rice flour is a good source of fiber. White rice flour is a very plain tasting flour. All these flours work well when combined with other flours in baking.

Sorghum Flour - This flour is good for baking when it is combined with other flours, especially bean flours.

Soy Flour - Available as regular or defatted, soy flour is a nutty flavored flour made from soybeans. The defatted flour works better in baking because of the lower fat content, and it stores well. Regular soy flour should be stored in the fridge. The flour

B. A. Smit

should be blended with other flours because of it's strong flavor, but works well in baking. Soy flour is a nutritious flour.

Tapioca Flour - Derived from the cassava root, tapioca starch flour is excellent for combining with other flours for baking and as a thickener. It is colorless and tasteless when cooked. This makes it a good choice for thickening sweet sauces and pies.

Whole Bean Flour - This flour is often made from romano (cranberry) beans. It has the most fiber and nutrients of all the gluten free flours. Because of how dense the flour is, it is best to use small amounts blended with other flours.

Note

There are a number of companies who mill bean flours. To ease the flatulent effects (gas), some companies treat the beans before grinding. Since the companies prefer to keep the method secret, phrases such as toasted, processed, precooked and micronized are used. Most people who have celiac disease should introduce the bean flour slowly, in small amounts, to their system. Most find the treated flours easier to digest than the untreated flours. Read labels.

I have mentioned blending flours for better results when baking. You may find a recipe on your own, or you can experiment with different flours to find a blend that works for you. A basic generic blend of flours and starch for baking can be premixed, placed in an airtight container and stored in the fridge until needed. With this blend that I have created, you do not need to add xanthan gum (or guar gum) to the recipe you are making, it will be in the flour blend. When you use a recipe that calls for several types of flour and starch, add up the cups in total that are needed for the recipe, and use that amount of your flour blend. Remember that corn, potato and tapioca flours may absorb more liquid, resulting in a drier texture, so use less of these flours. For more information on the Five Cup Blend and recipes, look in the Recipe section of this book.

Five Cup Blend

3 cups of one flour or a blend* of two types flours - brown rice flour
    (or your own choice of flour)   soy flour
                                           sorghum flour
* I use 2 cups brown rice flour and 1 cup sorghum flour

1 cup white rice flour
1/2 cup buckwheat, potato or corn flour
1/4 cup any bean or nut flour
1/4 cup corn or tapioca starch
1 tbsp + 2 tsp xanthan or guar gum

Mix until well blended and store in an airtight container in the fridge. Use in place of the flour, starch and gum in recipes. Add the amounts of these ingredients called for in your recipe and then use that amount of the five cup blend in your recipe.

Gluten Free Flours and Companies That Supply

I have tried to compile as much basic information that I could find on gluten free products. I hope that you will find the information useful.

Some companies manufacture gluten free products exclusively, while others use quality control to prevent cross contamination while manufacturing both gluten free products and foods that contain gluten. Companies can also change ingredients to improve flavor or for other reasons. Between human error, cross contamination and changed ingredients, you may not be guaranteed one hundred percent gluten free. Try to get into the habit of reading labels on a regular basis to ensure that your products continue to be gluten free.

Health food stores and grocery stores both have increased their selection of gluten free products. Keep in mind the risk of cross contamination when buying in bulk or from a commercial bakery. Cereals may be wheat free, but not gluten free. Many cereals contain malted barley extract, oat syrup or liquid barley malt. Remember that products containing kamut or spelt are not gluten free. Buckwheat flour, for example, may contain wheat flour, always check the labels to ensure one hundred percent pure flours.

Here are some gluten free flour and combinations of gluten free lentil, bean, pea and chickpea flours and companies that produce them. Some or all of these may be available in your area. If you cannot find the products you want, ask your local grocer if they could carry them, most are willing to bring in new products, especially for restricted diets. Again, forgive me if the list is missing some names, new and changing products and companies are often popping up.

Bean, Pea and Lentil Flours

Product	Ingredients	Company/Companies
Beans 'R Us Bean Combo	black-eyed peas, navy beans, soybeans	Gluten Free Pantry
Black Bean Flour	black beans	Bob's Red Mill
Chickpea Flour	garbanzo bean flour	Bob's Red Mill, Glutino, Authentic Foods, Gluten Free Pantry
Four Bean Flour	cornstarch, sorghum flour, garfava flour, tapioca starch	Bette Hagman through EnerG, Authentic Foods
Garbanzo Bean Flour	same as chickpea flour	
Garfava Flour	garbanzo beans, fava beans	Authentic Foods, EnerG, Bob's Red Mill
Green Lentil Flour	green lentils	Northern Quinoa Corporation

Product	Ingredients	Company/Companies
Green Pea Flour	green peas	Northern Quinoa Corporation, Bob's Red Mill
Light Bean Flour	cornstarch, tapioca starch, garfava flour	Bette Hagman through Miss Roben's
Mung Bean Starch Flour	mung beans	Miss Roben's
Romano Bean Flour	cranberry beans, whole beans	El Peto, Glutino, Kinnikinnick
White Bean Flour	white beans	Bob's Red Mill
Yellow Pea Flour	yellow peas	Northern Quinoa Corporation

Gluten Free Flours

Product	Company/Companies
Almond Flour	Gluten Free Pantry
Amaranth Flour	Northern Quinoa Corporation, El Peto, Bob's Red Mill
Arrowroot Starch Flour	Authentic Foods, Glutino, El Peto, Miss Roben's
Buckwheat Flour	Arrowhead Mills, Bob's Red Mill, Glutino, Miss Roben's
Corn Bran	Glutino
Corn Flour	Authentic Foods, Glutino, El Peto, Bob's Red Mill
Cornmeal	Arrowhead Mills, Kinnikinnick, El Peto, Glutino
Flax Seed Flour	El Peto, Gluten Free Pantry, Glutino, Bob's Red Mill
"Gourmet Blend" (white rice flour, potato starch, tapioca starch)	Bette Hagman's through EnerG

Product	Company/Companies
Hazelnut Flour	Bob's Red Mill
Millet Flour	Arrowhead Mills, Bob's Red Mill, El Peto
Potato Flour	Bob's Red Mill, Authentic Foods, El Peto, EnerG
Potato Starch Flour	Glutino, El Peto, EnerG, Authentic Foods
Quinoa Flour	Ancient Harvest, El Peto, Bob's Red Mill, Northern Quinoa Corporation
Rice Bran	Glutino, El Peto, Bob's Red Mill, EnerG
Rice Flour (brown)	Authentic Foods, Glutino, EnerG
Rice Flour (white)	EnerG, Arrowhead Mills, El Peto, Bob's Red Mill
Rice Flour (sweet)	Gluten Free Pantry, El Peto, EnerG, Authentic Foods
Rice Polish	EnerG
Sorghum Flour	Miss Roben's, EnerG, Authentic Foods, Bob's Red Mill
Soy Flour	Eden Foods, El Peto, Bob's Red Mill, Glutino
Sweet Potato Flour	EnerG
Tapioca Starch Flour	Authentic Foods, Bob's Red Mill, EnerG, El Peto
Teff Flour	Bob's Red Mill, The Teff Company

Cross Contamination - In the Home

You must watch that gluten free products do not cross paths with foods that aren't gluten free. This is especially important for people with celiac disease. The following tips can help, particularly in households where there are several people using the kitchen.

- Always store gluten free products in containers with a label to identify it as gluten free.
- Try to have an entire separate cupboard strictly for gluten free products.
- Keep one area of the fridge for a gluten free zone.
- Buy separate containers of foods, peanut butter, jam or mayonnaise. Spreading peanut butter on toast then dipping into the jam will contaminate the jam with crumbs from the toast containing gluten.
- Best to buy squeeze bottles of mustard, relish and ketchup. Squeezing rather than dipping can help to lower the risk of cross contamination.
- Have separate cutting boards, one exclusively for gluten free products.
- Have a separate butter dish for gluten free foods.
- Use a toaster oven or buy a separate toaster for gluten free breads. The rack in a toaster oven can be wiped down before using, helping to curb cross contamination.
- Always wipe down the counter before using to ensure it is free from crumbs or flour.
- Either use separate pots for gluten free foods or thoroughly wash before using.
- Have a separate set of utensils, bowls and bakeware for gluten free baking.

Cross Contamination - Outside the Home - Restaurants

- Avoid buying in bulk if you need to use a scoop. You don't know where the scoop could have been.
- Use caution when ordering french fries. The oil could have been used for frying something containing gluten, like batter.
- Always ask if the cook can clean the grill or pans before cooking your food. Keep your food separate from meals containing gluten.
- Buffets are also a source for contamination. The spoons could have been used for a food containing gluten.
- Try ordering steam vegetables, there is less risk of butter or other contaminates.
- Baked potato, plain, can be a safe option.
- Rice may not be safe, they could use a prepackaged rice that could contain gluten.
- Always order salads plain with oil and lemon on the side, dressings could have gluten or other problem ingredients.
- It is wise to carry your own snacks.

Tips for Baking Gluten Free

- Always take care to measure the amounts exactly.
- When baking a chocolate cake, muffins or brownies, try dusting the pan with cocoa powder instead of flour.
- If possible, bake items in the oven with a pan of water beside, above or below the baking. Check to keep water in pan (usually about one inch). This will help to add moisture to your baked goodies.
- When you use glass or teflon coated nonstick pans, lower the oven temperature by twenty five degrees. (my recipe temperatures are adjusted to this change)
- If possible, add extra flavorings to your baking. Chocolate or carob chips, dried fruit (apricots, dates, cranberries, raisins) or yogurt instead of milk.
- When using gluten free commercially made bread, it is best to toast it before eating, even with sandwiches.
- To help improve the texture, always sift your dry ingredients before and after measuring.
- Heavier flours like bean, dark buckwheat or nut flours should have more leavening than the lighter flours. I try to use at least two and one half teaspoons of baking powder for every cup of flour used.
- An extra sifting of heavier flours can also improve texture.
- Always bake in small sizes. Muffins and mini loaves work better than a full sized loaf or a 9" x 13" cake pan.
- Cold ingredients tend to result in a better quality of baked goodies.
- Cornstarch, arrowroot starch and tapioca starch are all excellent as thickeners in both sweet and savory sauces, pie fillings and puddings.
- For gravies, I use a mixture of rice flour, cornstarch and seasonings with water to give the gravy flavor and a smooth texture.
- When making meatloaf, buckwheat flakes, gluten free rolled oats, rice flour, bean flour, cooked rice or mashed potatoes can all be used with egg to bind the loaf.
- Rice, corn or nut flours, carob, nuts and tapioca starch work well as substitutes in most gluten free recipes.
- Gluten free breads and cakes need a little help to hold together and have the right texture when baked. Eggs and guar or xanthan gum help to solve these problems.
- Using the right balance of ingredients is important for each recipe to work out. Avoid changing or substituting ingredients unless suggested in the recipe. Dry ingredients for dry and wet ingredients for wet can work most times, but always try the exact recipe first to know how the recipe will bake up and taste. Dry for wet and wet for dry are not recommended as it will put the balance of the recipe off.
- Breads bake better in mini loaves than in full sized loaf pans.

- Try to use teflon, nonstick pans when baking. Let the muffins, breads, cakes etc. cool in pan about five to ten minutes before removing to rack to finish cooling completely.
- When you bake with eggs, separate the yolks and the whites. Beat the egg whites until stiff and set aside. When all the ingredients have been mixed, fold in the beaten egg whites. This will help the muffins, cakes and cookies bake lighter and fluffier.
- Two well beaten egg yolks can be used instead of one egg called for in recipes.
- When baking and cooking, use different starches to thicken sweet and savory. For sweet baking, cookies, muffins, cakes etc. use cornstarch, tapioca or arrowroot starch. For sauces and gravies, rice flour or cornstarch work best.
- When you measure honey or maple syrup, measure the oil first, then the sweetener. The sweetener will pour out easier from an oiled measuring cup.
- If you are using more than one pan when baking, keep the pans at least one to two inches apart in the oven. If you are using two racks, do not place pans directly on top of each other, off center, to ensure even air flow for even baking.
- While breads, cakes, muffins etc. are baking, avoid opening the oven door until they are nearly done. This could cause the baking to "fall" (go flat).
- Baked goodies taste better served at room temperature. Slice and freeze the breads or cakes, removing only what you need at a time. The same can be done with muffins and cookies. I microwave for thirty seconds to thaw and warm the goodies.
- Some breads made mainly with rice flour, and especially millet flour, may be bitter if the flavors are not balanced. These breads are best not stored in the fridge, but in the freezer. Cinnamon, spices, sweeteners and fruit juices will counteract the bitterness. Follow recipes without changing or substituting is best until you know the result of the recipe's flavor before making changes.
- Most quick breads can be baked in muffin tins instead of mini loaf pans. If you cannot fill all the cups with batter, use a little water in the empty cups while baking, (about half of the cup).
- To prevent a crumbly texture in baked goods, adding guar or xanthan gum will improve the texture. Remember to always add the gum to the dry ingredients and mix well before adding to the wet ingredients. The gums do not mix well in liquids.
- For most recipes, you will only use one quarter of a teaspoon of the gum for every cup of flour. This is only an estimate, each recipe can be different depending on the ingredients used.
- Combining flours, including some starch, for recipes will help to improve flavor and texture.
- Before you begin baking, read the complete recipe first. Bring out all the ingredients needed. After you have added them to the recipe, put them away. This will help to ensure you have included all the ingredients needed for the recipe.

B. A. Smit

Storage Tips

- Try to keep all flours in the fridge or freezer. With no preservatives, these flours, especially bean flours, can turn rancid quickly.
- Baked goods should be wrapped as soon as possible after baking to maintain the moisture.
- Breads should be kept in the freezer to keep fresh and avoid them drying out.
- Label and date items that you store in the freezer to ensure that you always know what you have and how long they`ve been in the freezer.
- A handy tip for your salt. Placing a few grains, about one tablespoon, of raw, regular rice into your salt shaker will help the salt to remain dry and not clump up.

Baking Ingredients - Gluten Free

Baking Powder

Baking Soda

Caramel Color

Cream of Tartar

Dairy and Egg

Carrageen Gum

Guar Gum

Xanthan Gum

Agar Agar

Carboxymethyl Cellulose

Lecithin

Maltodextrin

MSG

Tartaric Acid

Salts: Kosher
          Pickling
          Rock
          Salt Substitutes
          Sea Salt
          Seasoned
          Table

Starches: Arrowroot
          Cornstarch
          Potato
          Sago
          Sassafras
          Tapioca

Yeasts: Introduction
          Autolyzed Yeast and Extract
          Leavening
          Nutritional
          Torula

Baking Powder - Baking powders consist of an acidic ingredient like cream of tartar and an alkaline such as baking soda. These are usually mixed with a starch ingredient, most often white flour. Other additives are often used. Most supermarkets carry brands that contain wheat, corn, or both, as well as alum or other unlabeled additives. This is why most people with food allergies or intolerance cannot tolerate this type of baking powder. Health food stores carry wheat-free baking powder. The following recipe is made from ingredients that are easy to find. It is important to realize that homemade baking powder doesn't contain alum, long lasting or fast rising ingredients. For this reason, store your homemade baking powder in a dry, tightly sealed glass jar with a metal lid. Keep in a cool, dry cupboard. When using in a recipe, remember that once the wet and dry ingredients are mixed, bake immediately. If left, the baking powder may lose it's rise power. Use up this recipe amount within 2 - 3 months.

RECIPE
2 tbsp baking soda
4 tbsp tapioca starch
4 tbsp cream of tartar

Sift and resift 3 - 4 times to make sure all the ingredients are well blended. Follow storing instructions from previous paragraph.

Baking Soda - This is the alkaline ingredient used in baking powder.

Caramel Color - This is created by heating carbohydrates or heating carbohydrates with food-grade acids, alkalies and sometimes salt. It is produced commercially with food-grade nutritive sweeteners which include dextrose (glucose) fructose, sucrose, invert sugar and/or starch hydrolysates. In Canada, ingredients that contain gluten, mainly malt syrup (barley) and starch hydrolysates, are not used in the caramel color. Corn can produce a longer shelf life and a better quality to the food.

Cream of Tartar - This is the acidic ingredient used in baking powder. It is also used in some baking recipes, such as cakes and frostings.

Dairy and Egg - There are many dairy substitutes on the market. Rice, nut and soy are the most common. There are several choices that I have researched and are found in the dairy chapter of this book. Eggs, organic and free range, are the best for nutritive value. When baking and you use a substitute egg product, remember that one large egg is about one quarter of a cup, so measure your alternative choice with this in mind. Various packaged egg replacements are available. When using an egg replacer, try using a bit more than is suggested on the package. For each egg that is omitted, use 2 1/2 - 3 tsp powdered egg replacer and 3 1/2 - 4 tbsp water or other liquid.

Carrageen Gum - This originates from a very dark purple cartilaginous seaweed known as Irish Moss. It is found on the coasts of Northern Europe and America. This gum is often used as a suspension agent in frozen foods.

Guar Gum - This can be used instead of xanthan gum. It is extracted from the seed of an East Indian plant. It is used as a thickener and binder to help gluten free baked goods keep their rise and also as a replacement for eggs. It is not to be used in yeast recipes because it will hinder rising. Consuming large amounts is not advised as it is very high in fiber and may act as a laxative.

Xanthan Gum - Created from the fermentation of corn sugar, it acts as a binder and improves the texture of quick breads, cakes and desserts. Commercially, it is used to thicken sauces, dressings and baked goods. It is also used in gluten free baking at home because it improves texture and structure of the foods. Like guar gum, xanthan gum should not be used in yeast recipes as it will hinder the rising. Always mix xanthan gum with the dry ingredients before mixing with wet ingredients because it will not blend into liquids. Guar gum and xanthan gum both achieve basically the same results in a recipe, but the guar gum is more economical cost wise.

There are other gums that are derived mainly from plant sources that improve texture in gluten free products. Some of the more common are :

Algin	Carob Bean Gum	Cellulose Gum	Guaiac Gum
Karaya	Locust Bean	Tragacanth Gum	

Other products used to improve flavor and texture in gluten free foods include:

Agar Agar - An extract taken from certain algae.

Carboxymethyl Cellulose - A product made from cellulose.

Lecithin - Taken mainly from soybean oil, it can also come from vegetable seeds, usually corn, egg yolk or animal sources.

Maltodextrin - A concentrated, purified, unsweetened, nutritive mixture, usually a white powder. It can sometimes be a concentrated solution created by partial hydrolysis of potato, corn or rice starch with safe enzymes and acids. Maltodextrin is used as a free-flowing agent, an anti-caking agent, processing or formulation aid stabilizer, bulking or surface-finishing agent. It is also used as a thickener.

MSG (monosodium glutamate) - Sodium salt taken from gutamic acid, this is used as a flavor enhancer.

Tartaric Acid - This is a chemical used as a pH adjuster in baking powder.

Salts

Kosher - Coarse grained sea salt. This has natural iodine and minerals which gives it more flavor than table salt. Chefs prefer to use kosher salt when cooking because of the granules size and it's pronounced flavor.

Pickling - Fine grained salt that is pure, with no additives. It is used for making pickles because it leaves no cloudy residue.

Rock - Coarse grained salt that comes in a block or chunk form. It is used in recipes for oysters and clams as well as in making ice cream in home machines.

Salt Substitutes - These substitutes have the sodium replaced with chloride compounds, such as calcium or potassium. They should not be used on a daily basis.

Sea Salt - Taken from dried sea water, this salt contains the natural minerals that are refined out of earth salt. It is easy to digest and contains no chemicals or sugars. Because it is saltier than table salt, use 2/3 tsp when 1 tsp table salt is called for in a recipe. Vegetable sea salt has dried, ground vegetables added, which add both flavor and extra nutrients. Vegetables usually used include celery, spinach, carrot and watercress.

Seasoned - This is simply table salt with various combinations of monosodium glutamate, sugar, spices, starch, onion, garlic and herbs added.

Table - Fine grained, it contains forty percent sodium chloride, with magnesium carbonate or sodium to make it free flowing. Some types add potassium or sodium iodide and are labeled iodized.

Starches

Arrowroot - Starch or flour, this comes from the root of a tropical plant, which has been dried. It is excelllent when used as a thickener. It can be substituted for cornstarch and unlike cornstarch, it is all natural. This makes it easy to tolerate for those with allergies and does not cause constipation or diarrhea.

Cornstarch - This starch is obtained from endosperm, a part of the corn kernel. It is used as a thickener in sauces, gravies and puddings. It is also used in baking. When combined with flour, it gives a finer, drier, more compact texture to cakes.

Potato - Though often thought of as the same as potato flour, the starch has a finer texture. It is the residue that remains after the potato is ground to a pulp and freed from it's fibers. It is used the same as cornstarch, but it expands more than other starches, so don't use large amounts in baking or a dry, crumbly texture may result. It is used in sauces and puddings and does not give a raw flavor when cooked for only a short time as cornstarch does. Remember that when potato starch is boiled, it will thin out when cooled. Serve sauces at once as the starch has little holding power. One and a half teaspoons of potato starch equals one tablespoon of flour. Therefore, it is good when used in gravies. This starch is not mixed with other fillers, so it is gluten free.

Sago - This is a starch taken from the trunk of the sago palm, as well as various other tropical palms. It is used mainly in the South Pacific for soups, biscuits and puddings. North Americans occasionally use it to thicken sauces and puddings. When using sago in cooking, it must be soaked for about one hour before using.

Sassafras - A tree belonging to the Laurel Family, one variety is native to North America. The leaves are dried, then ground. It is used as the prime ingredient of file', the seasoning and thickening base for gumbo.

Tapioca - This comes from the cassava root. It is gluten free and grain free. A white powdery flour, it is both lightly sweet and starchy. It works well when combined with rice flour in baking or alone to thicken puddings.

Yeasts

Nutritional yeasts are not the leavening yeasts that are used in baking. They may be eaten or used in cooking as a mock cheese flavor. Varieties are known as brewer's, engevita, primary or torula. They are very nutritious and high in vitamin B. Torula and brewer's yeasts are often used in protein drinks. The engevita and primary yeasts are used in cooking. Those with allergies and Candida should avoid all types of yeast.

Autolyzed Yeast and Extract - Derived from baker's yeast, it is created by a process which causes the yeast to be broken down by it's own enzymes. This creates compounds used as flavoring agents.

Leavening - These yeasts are used in baking to make dough rise, as in breads, pastries and pizza crusts. When added to water, yeast becomes a beige colored glob of fungi that creates fermentation. It can be found in granule form, dried into flakes or compressed into small cakes. This yeast can be used in various ways to activate the fermentation. Single use premeasured packets, or a tin that you measure out the amount needed, is sprinkled over very hot water and left for a set amount of time. You then would use it in your recipe. For the compressed form, lukewarm, never hot water, is used. The recipe you are using or the yeast package will have detailed instructions to follow.

Nutritional - This type is made from an inactive form of baker's yeast. It is grown on a sugar beet molasses mixture that is fermented, washed, pasteurized, then, at very high temperatures, dried. This yeast is available in flake, powder or pill form. Popular as a dietary supplement, it is rich in protein, fiber, minerals and vitamins.

Torula - This yeast is grown on wood sugars that give it a hickory smoked flavor. It is a by product of waste from paper mills.

Dairy and Dairy Substitutes

Lactose Intolerance

Lactose Free Products:	Lacteeze and Lactaid Products
	Beverages That Contain Gluten
	Soy Beverages - Gluten Free
	Rice Beverages - Gluten Free
	Other Gluten Free Beverages

Yogurt

Cheese: Introduction

Fresh Cheese -	Bucheron	Montrachet
	Chèvre	Mozzarella
	Feta	
Soft Cheese -	Brie	
	Camembert	
Semisoft Cheese -	Fontina	
Hard Cheese -	Cheddar	
	Gjetost	
	Marchego	
Grating Cheese -	Ricotta Salata	
	Romano	
Blue Cheese -	Blue or Bleu	
	Roquefort	

Culture: Sour Cream
Crème Fraiche
Buttermilk

Ice Cream

Lactose Intolerance

The enzyme lactase, found within our digestive system, digests lactose into simple sugars, galactose and glucose. Lactose is the natural sugar found in milk and milk products. When a person lacks enough of the enzyme lactase, he or she is considered lactose intolerant.

The symptoms include gas, nausea, bloating, cramps, diarrhea and headaches. The symptoms may occur within minutes of consumption, or can take several hours to appear.

Primary deficiency of lactase may increase with age. As much as seventy percent of the world population grow intolerant with age. Secondary deficiency is often a temporary intolerance due to gastrointestinal tract conditions. Examples are surgery, inflammatory bowel, celiac disease or infection. The damage to the intestinal tract leaves a person lacking enough of the lactase enzyme. As the tract heals, such as a gluten free diet for celiac patients, the lactase enzyme may return to normal.

When you feel stable enough to try reintroducing milk, do so gradually, with guidance from your doctor or dietitian. Try small amounts of milk with meals. Avoid drinking on an empty stomach, and don't drink more than one quarter to one half of a cup at one time to start. Heating the milk may help the body to digest the milk. When the fat content in milk is higher, like whole milk, the longer it takes for the body to digest it. This slower digestion may be easier to tolerate than the quicker digestion of two percent and especially one percent skim milk. Buttermilk and acidophilus milk work in the same way as whole milk, they take longer to digest, and may be easier to tolerate.

When choosing a yogurt, look for brands containing "live" or "active" cultures. It is strange, but those who are lactose intolerant can often tolerate yogurts. These yogurts contain lactose, but the lactase enzymes within the active cultures digest the lactose, making it easier to tolerate.

Cheese is also important for it's calcium and nutrients. Mozzarella, edam and cheddar are aged, natural cheeses containing very little lactose. During the cheese making process, the majority of lactose is removed with the whey. The remaining small amount is broken down during the aging process. Ricotta, quark and creamed cottage cheese are considered fresh cheeses and their lactose content will vary. Dry-curd cottage cheese contains less lactose than the fresh cheeses. Processed cheeses have about equal amounts of lactose as the aged cheese, but often other dairy products are included with the processed cheese, especially cheese spreads, therefore increasing the lactose content. The light varieties of cheese can be very high in lactose.

There are many products available for those who are lactose intolerant. Read labels to ensure that the product is right for your diet.

B. A. Smit

Lactose Free Products
Lacteeze and Lactaid Products
Lacteeze Milk - This is a milk product available in skim, 1% and 2%. It is a lactose reduced milk. The lactase enzyme is added to the milk with almost ninety-nine percent of the natural lactose changed to easily digested sugars. It is sweeter than regular milk, but is nutritionally equal. It can be used in baking and cooking. Lacteeze Milk can be found in the dairy section of most grocery stores. An Ultra High Temperature (UHT) variety is available in shelf-stable packages. They must be stored in the fridge after opening.

Lactaid Milk - Like Lacteeze Milk, this is another brand of lactose reduced milk. In Canada, it is available as either skim or 2%. It also has a shelf-stable 2% variety that must be stored in the fridge after opening.

Lactaid-Drops and Lacteeze Enzyme Drops - These are available at most drug stores. These drops contain enzymes which, when added to liquid dairy products, make digestion easier. About seventy five to ninety five percent of the lactose is broken down, depending on how many drops you use. The average is five to ten drops. There are also Lacteeze 4000 Tablets, which contain extra strength natural enzymes. They are taken just before meals or snacks that contain lactose. A strawberry flavored children's tablet is also available. Both of these Lacteeze Tablets are found at most drug stores.

Lactaid Tablets - These are another brand of enzymes, available in a variety of strengths, regular, extra-strength and ultra-strength caplets. They also have a chewable vanilla flavored tablet.

Lacteeze also makes swiss-styled yogurt in fruit flavors. About ninety percent of the lactose is converted into digestable glucose and galactose. With their regular styled yogurt, about forty percent of the lactose is converted. Lacteeze also makes several flavors of ice cream.

Beverages That Contain Gluten
Soy beverages are available in a number of flavors, but not all are enriched with calcium and vitamin D, and not all are gluten free. Several brands of soy milk contain barley malt or oats. Read labels carefully. Some soy brands that are not gluten free are listed here.

EdenSoy - with exception of Eden Blend
NutriSoy - both Original and Vanilla flavors
President's Choice - Fortified and Lite flavors
Vitasoy
Westbrae West Soy - Organic, Organic Original, Unsweetened, Low-Fat Plain and
                          Low-Fat Vanilla

Rice beverages are most often gluten free. However, Imagine Food's "Rice Dream", all flavors, is processed using a barley enzyme. This is discarded after processing, but the final product may contain a very small amount of the barley protein, about 0.002%. This may affect some people who are gluten intolerant.

Pacific Foods Original Naturally Almond Non-Dairy Drink, Original Non-Dairy Multigrain Beverage and both the **Original** and **Vanilla Non-Dairy Oat Beverage** are **NOT gluten free.**

Pacific Foods does produce gluten free, shelf-stable:

> 100% Lactose Free, Fat Free Milk
> 100% Lactose Free, Reduced Fat Milk
> Lactose Free, Low Fat Milk and Soy Blend
> Lactose Free, Reduced Fat Milk and Soy Blend

Soy Beverages - Gluten Free

Other companies also make gluten free soy beverages. For easy reference, here is a list of the most common companies. Note that in Canada, enriched includes calcium, vitamins A, D, B12, B2 and zinc. On the west coast, there can be different names and products than on the east coast, so this is just a guide to show you the variety that can be available. Check your favorite stores and with this knowledge, you will be able to make proper choices for your dietary needs.

EnerG Soyquik - powder

Imagine Foods - Soy Dream Non-Dairy Beverages - shelf stable packages, 8 oz., 32 oz.:

> Soy Dream Regular -   Original, Carob, Vanilla
> Soy Dream Enriched - Original, Chocolate, Vanilla
> Soy Dream Enriched - Original, Vanilla, Chocolate
> > (is also available refridgerated)

Pacific Foods Non-Dairy Soymilk Drinks - shelf stable package:

> Original - Unsweetened
> Select Soy - Vanilla, Plain
> Enriched Soy (calcium, vitamins A, D, B2)
> > Plain, Vanilla, Cocoa
> Fat Free Soy - Plain, Vanilla
> Ultra Soy - Plain, Vanilla with calcium and
> > vitamins

Soya World - "So Good Fortified" - shelf stable package:

> Original, Chocolate, Vanilla
> fresh:
> Original, Chocolate, Strawberry, Vanilla Fat Free

"Soy Nice Soyganic" - shelf stable package:

> Natural, Original, Chocolate, Vanilla
> fresh:
> Natural, Original, Chocolate, Vanilla, Mocha

In Canada, most of the Soya World products are fortified with vitamins, calcium and minerals. Check the labels for a complete list.

Sunrise Soya Beverage - Non Fortified, available in both fresh and shelf stable
packages, sweetened and unsweetened

White Wave Silk Soy Beverages - Canada - fresh: Plain, Vanilla, Chocolate
fresh: Enriched - Mocha, Chai
White Wave Silk Cultured Yogurts - enriched with calcium - a variety of fruit flavors,
Plain, Vanilla

Rice Beverages - Gluten Free
Pacific Foods Non-Dairy Rice Drinks - non-enriched, shelf stable package:
Fat Free Rice in Plain and Vanilla

Rice Choice Fortified Rice Beverages - (calcium, vitamins, zinc)
shelf stable package and fresh:
Original, Vanilla

Westbrae Rice Drinks - shelf stable package:
Plain, Vanilla

Imagine Foods does carry several non-dairy varieties, such as Rice Dream, but they
may contain trace amounts of gluten. Read labels.

Other Gluten Free Beverages
Blue Diamond "Simply Almond" Non-Dairy Beverage - shelf stable package:
Enriched (calcium and vitamins) Vanilla, Chocolate, Original

Eden Foods "Eden Brand" Brown Rice and Soy Beverage - shelf stable package

EnerG "Nutquik' Powdered Almonds

Whyte's DariFree Beverage (potato based) - shelf stable package:
Regular, Chocolate
fresh:
Regular

Tayo Foods Non-Dairy Drink (potato based) - fresh: Original, Chocolate, Vanilla

When you are lactose intolerant, replacing the nutrients found in milk, especially calcium,
is vital. Calcium is important for the development and continued strength of bones.

Milk is most nutritious when the cow, goat or sheep have been given proper feed.
Organic ensures a better quality of feed, which makes the milk or other dairy product
healthier.

Goat's milk is a good substitute for cow's milk. Soy, rice, and nut milks, and even
milk made from potato, are also excellent substitutes. Most of these substitutes are
fortified with calcium and vitamins.

Yogurt

When the balance of good and bad bacteria within the intestines and digestive tract is not even, numerous health problems can arise. For many years the balance has been stabilized with yogurt. The live "helpful" bacteria, such as Bulgaricus Bifidobacteria, Lactobacillus Acidophilus or Streptococcus Thermophilus, are cultures that are added at the starting point of pasteurized milk, which is how commercial yogurt is created.

There are a number of yogurts, especially ones with long "sell-by" dates, that are pasteurized after the yogurt is made. These yogurts contain no beneficial bacteria which makes them so unique. These yogurts contain chemicals, artificial colors and flavors, excess sugar or artificial sweeteners, preservatives, stabilizers and emulsifiers. Some of the healthier yogurts contain some of these ingredients also. Read labels.

Live yogurts help to restore balance in the body's system. Eating healthy soy, goat or lactose free yogurt as a substitute when real dairy yogurt is not tolerated, can help to restore health.

Those who are dairy intolerant lack the enzyme lactase, which is vital to digest the milk sugar lactose. The fermenting process of yogurt creates a thicker curd, which can be held longer in the digestive tract than ordinary milk. The result is that the smallest amount of lactase is given more time to digest the lactose.

The nutrients in yogurt are essential to keep the body healthy and balanced. Yogurt contains calcium and vitamin D, which is important for the absorption of calcium. Try the alternative sources like soy, goat or lactose free yogurt when you must avoid the real dairy made yogurts.

An important fact to remember is that people who are afflicted with sinus problems, eczema, asthma and rheumatoid arthritis, can have their symptoms aggravated by cow's milk and cow's milk products. Before you stop all dairy or try substitutes, consult your doctor or dietitian, you need to ensure that you do not develop a calcium deficiency or other related side effects.

B. A. Smit

Cheese
Introduction

Cheese can be made from several sources of milk; cow, sheep, goat or buffalo. The process of making cheese is simple. A starter such as rennet (an extract from the animal's stomach, used to curdle the milk) that contains an enzyme, or an acid, like lemon juice or tartaric acid, will cause the milk solids to coagulate into curds. The liquid that is left is called the whey.

There are several ways to process the curds resulting in a variety of cheese types. Fresh cheese is drained and used right away. For brick style, the curds are pressed, shaped and aged. Whey is sometimes used to make cheese.

Natural cheeses are similar to wine. They are both considered living, so the cheese will continue to develop or age until it over ripens and spoils. Pasteurized or processed cheese do not ripen, therefore their character never changes. The groups of cheese types are fresh, soft, semisoft, hard, grating and blue veined.

Fresh types include cottage cheese, mozzarella, ricotta and fresh goat cheese. These types are soft and moist, with a mild flavor. Goat and sheep cheese may taste stronger.

Most cheese made from goat's milk is eaten when it's still young and soft in texture. As the cheese matures, it becomes firmer with a characteristic zip to the flavor. Overall, goat cheese is a mild tasting cheese that can often be tolerated by people who are lactose intolerant.

Cheese from sheep's milk is also mild in flavor, becoming firmer and stronger in taste as it ages. The Italian, Spanish, Greek and French all make excellent firm, full flavored sheep's milk cheese. The cheese from sheep, like goat cheese, is lower in lactose and fat than cow's milk cheese and can often be tolerated by those who are lactose intolerant.

Soft cheese will usually have a surface mold. This cheese ripens from the outside to the center. Fully ripe, this cheese would be runny with a bold, full flavor. Camembert and Brie are good examples of this type of cheese.

To preserve the moisture and extend the life of semisoft cheese, they have an edible wax rind covering the cheese. These varieties can be sliced, but are too soft to grate. Muenster and Edam are the most popular types. Semisoft cheese does not age as long as hard cheese.

Hard cheese has a drier texture with a firm consistency. This makes slicing and grating easy. Cheddar is the most well known hard cheese.

Parmesan and Romano cheeses are both grating cheeses. The texture is hard and tends to crumble, so slicing is often not used for these varieties.

A special type of mold is injected into blue-veined cheese before it is ripened. This results in a smooth and creamy texture to a crumbly and dry texture, depending on the variety of ingredients. Roquefort, Bleu Cheese and Gorgonzola are popular blue-veined cheeses.

For many years cheese has been very basic, but today there are many new varieties emerging from sources other than cow. Read labels. Lactose intolerant does not always mean no cheese. Here is a small example of cheese made from goat, sheep or buffalo.

Fresh Cheese
Bucheron - This is made from raw goat milk. It is a creamy white, log shaped cheese that is mild but tangy in flavor.

Chèvre - Also from goat's milk, this cheese is usually shaped in a log, often flavored with herbs or peppercorns. Depending on how long it is aged, this is a mild cheese that is often served with crackers.

Feta - This cheese is most famous as a topping on Greek salads. It can be made from goat or sheep's milk. This cheese has a salty, tangy flavor that is available in blocks that can be easily crumbled over salads or into other foods.

Montrachet - A soft, creamy, raw goat's milk cheese that is shaped into a log. It is white in color.

Mozzarella - This cheese can be made from either goat or buffalo milk. It is a mild flavored, easy to melt cheese that is popular on pasta, pizza or toasted sandwiches.

Soft Cheese
Brie - This cheese can be made from goat's milk. It has a soft, edible rind covering the cheese. It is a light yellow color with a sharp, distinct flavor.

Camembert - Similar to Brie, it has a creamy texture but is less intense in flavor. It can be made from goat's milk also.

Semisoft Cheese
Fontina - A firm cheese with a smooth texture. This cheese can be made from sheep's milk. It has a medium yellow color with a strong aroma and nutty flavor.

Hard Cheese
Cheddar - The most common variety of cheese, it can be made from goat's milk. The goat milk variety is white in color, shaped like a brick, with a slight tang to the flavor.

Gjetost - This is made from goat's milk. The cheese has a light tan color and hard texture, but a mild flavor.

Marchego - This variety can be made from sheep's milk. The cheese is a pale yellow color with a full flavor.

Grating Cheese
Ricotta Salata - A cream colored cheese made from sheep's milk. Because whole milk is used to produce this cheese, the result is a strong flavored, hard cheese.

Romano - This variety can be made from either sheep or goat's milk. It is similar to Ricotta Salata, a hard texture and strong flavor.

Blue Cheese

Blue or Bleu - This cheese can be made from goat's milk. It is a white cheese with blue/green veins running through it. A very distinct flavor that many cannot adjust to.

Roquefort - Made from sheep milk, this cheese is very similar in taste and texture as Bleu Cheese. The two are interchangeable.

Culture

Culture is achieved by placing a bacterial body into the cream to begin the fermentation process. This will thicken and sour the cream. The result is sour cream, crème fraiche and buttermilk. Yogurt is created by the same method.

Sour Cream is cultured sweet cream. It contains 16 - 22% fat. Low fat sour cream is also available. This can be blended into many dishes or served on top, like in Mexican dishes. This product is not recommended for those who are lactose intolerant.

Crème Fraiche is used in many dishes, sweet and savory. It is very similar to sour cream, but less tangy in flavor. Crème fraiche blends into hot dishes easier than sour cream. It is not recommended for those who are lactose intolerant.

Buttermilk is a nonfat milk that a bacterial strain has been added. In European countries, it is often poured into a dish and sipped with a spoon as a dessert. It can also be used in baking, like pancakes and muffins. Again, it is not recommended for lactose intolerant people.

Ice Cream

This can be a wonderful treat, especially if your diet is restricted. There are a number of alternative ice cream products. Many have ingredients that may cause problems for those on a restricted diet, read the ingredient list carefully.

Some ice cream, like sherbet, have more fats, sugar and even egg to improve texture and flavor. Sorbets are typically made without any milk ingredients, but can be high in sugar.

Soy, yogurt and rice are all common substitutes for making ice cream treats. Some of these products can contain stabilizers, so again, read labels.

If possible, purchase an ice cream maker and experiment using your substitutes for the ingredients in the recipes provided by the manufacturer. I found that using my milk and sugar substitutes still resulted in a good ice cream. It can be worth the time and investment.

B. A. Smit

Eggs and Egg Substitutes

There is a difference between dietary cholesterol and blood cholesterol. Blood cholesterol is what the body manufactures from high intakes of saturated animal fat. This is what can cause coronary heart disease. The cholesterol in foods such as eggs does not get added to blood cholesterol. Unless you suffer from very high cholesterol, allergy, or you have a hereditary disease which can cause you to manufacture too much cholesterol, you should include eggs as part of a healthy, balanced diet.

Eggs are an ideal source of protein, zinc, vitamins D, E, A and B, including B12. Egg yolks are also a source of lecithin, an important element of the body's metabolic process. It can protect against heart disease, gall stones and helps to speed the conversion of body fats into energy.

The nutritional value in eggs varies little from one type to another. Hen, quail, goose or duck, nutritionally, they are all similar. Free range eggs are the best type to purchase. The hens are in a happier environment and eat healthier, making their eggs nutritionally better than factory farmed hens who have so many additives in their feed.

Eggs are available in sizes ranging from pee-wee to jumbo. Small eggs usually come from younger hens, which makes them a better quality than larger eggs. The medium size often has the best look, making them the preferred for breakfast meals. When looks are less important, like in baking and cooking, the larger egg is often used.

Eggs are also available in processed form. Bulk, whole egg (which can have added yolk to improve a certain blend), egg yolks or egg whites, are the most common varieties. When producing salad dressings, desserts, or egg nog, pasteurized eggs are now used where raw eggs were used in the past. Pasteurized egg is available in both frozen and liquid form.

Dried, powdered, or egg substitutes can be used in place of fresh eggs, especially in baked goods, see under Baking Ingredients for more information. Egg substitutes may contain no real egg, or can be made with dairy or vegetable products and egg whites. Read labels to find the right substitute if eggs are not recommended for your diet.

Fish and Shellfish

Introduction

Fish:	Anchovy	Flounder	Snapper
	Bass	Halibut	Sole
	Catfish	Monkfish	Trout
	Cod	Perch	Tuna
	Dolphin Fish	Salmon	
	(Mahi Mahi)		

Shellfish:	Abalone	Crab	Oysters
	Calamari	Lobster	Scallops
	Clams	Mussels	Shrimp
			Snails

Introduction

This category of food is essential for a balanced diet. Fish and seafood are a healthy source of important nutrients and omega 3. There are many varieties of fish available in many forms. Fresh is probably the best for flavor, but fish can be found canned, frozen, salted and smoked. Due to the increase in popularity, fresh, wild fish are becoming harder to find. What was once plentiful and economical, has waned for numerous factors. Demand has lessened availability, pollution of fishing beds and restrictions in areas used for commercial fishing, all contribute to an increase in price, decrease in availability and the advances in fish farming. Fresh fish is available in a number of forms.

Whole Fish is untouched after being caught. The entire fish from head to tail is completely intact.

Drawn Fish is a whole fish that has the guts (insides) removed.

Dressed or Pan Dressed Fish are fish that have scales, fins and guts removed. In some types of fish, the head and tail are also removed.

Fillets are boneless pieces of fish taken from either side of the backbone. You can cook these with or without the skin.

Steaks are best from large, round fish. The fish is sliced in cross sections, including a section of the backbone in each steak. Most often, the skin is left intact. The most popular fish steaks are from salmon, halibut, tuna or swordfish.

With all types of fish there are several ways to ensure freshness and quality before purchasing. Check the market or deli counter to see how the fishmonger (seller) operates. He or she should correctly handle the ice, fish and most importantly, the displays with care and expertise. He or she should answer questions with an informative ease. They should know the origin of the fish, whether it is lean or oily, firm textured or delicate. They will also be able to explain the best method of cooking; moist heat, frying or grilling.

To ensure freshness, check the fish for odor. If it has a strong, pungent odor, it is not fresh. Fresh fish leave a crisp, subtle sea air aroma. The eyes should be clear, not cloudy, and rounded. Older fish have the eyes sunk into the head and are drier. The skin should be moist, the flesh firm and slightly elastic, leaving no dent when pushed gently with your finger. The fins and tail will be full, moist and flexible. The scales will be firmly attached to the body. The body should be intact with no gashes or tears. Regardless of passing all these points, if the fish smells foul, do not use it.

Ideally, you should purchase fresh fish and seafood the day you plan to use it. Keep it stored in the fridge wrapped and in a container or cover completely with ice in a container that allows the water to drain from the fish. Frozen fish are best used within three to four months of freezing. When you purchase fish to freeze, cut into serving portions, wrap in tin foil and freeze. Whole fish should be put into a container with water and frozen. Thaw the ice under running water before cooking the fish.

B. A. Smit

Fish

There are so many types of fish worldwide. With new technologies with storage and shipping, it is possible to sample fish from almost every corner of the world. I have included only a few of the most common fish here.

Anchovy - These small fish are the important ingredient added to caesar salad and pizza. The flesh is firm but fatty. Anchovies are most commonly found as fillets that are packed in oil, sometimes with capers. Fresh, smoked and anchovy paste are also available. Anchovies are often added to seafood dishes, sauces, salads, dressings and dips.

Bass - This fish can be found in both the Pacific and Atlantic Oceans. They are small, usually under three pounds, with a firm texture and only a small amount of fat. There are numerous varieties, including Pike, Sea and Striped Bass, as well as Red Snapper. Bass can be cooked in all ways, baked, steamed, grilled or poached. Some varieties are found in fresh waters but are not as well textured or flavored as the sea bass.

Catfish - These are not as commonly used as cod or halibut. They are available as farmed with strict guidelines when marketed. The fish is light in flavor, firm in texture and must be skinned before cooking. Catfish can be cooked by any method. The most common method is to dip the fish in cornmeal and pan fry.

Cod - This fish is often associated with fish and chips. The flesh is firm, white in color and has a mellow flavor. The cod family has a number of species, each with their own markings. Among the most common cod species are Haddock, Atlantic Cod, Cusk, Whiting and Pollock. Boneless fillets are battered and deep fried. Cod can also be poached, baked or pan fried. It is also good in seafood chowders. Salted cod is used in a variety of specific dishes.

Dolphin Fish - Also known as Mahi Mahi, it is becoming popular worldwide. It is harvested in both the Pacific and the Atlantic Oceans. This fish should not be confused with the mammal dolphin. It is a round fish with a light flavor and firm texture. The skin should be removed before cooking. This fish can be cooked in a variety of methods. Grilling, poaching or pan frying are the most common methods.

Flounder - This fish is often sold in North America as Sole. Gray Sole, Lemon Sole and White Sole are all Flounders. It is a flat, round shaped fish that is distinct because both eyes are on the same side of the head. Dab, Sand Dab and Roughback are known as Plaice, a species of Flounder. This fish is light in texture and flakes easily. It is best to poach in a shallow amount of liquid or steam. Flounder is a common fish that is available whole, skinned or cut into fillets.

Halibut - Best known for it's use in fish and chips, the fish has a firm texture, pale white flesh and a mild flavor. Most halibut can be over two hundred pounds. This makes cutting them into steaks or fillets so common. Halibut can be battered and deep fried, pan fried, steamed or added to chowder. It is a versatile and economical fish that can be served as a casual or fine dining meal.

Monkfish - This fish is known for it's tail. It is a fish with few bones that is used in many soup and chowder dishes. The dense texture and subtly sweet flavor makes it ideal for any cooking method. Monkfish is also known as Lawyer, Goose, Belly or Angler fish.

Perch - Found in fresh waters, lakes and reservoirs, it has a light, lean texture and mild flavor. Small perch are usually kept whole and pan fried or deep fried. Larger perch are cut into fillets and steamed, fried or baked.

Salmon - This is a very common fish and is readily available smoked, cured, frozen, canned and fresh. The flesh is slightly oily, but firm with a light pink to a deep orange/pink color. There is a variety of species that are available.The most common are the Sockeye, Coho, Pacific, Pink, Atlantic and King. Though some are still available wild, farmed salmon is becoming more common. Salmon is available as steaks, fillets or whole. They can be cooked by many methods, often poached, baked or grilled. Canned salmon is often used in salads, sandwiches and casseroles.

Snapper - The true Red Snapper from the Gulf of Mexico and the Atlantic Ocean is becoming harder to find. Snapper is available by a number of species. They have firm but finely textured flesh. Other common varieties include Mutton, Gray, Pink, Silk and Yellowtail. This fish can also be cooked by many methods, the most common being baked or pan fried.

Sole - There are many varieties of flounder called Sole, but the truest is known as Dover Sole. It is a flat, oval shaped fish with a firm texture and a light flavor. Dover Sole is used in hundreds of recipes because of it's reputation as a superior flavored fish. It is available fresh or frozen and can be cooked in so many ways, which keeps it an economical and versatile fish to buy.

Trout - The trout is often found in lakes and rivers. The flesh and texture are both light and the flesh is a peach tone. Steelhead and Rainbow are popular species. Trout are usually kept whole and either pan fried or broiled. For restaurants, trout is raised in commercial hatcheries.

Tuna - These are a member of the Mackerel Family. The flesh is slightly oily but firm and has a noticeably darker shade of flesh along it's back. The flesh has a deep coral-beige tone that deepens in color in some fish. The most common source of tuna is canned, either packed in oil or water. There are a number of species of tuna. Albacore, Skipjack and White are the best known. Fresh tuna is usually cut into steaks and grilled or baked.

B. A. Smit

Shellfish

There are many varieties of shellfish. They are divided into four basic categories.

Univalves are single shelled, like abalone and sea urchins.

Bivalves are shellfish with two shells attached by a hinge. Oysters, scallops and mussels are examples of this group.

Crustaceans have jointed exterior skeletons or shells. Shrimp, crayfish and lobster are the most common in this category.

Cephalopods are squid and octopus. These shellfish have tentacles attached to their heads.

Care must be taken when purchasing shellfish. Live shellfish like crabs and lobster should be active and move about when touched. Other shellfish like clams and oysters will have tightly closed shells. The shell will begin to open as the shellfish ages. When tapped, the shell should snap shut, if it doesn't, discard it immediately. Lobster and crabs, if purchased live, should be cooked the same day. Putting them in fresh water will kill them. Keep wrapped in the container used when purchased and store in the fridge until ready to cook.

There are so many varieties of shellfish that I have chosen a few of the most common to detail in this book. If you have any questions about shellfish, ask the person you are buying from, they should be most helpful.

Abalone - These have one shell plus a suction cup that attaches to rocks. It has a firm hold onto the rock, so when harvested, it must be pried from the rock. The majority of abalone is available within the waters of California. The state laws do not allow live abalone to be exported, so the majority of the world's abalone is either canned or frozen. The meat is cut into steaks, often pounded flat, then grilled or fried. Abalone can become very tough if it is over cooked.

Calamari - Better known as squid, calamari is very popular in Mediterranean and Asian cooking. Popularity is growing for these once ignored seafood. Calamari, now the common name for squid, is usually cut into rings, battered or breaded, then fried. It is served with a tangy sauce that is either the Greek sauce tzatziki, or a similar one. Once only readily available in restaurants it is now found in grocery stores fresh or frozen. Calamari can also be stuffed and baked whole. There are a number of varieties and sizes to choose from, but calamari rings are the most common type eaten today.

Clams - Readily available fresh, shucked (removed from the shell) then frozen, or canned, clams are very well liked by many people. Clams are used in chowders, appetizers and as a part of the main course. They are versatile and can be eaten raw or cooked. When purchasing fresh clams, make sure the shell snaps closed when touched and it has a slightly sweet aroma. Clams can be marketed by the name of the bed they were harvested from. Bed is the term used for the area of shoreline where the clams are raised. Hard shell clams are small in size. Littlenecks are usually eaten raw on the half shell. Cherrystones are slightly larger, but again, often eaten raw. If the clams are more than three inches in size, they are referred to as quahog. This type is used mainly in chowders or fritters. Soft shell clams are steamed or battered and fried as fritters.

Crab - There are many species, some more common than others. Dungeness, King, Blue and Spider are the most popular. Blue Crab is available on the Atlantic Coast. In the spring when the crab molts it is known as soft shell crab. This crab is either sautéed or pan fried. Crab can be purchased fresh, live, frozen or canned. The hard shell crab is often steamed or boiled. The Pacific Ocean is host to the Dungeness Crab. The Spider and King Crab are mainly used for their legs. Fishermen will remove the legs and return the crab to the ocean where it will grow new legs. Stone crab is harvested from the Florida coast of the United States north to Nova Scotia in Canada. This crab meat is excellent for crab cakes. Crab meat, whether fresh, frozen or canned, is good when used in many seafood dishes. Crab legs are often steamed then served. Other methods of cooking include pan frying or sautéeing.

Lobster - Considered a delicacy, lobster is often included in fine dining meals. There are a number of varieties, but in all varieties, the tail is most commonly the part eaten. Lobster is included in seafood chowders, pan fried, added to soups or a part of seafood cakes. New England in the United States and Nova Scotia in Canada are both well known for their lobster. It is sold live, fresh and the tails are available frozen. The entire lobster inside the shell is edible, though lobster with visible egg sacs are not allowed to be harvested. Lobster tails are often boiled or steamed just before serving.

Mussels - These are becoming more popular. Whether you purchase wild or farm raised, if fresh, ensure that the shell shuts when touched. Remove the beard (tufts of fiber like strands) from the shell and steam. Wine, lemon and garlic are often added to the liquid for steaming. Mussels are also available frozen or canned.

Oysters - Very popular and available worldwide, oysters are sold and cooked in a similar manner as clams. They are available fresh, canned, smoked or frozen. Like clams, they are often sold by the name of the bed they were harvested from. Oysters are often eaten raw on the half shell. With any seafood, fresh is best, but buy from a reputable source and eat as soon as possible to reduce the risk of poisoning by tainted shellfish.

Scallops - This shellfish is also very popular and available worldwide. There are three main species, Bay, Calico and Sea Scallops. The two species, Bay and Calico, are smaller than Sea Scallops, usually under two inches. Bay Scallops are divided into two categories, northern and southern. They are thought of as superior in flavor and quality than the Calico species. Sea Scallops can grow to about three inches in size. Most scallops are available shucked. Farm raised scallops can be found in the shell. Scallops can be found fresh, frozen or canned. They are a tasty addition to many seafood dishes. Scallops are usually pan fried.

B. A. Smit

Shrimp - These are a versatile and affordable seafood. They are the most readily available seafood, whether fresh, canned or frozen. Fishermen often remove the head and flash freeze the shrimp on board their boats while still at sea. This maintains the flavor and quality of the shrimp. There are both salt water and fresh water shrimp, varying in size, depending on the species. Shrimp are extremely delicate and will perish quickly, so only buy fresh what you need, when you need, or use frozen or canned. Shrimp can be battered and fried, sautéed, steamed or baked. Shrimp can be purchased by the pound. A certain number of shrimp per pound is known as the count. Fresh shrimp must be peeled and deveined before eating (there is a vein that runs down the back that is removed). You can purchase shrimp ready to eat, which is more convenient for most people. Shrimp can be colossal, jumbo, regular or small in size. The count can vary depending on the size. Colossal have less than fifteen per pound and the small can yield up to fifty or sixty per pound. The smaller shrimp are best in salads, appetizers and seafood dishes and sauces. The larger size is best for grilling and sautéeing. Prawns are the same as shrimp both in purchasing and cooking. They are medium in size compared to shrimp.

Snails - These are not your household garden variety. These shellfish are usually imported fresh from France. They are known as Escargot. There are about thirty to thirty three snails per pound. As an appetizer, they are often served in their shell with garlic butter. Although Escargot are also available canned and frozen, fresh is far superior in quality, flavor and texture.

Flavorings Other Than Herbs and Spices

When you have a restricted diet, it doesn't mean that your food must be bland. Experiment with flavorings to enhance the flavor of your food. Whether it is main dishes, desserts or baking, when extra flavor is added it will improve your food's flavor.

The most popular flavorings include vanilla, maple, peppermint, almond and lemon. Extracts made from alcohol and pure oils are true essences. Artificial extracts are usually made with synthetic sources, not true flavor. This makes true essences stronger in flavor thus requiring less in the recipe. Maximum flavor is obtained when true essences are added after cooking. For sauces, custard sauces etc. this is fine, but impossible in baked dishes. Fats retain the flavors well, so adding directly to the fat before baking, as in cakes, works well.

MSG - Monosodium glutamate appears under many names. This is a chemical that enhances the flavor of foods. It does not have a flavor of it's own. Used mainly on meat, fish and vegetables, only a small amount is needed, about one half of a teaspoon for a recipe to serve six people.

Wine - Cooking with wine can add flavor to many dishes, use about two tablespoons of wine for each cup of liquid. Wine is good in soups, sauces, stews, gravies, as well as for fowl, beef and lamb. Bring liquid to a boil to evaporate the alcohol. To flame the alcohol improves the flavor of the food. When alcohol is not an option, fruit juice can be a good substitute. Apple or berry are the most common and though they do not flame, the juice adds flavor.

Liquor - The dark rum is often used for Christmas pudding, baked bananas and apples. Light rum is used for pineapple and fruits, brandy for crepes, meat and cherries jubilee. Kirsh adds flavor to strawberries or mixed fruits.

To warm liqueur, use a small stainless steel warmer or a metal ladle. Just before serving, pour a small amount of liqueur over and around the food. Light about one teaspoon of liqueur in a ladle and use the ladle to light the liqueur on the food.

Marinate fruit in wine and serve chilled. This makes a good dessert in the summer.

Vinegar

Vinegar is a condiment used to flavor food, or an ingredient in brine used for pickling. If you are sensitive to fermented products, it is best to avoid all vinegars. If unopened, the vinegar will last indefinately, but once opened, it must be kept in a cool place and used within four to six months, this applies to all types of vinegar.

Vinegars are created from various ingredients. Distilled vinegars are gluten free. The process of distilling removes the gluten. Malt vinegar is made from barley and is fermented, not distilled, therefore it is not gluten free. Other ingredients used to make vinegars include grapes - balsamic vinegar, corn - white vinegar, rice - rice vinegar, apples - cider vinegar and red wine - wine vinegar. Read labels to ensure the vinegar is compatable to your diet.

When making your own salad dressing, try to avoid using regular distilled white vinegar. This can be a bland addition, try lemon or lime juice instead. This will enhance your salad dressing flavor. Use less juice than the amount of vinegar called for in the recipe and taste. Adjust the amount of juice used based on your taste.

Recipe - Flavored Vinegar
1 cup fresh berries, raspberry, blackberry, your choice
2 cups rice or cider vinegar

Place ingredients into a stainless steel or glass pot, aluminum would be reactive with the vinegar. Bring to a boil over medium heat. Remove from heat and let cool. Store in a cool place for up to four days, two at the least. Strain into a bowl, pressing the berries to release the juices. Discard the fruit, pour into a sterilized glass jar with a tight fitting lid. Store in a cool place and use within four months.

Balsamic - This vinegar can be strong in flavor. It is made using concentrated white grape juice. The vinegar is boiled down then aged in barrels for up to ten years, occasionally longer. This is what makes true balsamic vinegar so expensive. There are several less expensive varieties but the quality is not the same as the original. Balsamic vinegar can be simmered down to use in main dishes or can be used in marinades or salad dressings. The strong flavor is not recommended to be used alone on salads. This vinegar is best when blended with other ingredients.

Cider - This is made from apple cider or apple wine and is less acidic than malt vinegars. It is used mainly to flavor salad dressings.

Flavored - These vinegars usually have fruits, herbs or spices infused into them. They can be acidic, but are a nice addition to salad dressings. Raspberry, thyme and rosemary are examples of flavored vinegars.

Malt - This is made from fermenting malted barley and yeast. It often has acetabactor cultures and caramel coloring added. Distilled malt vinegar is a clear distillation of malt vinegar without colorings added. This is not recommended for gluten free diets.

B. A. Smit

Rice - This is the best choice for gluten free diets. Made from rice or rice wine, it is less acidic than other vinegars and is a light addition to foods. It is often used in cooking, as an accompaniment with sushi dishes and in salad dressings. The Asian style of cooking use it as a seasoning. Rice vinegar is available in various colors and strengths. You may want to try this vinegar in salad dressings or in sweet and sour sauces.

Synthetic - This vinegar is also known as NBC, nonbrewed condiment. It is not fermented and not a true vinegar. It has artificial flavorings, color, sugar and salt. Synthetic vinegar is a cheap product from a chemical beginning. It is best to avoid this type of vinegar.

Wine - This vinegar begins with red, rose or white wine, and cultures are then added to make the vinegar complete. These vinegars, with balsamic the exception, can have additional flavors added. You can experiment with garlic, chilies, herbs and fruit to infuse (mix into and let flavors develop) with the wine vinegar to add more flavor to your food.

Fruits

Introduction

Apples:

Crabapples	Jonathon	Rome Beauty
Golden Delicious	McIntosh	
Granny Smith	Red Delicious	

Pears:

Bartlett	Comice	Sekel
Bosc	D'anjou	William

Rhubarb

Grapes:

Black	Concord	Thompson
Black Corinth	Red Emperor	

Berries:

Acai'	Cloudberries	Mulberries
Blackberries	Cranberries	Raspberries
Blackcurrants	Elderberries	Red Currants
Blueberries	Goji	Strawberries
Boysenberries	Gooseberries	

Freezing Berries

Citrus Fruit:

Citron	Kumquats	Oranges
Clementines and Satsumas	Lemons	Persimmon
Grapefruit	Limes	Ugli

Dried Fruit:

Dates	Prunes
Figs	Raisins

Stone Fruit:

Apricots	Nectarines and Peaches
Cherries	Plums

Tropical Fruit:

Bananas and Plantain	Mangos	Quince
Guavas	Papaya	Tamarind
Kiwi	Pineapple	

Melons:

Cantaloupe	Gallia	Persian
Casaba	Honeydew	Watermelon
Crenshaw	Muskmelon	

B. A. Smit

Introduction

Fruit is a very important part of nutrition and today there are so many fruit varieties available from all over the world. I am including some of the basic, well known fruit as well as some that you may not be familiar with.

Fruit is divided into several groups, including berry, citrus, dried, stone and tropical. With this information you will be able to try new fruits and expand your tastes from basic to fascinating.

Apples

Probably the most common and versatile fruit, there are hundreds of varieties worldwide, with as many uses. Some are eaten fresh, raw, others are best in pies, and certain varieties simmer down well and are excellent for applesauce. A mixture of varieties are used in apple cider to give a balanced fresh flavor. Apples can be stored for several months in a cold, dry place. Dried apples, frozen, canned and fresh give versatility to availability.

In general, apples are a good source of vitamin C, a fair source of fiber, and are good for circulation and the heart. Apples are also beneficial for diarrhea and constipation, and you are encouraged to try and eat at least two a day. They are high in a soluble fiber called pectin and helps the body to eliminate cholesterol and protects the body from environmental pollutants. Pectin is also important to the body because it merges with heavy metals such as mercury and lead, and aids the body to eliminate them.

Research has concluded that eating two apples a day may lower your cholesterol level by up to ten percent. Malic and tartaric acids help digestion, especially with rich fatty foods, and both are found in apples. The amount of vitamin C in apples helps boost the immune defences within the body. The sugars in apples are mostly fructose, which is simple sugar that breaks down slowly, helping to keep the blood sugar levels even. Apples are an excellent food for people with gout, rheumatism, arthritis, colitis and diarrhea. To gain the most nutrients, apples are best eaten raw or gently simmered.

When apples are cut open, the exposed flesh may turn brown. If you are preparing a quantity of apples, soak the cut pieces in water that about one tablespoon of lemon juice has been added. This will help to slow the browning, which does not change the flavor of the apples.

When freezing apples, just peel, core and slice. Place into freezer bags and label, date and place in the freezer.

There are so many varieties that were often found only in certain regions of the world, but now can be found at your local market. Often brochures or information sheets can be available near the apple section. With all of their nutritional value, apples should be included in your diet.

Crabapples - These are available in the fall. The most common use is for types of canning, sauces, relishes and jams. They are small, red in color, with a tinge of white or yellow in the flesh. Crabapples are tart in flavor.

Golden Delicious - These apples are most abundant from May to September. Their crisp, sweet, juicy flesh makes them refreshingly popular. The skin is speckled yellow to green toned. These apples can be used in a variety of dishes and don't brown as quickly as most varieties of apples.

Granny Smith - This variety is a baker's favorite for pies. With a fine textured, crisp flesh, these apples have a subtle tart flavor. The skin is green and the flesh white, which makes them a colorful addition to salads. The best time to purchase Granny Smith apples is between April and July.

B. A. Smit

Jonathon - These apples have yellow speckles on a bright red skin. The flavor has a tartness which makes them good in sauces and pies. They also freeze well. Jonathon apples are available September to January.

McIntosh - This is a well known name in apples. Similar to Jonathon, these apples are red in color, streaked with yellow to green tones. The flesh is a clean, bright white color. Most commonly eaten fresh, they can be used in baking and freeze well. These apples are available from September to June.

Red Delicious - These apples have yellow speckled, bold red skin. The flesh is a yellow to white blend with a firm texture and compared to most apples, are quite sweet. Available between September and June, Red Delicious apples are versatile and can be used in many ways.

Rome Beauty - This variety has a very bright red skin, firm flesh, sweet flavor, with a little tartness. From October to June, these apples are available and at their best. Rome Beauty apples can be eaten fresh, baked or made into sauce.

Pears

Pears are very popular and are often prepared in the same ways as apples. Like apples, they will turn brown when cut so use the same method of placing in water and lemon juice when slicing a quantity of pears. The most common varieties are Bosc, Bartlett, Comice, D'anjou and Sekel. When ripe, pears can be fragile and bruise easily. This is why they are shipped before they are ripe. Given a day or two at room temperature, they will ripen. To slow the ripening, place the pears in the fridge.

This fruit is good for constipation, lowering cholesterol, renewing energy and aiding in restoring health. Pears are most enjoyable when eaten raw or dried. They are a nice dessert fruit. The nutritional aspect of pears is often ignored. Pears are an ample source of the soluble fiber, pectin. This is vital for the regulation of bowel functions and helps the body to eliminate cholesterol. Pears contain vitamin C and A, with a small amount of vitamin E and potassium. Dried pears contain vitamins A and C, iron, protein, potassium and fiber. Pears are easily digested so they are preferred by those regaining their health.

Bartlett - These pears have a green skin, with some varieties a red skin. The flesh is either white or cream. The skin will lighten to yellow when ripened. The fall is the best season for this variety. They can be eaten fresh, poached, or made into many kinds of desserts. Bartlett pears are typically oval shaped, which makes them a favorite choice for some dessert dishes.

Bosc - The shape of these pears is slightly different than the Bartlett. They have a longer neck than the Bartlett variety, with a dark maroon skin. This color changes to brown as it ripens. These pears are best in the late fall, and can be eaten and cooked the same as other varieties of pears.

Comice - Compared to the Bosc, this pear has a rounder shape with a shorter neck. The skin is a yellow to green color, with some pears having a reddish tint. Comice pears are very juicy and sweet, therefore they are popular for desserts and salads. This pear is available from late summer to early spring.

D'anjou - These pears are very similar to the Bartlett pear. They have the same green skin that will turn yellow as the pear ripens. D'anjou pears are known to have brown scarring on the skin. The best time to purchase these pears is in the fall. Again, this variety can be used the same as other pear varieties.

Sekel - The Sekel pear has a red tint to it's green skin. These pears are crisp, sweet and small in size. This variety is often eaten fresh and are at their peak season in the fall.

William - This is a less known variety of pear. They have a long neck, yellow skin and a distinct aroma. William pears are most often used in jams.

Rhubarb

Originating in China and Tibet, it now grows worldwide. Centuries ago the plant was used for medicinal purposes and the Greek grew medicinal varieties, using the roots not the stalk. It was used mainly to treat constipation.

Rhubarb is really a vegetable, but is often referred to as a fruit. The plant grows in long stalks with big curly leaves. The leaves contain high amounts of oxalic acid, which is a toxic compound. Therefore, the leaves must not be eaten.

Rhubarb has no sodium, but is a good source of maganese and potassium. It also has vitamins C and A. With a large amount of calcium, rhubarb stalks also contain some oxalic acid, which interrupts the calcium absorption.

The stalks are a deep red and green tinted color, but can be very sour. Rhubarb stalks are traditionally cut into small pieces, cooked and sweetened before eating. This vegetable/fruit is used in desserts, pies and jams.

Grapes

Grapes are considered berries, but because there are so many varieties and uses, they are put into their own category. Grown in clusters on vines, grapes can be eaten fresh, as in table grapes, dried into raisins or made into wine, jam or jelly. Grapes are available year round, with some varieties being seedless.

Grapes often are best eaten raw. They help in anemia, fatigue, weight loss, cancer prevention and healing. The Okanagan in British Columbia, Canada, and the Napa Valley in California, United States, are prime examples of how cultivated the grape vine has become. They have been used for centuries for wine making. Grapes are also known for grape jelly. This small, tasty fruit is strengthening, cleansing and regenerative. Grapes are also helpful for gout, rheumatism and arthritis. There are large amounts of aromatic compounds in grapes. The most vital of these are astringent tannis, linalol, geraniol, nerol, flavones and red anthocuanins. Combined, all these help prevent cancer.

Grapes can be sprayed with insecticides during growth, so wash the grapes well before eating. Naturopaths believe grapes should be eaten alone, not with a meal, since they can rapidly ferment in the stomach.

Some of the more common varieties are listed here.

Black - These grapes have dark purple/black skin and can often be found seedless. They are good eaten fresh or on cheese platters.

Black Corinth - These grapes are small in size with a purple/red colored skin. Like the black variety, these are often eaten fresh.

Concord - A well known grape, they can have white, deep purple or red colored thick skin. This skin peels easily from the flesh. These grapes are popular for jellies, preserves, juices and syrups.

Red Emperor - This variety has a red tinged, thin skin that is secured firmly to the flesh. There are seeds in this grape. It is considered a table grape, best eaten fresh. Through importing, this variety is available year round.

Thompson - These are probably the most common and well known of all grape varieties. They are popular for their flavor and the fact that they are seedless. With a thick green skin and a juicy flesh, these grapes are most often eaten fresh or dried into raisins.

Berries

Berries can be found year round. Spring and summer provide fresh berries and frozen berries are available year round. Berries can bruise easily and rot quickly, so check them carefully before buying. It is always best to wash the berries just before using. Place berries in a strainer and rinse with cold water. Drain well and store in the fridge. Use them within three to four days.

Acai' - Pronounced "aw saw ee", this is a small berry, similar in size and color as the blueberry. It grows on a palm tree, primarily in the South American Amazon. They are becoming very popular because this tiny berry is loaded with many nutrients. Acai' berries contain antioxidants, protein, fats, vitamins, including B vitamins, plus minerals, calcium, potassium and iron to name just a few. These berries also contain fiber and are available as dried, fresh or most commonly, as juice. The pure juice may be very expensive, but you will still get many nutrients from fruit juices that contain acai' juice. This berry is excellent for overall good health.

Blackberries - These small, dark berries grow wild throughout British Columbia, Canada, as well as other select areas worldwide. Nicknamed brambles in British lore, they are named in the Bible and the ancient Greek used them as a remedy for gout. Blackberries are gaining popularity, even being cultivated, especially to tame the sharp thorns on the branches. They are high in vitamin E, which is useful for the treatment and prevention of circulatory and heart conditions. Also, blackberries are rich in vitamin C, making them a strong antioxidant, and a protectant against infection, degenerative disorders and cancer. Blackberries also contain potassium and the soluble fiber, pectin. The blackberry leaves contain tannin, useful in a mouthwash to combat gingivitis and infection. It is also used as a tea to help sore throats and diarrhea. Blackberries blend well with apples and other berries, making them both versatile and popular for dessert dishes.

Blackcurrants - This tiny fruit encourages the immune system to be stronger, fighting the flu, sore throats and colds. It is beneficial in cancer prevention, stress and anxiety, fluid retention and high blood pressure. Blackcurrants also help diarrhea. Most often a juice or jelly, blackcurrants are nutritionally a wise choice. High in vitamin C, this berry is an antioxidant protecting against heart disease, infections and circulatory problems. They are also a good source of potassium and contain almost no sodium. Within their dark skin is a pigment called anthocyanosides, which has both anti inflammatory action and bactericidal qualities, excellent against sore throats. Sipping hot blackcurrant juice is the remedy.

Blueberries - This tiny berry is actually purple with a blue hue. It grows on shrubs native to both North America and Europe. Blueberries are available wild or farmed, ready to pick late in the summer. Other names for this fruit include bilberries, whortle berries, huckleberries and whinberries. Blueberries are helpful with diarrhea, food poisoning and as an antibacterial. They can also be helpful for urinary infections and varicose veins. Blueberries can be eaten raw from the bush, but their fruit-sugar content may cause diarrhea if too many are eaten at one time. Nutritionally, blueberries offer a small amount of vitamins C and B1, beta carotene and potassium. They contain natural chemicals, antibacterial anthocyanosides, which provide a tonic effect on blood vessels, specifically with helping varicose veins. Combining with vegetable mucilage which lines the urinary tract, blueberries antibacterial benefits prevent bacteria from attaching to the bladder wall, thus preventing urinary tract infections. Blueberries are available fresh, frozen or dried. They are excellent in muffins, pies and other baked goodies.

Boysenberries - These are a mix of blackberry, loganberry and raspberry. This fruit is versatile and used in many of the same recipes as other berries, including wine, syrup and jam. They can be found fresh or frozen year round.

Cloudberries - This fruit is very similar in looks and flavor as raspberries, but are a tinged orange and red in color.

Cranberries - These tiny berries are grown in bogs. Originating in North America, the Native Indians used cranberries for medicine as well as food. Like the blueberry, they have antibacterial qualities that stop bacteria from attaching to the bladder wall, helping to prevent urinary infections. A sauce made from cranberries is traditionally served with roast turkey dinners. The nutrition within this tiny berry helps the immune system. Researchers have concluded that drinking one eight ounce glass of pure, unsweetened cranberry juice a day greatly improves the health of your body. Cranberries are available fresh in the fall and dried or frozen year round. For those who don't eat raisins, dried cranberries are an excellent substitute. These tart, tiny, red berries are used in relish, jellies, sauces and baking.

Elderberries - Small, black with a purple tint, these berries are used mainly for jams, jellies, wine and liqueur.

Goji - Another small berry that is gaining popularity in North America, goji berries are often found dried. The dried berry can be added to many foods, granola, trail mixes or muffins. It can also be found as a juice. Known in China as gouqizi and as kukoshi in Japan, goji, pronounced "go gee", is grown on vines mainly in Asia. They have been used for centuries throughout Asia. Antioxidants, vitamins and minerals are abundant in this berry. Try to purchase products that contain organic, whole berry, not just pulp or skin. Dried berries and organic pure juice are the best for nutritional value.

Gooseberries - Cultivated in Northern Europe and Britain for over five hundred years, gooseberries are smooth skinned and can range in color from green to red to white. Gooseberries have not been popular in North America as they are a known host of white pine blister rust and is a threat to the forestry industry. The name comes from the french root groseille. They are high in vitamin C and contain malic acid which helps in the treatment of urinary infections. The gooseberry is a popular fruit in both England and France. Somewhat tart, these berries are eaten raw, made into sauce or wine, canned, frozen, cooked into pies or made into jam.

B. A. Smit

Mulberries - These look quite similar to raspberries, but are not related to that family. They are usually used in wines and syrups.

Raspberries - Clusters of tiny drupes (fruit), each having a seed, make up each berry. They are most commonly red, but can also be white or black. They are grown on canes and are very nutritious. Loaded with vitamin C, a good source of the soluble fiber, pectin and iron, calcium, potassium and magnesium, raspberries are vital for a healthy body. Raspberries are also helpful for heart ailments, depression and fatigue. They are a delicate fruit, so they are best fresh, but can be found frozen or canned. This fruit is most famously used in jams, pies and jellies. In recent years, raspberries infused into vinegar for salad dressings has become very popular.

Red Currants - This fruit is a good boost for the immune system. The red currant is a close relative of the black currant, though nutritionally they are different. The plant is hardy, surviving the climate from Britain, Siberia, Europe and North America. Red currants contain only one quarter of the vitamin C than the black currant. They also have potassium, iron and fiber. Red currants are important for the natural function of the immune system and with their vitamin C, help to aid the body in healing itself. These berries can be used in many recipes calling for other berries.

Strawberries - These are red heart shaped berries with their seeds on the skin of the fruit. Once only grown wild, strawberries are now a cultivated crop. They are good for arthritis, gout, anemia and help with cancer prevention. For arthritis, strawberries can help the body rid itself of uric acid, an irritant of joints. They also help reduce high blood pressure. Along with vitamin C, strawberries also contain iron, which is helpful for the treatment of anemia and fatigue. Strawberries are abundant with the soluble fiber pectin, which aids in the reduction of cholesterol. Because of their antioxidant properties, these berries help combat circulatory and heart disease. Strawberries are available fresh, frozen and canned. They mix well with other fruits, rhubarb being the popular choice. Strawberry shortcake is a very famous dessert used at social functions. Jams, jellies and fruit desserts are all uses for these berries.

Freezing Berries

When you have berries to freeze, it is best to freeze in single layers before bagging. Wash the berries by placing them in a strainer and running cold water over them. Gently shake the excess water from the berries. Place a layer of parchment paper on a cookie sheet and place the berries onto the paper. Spread over the whole sheet in a single layer. Place in the freezer overnight. Scoop frozen berries into freezer bags. Label, date and return to the freezer. When you need berries, you will be able to take the amount needed without having one large mass of berries to thaw before using.

Citrus Fruits

This group of fruit is distinguished by being very juicy, the flesh is segmented and the skins contain very aromatic oils. The most common citrus fruits are limes, lemons, oranges and grapefruits. The flavor can be sweet as oranges to very tart like lemons. It is best to eat fresh, raw citrus fruit. Try to include some of the pith and membranes surrounding each segment. This is rich in vitamin C and certain protective phytochemicals, but lacks the fiber, pectin. When you think of all the foods used for their medicinal properties, citrus fruit is the most important. The large amount of vitamin C prevents the disease scurvy, boosts natural resistance to viruses and bacteria and helps to prevent some cancer. The majority of fruits are grown in the Mediterranean and Brazil. The United States and Mexico are also major contributors. Most fruit is shipped whole, but some areas like Brazil will convert the fruit to a juice concentrate, freeze it, then ship it worldwide. Those who suffer from migraine headaches can be sensitive to citrus fruits. Simply inhaling the zest can trigger an attack. Many citrus crops are sprayed with toxic antifungal and insecticidal wax before shipping. It is much better to buy organic fruit whenever possible. Wash all fruit well before eating.

Citron - This fruit resembles a lemon, but grows to a length of six to nine inches. It has a tough green to yellow colored peel. Citron is cultivated exclusively for it's peel, which is used in many baked goodies. The peel is treated with a brine to remove it's bitter oil, enhance the flavor and prevent spoilage. It is then candied with sugar and glucose.

Clementines and Satsumas - Both of these fruits are part of the Mandarin Family. The Mediterranean mandarin, the satsumas and the common mandarin are the hybrids. Compared to grapefruit, limes and lemons, the satsumas and clementines are less acidic. Both of these fruits contain a good supply of folate, a small amount of potassium and the B vitamins. Included in this family are tangors, orange, mandarin and tangelos, pommelo and grapefruit. Clementines and satsumas are easy to peel like the mandarin.

Grapefruit - Somewhat tart, grapefruit is a refreshing favorite to eat at breakfast or by the glass, juiced. There are three basic varieties, pink, red and white. The pink and red both have a yellow skin, the flesh being either pink or red. The white grapefruit has a pale yellow flesh and some varieties are seedless. Sixty percent of your daily vitamin C can be found in one grapefruit. Red or pink grapefruit is slightly more. Grapefruit also contains potassium and within the pith, beta carotene. The cell walls dividing the sections contain bioflavonoids and pectin.

Kumquats - These are the smallest fruit of the citrus family. They are oblong, but smaller than a plum. Kumquats have a thick, golden orange, spicy flavored rind with a dry flesh containing tiny seeds. The fruit is often cooked whole, in a sugar syrup, candied or made into jam. They are sweet, with a taste similar to mandarin oranges, but are best cooked before eating, unless very ripe. Kumquats are good in salads, fruit cups or added to fruit compotes.

B. A. Smit

Lemons - Long before the reason was known, lemons were reputed to cure scurvy. It was actually the abundance of vitamin C. Lemons have some B vitamins, vitamin E, phosphorus, magnesium, potassium and calcium. Also, lemons have trace minerals, manganese, zinc, iron and copper. They are known to trigger white dorpuscle activity, thus activating the immune system. Lemons are abundant in limonene, bioflavonoids and mucilage, which is helpful to the lining of the digestive tract and stomach. Researchers thought that the highly acidic lemon was harmful for rheumatism, but in actual fact, the acidity is caused by organic acids that are metabolized during digestion, which produce potassium carbonate. This aids in neutralizing excess acidity and also relieves the pain of rheumatism and arthritis. Lemon juice has been effective in protecting the mucus membrane lining of the digestive tract. It can also stimulate the liver and the pancreas. For mouth ulcers, sore throats or gingivitis, the antibacterial activity of lemon juice is often used. Dilute half and half with water and gargle. There are a number of varieties of lemons available. Meyer lemons are a lemon/orange cross with an orange tinted yellow flesh. The juice is sweeter than regular lemon juice. Lemons are commonly deep yellow in color and extremely tart. They are used in a variety of cooking recipes, as garnish, or as a flavoring in desserts. Lemon meringue pie is a famous dessert. Lemon is used in salmon and other seafood dishes to both flavor and garnish the dish. Popular in hot weather, ice cold, fresh lemonade is made from lemon juice.

Limes - These green fruits are a bit smaller than lemons. Limes are the most acidic citrus fruit. They have more vitamin C than grapefruit, but less vitamin C than lemons and oranges. Many citrus fruits, including limes, have high amounts of bioflavonoids. Limes are grown for their juice more than their fruit. The juice is popular in drinks and certain savory dishes. Two varieties of limes are the Persian and the Key. Persian limes have smooth, dark green colored skin. These limes are tart in flavor and seedless. Key limes are light green in color and are most often used for Key Lime Pie, a famous dessert pie that originated in the Southern United States. Limes can also be used for medicinal practices.

Oranges - There are four categories of oranges. Eating, juicing, mandarin and bitter. Eating oranges include the naval orange, which is often larger in size, seedless and easy to peel. Juicing oranges, like the velencia, are very juicy, sweet and plump. They have a smooth skin that is hard to peel, which makes them ideal for juicing. Mandarin varieties include the clementine and tangerine. The clementine often have few, if any seeds, and peel easily. Tangerine oranges have a lightly tart, sweet flavor and are easy to peel, but contain a lot of seeds. The mandarin varieties are smaller than the naval. Oranges are very important to maintain a healthy body. They help to fight illness, infection and general poor health. They have beta carotene, and within the pith and segment walls, bioflavonoids. These chemicals are also known as vitamin P or C2 since they increase the activity of vitamin C and fortify the walls of the tiny blood capillaries. Orange juice can provide vitamins C, B6 and A, calcium, iron, folic acid, thiamin, magnesium, protein, phosphorus, riboflavin and nicotinic acid. Oranges are high in potassium and very low in sodium. With all the nutrients in oranges, they are an excellent fruit for those with high blood pressure, heart disease and fluid retention.

The flowers and the peel of oranges are used in herbal medicine. The peel provides limonene and hesperidine, which can help with chronic bronchitis. Oranges should be washed before eating. They can be used in dessert dishes and a jam called marmalade is made from oranges.

Persimmon - This warm weather fruit has two main varieties. The American, or common persimmon, is native from Connecticut and Southern Iowa, to Florida and Texas in the United States. It is a small fruit between one and one half to two inches in diameter. Persimmon are yellow to orange in color with reddish cheeks. There are large seeds imbedded into the flesh. The second variety is known as Oriental or Japanese persimmon. This variety can grow to three inches in diameter. Some have large seeds, others, no seeds. When ripe, the fruit resembles a tomato in size and texture. The taste is sweet, but the fruit must be very ripe before eating raw. Persimmon can be found in salads, puddings and jam.

Ugli - This is a hybrid (mixed origin of fruit) with a wrinkled, greenish yellow skin and a pink seedless flesh. This fruit is also known as uniq fruit and is eaten raw.

Dried Fruits

Many fruits are available dried. From berries to tropical fruit, the options are plentiful. Dried fruit can be added to hot or cold cereal for breakfast, added to salads, or on their own as a snack. They also make a tasty, nutritious extra when baking muffins or quick breads. Some dried fruit is sweetened and some may have additives to enhance flavor and increase shelf life. Remember to read labels. I have included just a few of the most common for you.

Dates - These have been grown in the Middle East for over five thousand years and have both nutritional benefits and many culinary uses. These Middle East delights are good for chronic fatigue syndrome, anemia and postviral fatigue syndrome. They are also beneficial as a quick pick me up after physical exercise, and help when constipated. Dates are excellent as a snack, in baking, or included in main dishes. Dates are used as a sugar substitute, in alcoholic drinks and they can also be ground into flour. Most dates are dried or semi dried, but it is possible to find fresh dates. Fresh dates are more nutritious, with fewer calories than dried dates. Depending on the variety, dates have iron, fiber and potassium. They all contain vitamin C, some B vitamins and folate. The iron content combined with their available energy make dates an ideal snack for those affected by illness, anemia and chronic fatigue syndrome.

Figs - There are over eight hundred species of figs within it's family. They grow in Greece, Turkey, India, the Middle East and the Mediterranean. The fig tree is often thought of as sacred. Figs are a good source of the anticancer agent benzaldehyde, the healing enzyme, flavonoids and ficin, which are beneficial for digestion. Figs also contain potassium, beta carotene, iron, energy and both soluble and insoluble fibers. It is best to eat figs raw whenever possible, or dried.

Prunes - This fruit is ideal for lethargy, fatigue, constipation and high blood pressure. Prunes are best eaten when soaked, cooked, or as juice. Prunes are grown on a plum tree, the most famous grown in France. This fruit has been a part of history since the Crusaders brought them to England from the Middle East. California, U.S.A. cultivates about seventy percent of the world crop. The prune is high in potassium, fiber and iron. It contains vitamins A and B6, plus niacin. Prunes are known as a gentle laxative. The prune contains a chemical, hydroxphenylisatin, which encourages the muscle of the large bowel to work. Cultivated prunes are often treated with sulphur and mineral oil to keep them shiny and soft, and help to prevent them from sticking together. Wash prunes carefully before using.

Raisins - These are grapes that have been dried. The best are dried naturally while still on the vine. Raisins are excellent for high blood pressure, anemia, low energy and constipation. They are best if washed well and eaten as a snack. Raisins are a nutritious addition to salads, baking and some main dishes. For over five thousand years, fruit has been dried naturally by the sun. Even modern cultivation in California, U.S.A. and Australia use covered, open-sided sheds for drying. The nutrition of grapes is concentrated into raisins, including energy from the natural sugars, fructose and glucose. Raisins are an excellent food for hikers, athletes and those who suffer from chronic fatigue syndrome. They are high in fiber, selenium, iron and potassium. Raisins have a small amount of vitamin A and the B vitamins. Because they are treated with sulphur and mineral oil to prevent them from sticking and keep them soft, remember to wash the raisins well before using. For those who cannot have raisins, a good substitute would be dried cranberries.

B. A. Smit

Stone Fruits

Stone fruits are a collection of fruit that has one large stone or pit in it's center. Plums, peaches, cherries, apricots and nectarines are in this group. The flesh can be fragile and bruise easily, so care in handling is important. Most of these fruits are available fresh spring through summer. Stone fruits can be found frozen, canned or dried year round. They are also made into many varieties of desserts, preserves and wine. When freezing this type of fruit, you should follow the same procedure as with berries. Peel, slice and wash using a strainer. Shake off the excess water gently then lay in a single layer on a parchment paper lined cookie sheet. Place in the freezer overnight then package, label, date and return to the freezer. I am including just a few of the most common stone fruit, but you can find many more varieties at your local grocer.

Apricots - These are a close relative to the peach. They are smaller, less juicy and have a fuzzy skin like the peach. Apricots vary in color, but most are a yellow to yellow/ orange. This fruit is popular dried and is also great for jams and desserts. This fruit tastes best when eaten raw or dried. Either way, apricots are helpful to cancer patients and exceptional for skin and respiratory ailments. Dried apricots aid in anemia, high blood pressure, fluid retention and constipation. There is an abundant amount of beta carotene within apricots. The body will convert it to vitamin A. For people who suffer from skin ailments, infections, or are at a risk to develop cancer, apricots should be eaten daily. Dried apricots are high in fiber, which can help with constipation, but most dried apricots are high in sugar and diabetics should eat them with caution. Commercially dried apricots use sulphur dioxide as a preservative. This can trigger asthma attacks, so it is best to rinse before eating. Dried apricots are a good source of iron and the potassium helps rid the body of excess salt and water.

Cherries - There are many varieties that range from bright red to dark, almost purple/ black in color. The flesh can vary from crisp like an apple, to soft like a plum. Some varieties are sweet, others sour, and depending on the variety, some are juicier than others. There are both sweet and sour cherries. The sweet varieties are best when eaten raw, and the sour cherries, like morellos, are excellent for cooking, turning to juice or liqueur. Cherries can be found fresh, dried or canned. Some varieties are candied for baking. Cherries are popular for many types of pastries and desserts. In the past, the bark of the cherry tree was used in medicine. Now the dried fruit stalk and fruit are used. The ancient Greek physicians valued cherries for medicinal use. It is thought that cherries originated from orchards of Mesopotamia, prebiblical times. These small round fruits are good for the joints, helpful in the prevention of cancer and a useful diuretic. Cherries have no sodium and a small amount of potassium. They have vitamin C and generous amounts of bioflavonoids, making them an excellent antioxidant. This fruit is also a cancer protector, ellagic acid inhibits the carcinogenic cancer cells, and this acid is found in cherries. Cherry pie is the most popular dessert from this fruit.

Nectarines and Peaches - Most experts describe nectarines and peaches as different varieties of the same fruit. In actual fact, nectarines are a genetic variation of the peach. They both are part of the Prunus Family, which includes apricots, prunes and plums. Both fruits are good during pregnancy, work as a laxative, are helpful for low salt diets and for people with high cholesterol. Dried peaches are good for constipation, fatigue and anemia. Nectarines and peaches have the best flavor when they are ripe and eaten raw. It is believed that peaches originated in China, and traveled with the traders to Persia. Today, the United States and Italy are the top producers of about half of the worldwide crop. Nectarines and peaches are nutritionally equal. Both have vitamin C, calories, minerals, beta carotene and fiber. Dried peaches have a whole day's requirement of iron, and one third of your daily potassium need. Canned peaches lose their vitamin C, and when packed in syrup, they have many unnecessary calories. Peaches and nectarines are excellent fruits for people with high blood pressure or cholesterol problems, since they are sodium and fat free. Nectarines are the same shape as peaches, with a similar flavor and are classified the same as peaches, freestone or clingstone. The skin is smooth and the flesh is the same texture as plums. Though not as varied in uses as apricots or peaches, nectarines are tasty eaten fresh, in jams, wines or desserts. Peaches are available in a number of varieties. The two main categories are clingstone, where the flesh clings to the stone and freestone, where the flesh separates easily from the stone. All types of peaches have a fuzzy skin, which is a soft orange color. All peaches are sweet and juicy. The flesh varies in color, from white, yellow, creamy orange to red tinged. They are available fresh, frozen, dried or canned. This is a popular fruit for desserts, pies and jams.

Plums - Varieties are numerous, and those in Britain are hybrids of the cherry or sloe plum. Originating in eastern Europe, plums have been used throughout Europe for centuries. During the seventeenth century, fruit expert Luther Burbank introduced the Japanese plum to North America. Plums range in size from small like the apricot, to as large as the peach. The color of the skin can be green, purple, red, or shades of these colors. Ripe plums are often sweet and juicy, though some varieties have a tart flavored skin. Plums are placed into two varieties, cooking and dessert. The cooking plums are often more acidic and drier, but both varieties can be eaten raw. Damson plums are purple skinned and are known as cooking plums. They are excellent in pies and jams. Greengage plums have green skin and flesh. These sweet plums are a common dessert choice. Santa Rosa plums have red skin and a yellow flesh. Black Friar plums are dark purple skinned, with a maroon, almost purple flesh. Both of these varieties are excellent when eaten fresh. Prune or Italian plums are small, purple colored with green flesh and are not as juicy as other types of stone fruit, but the flesh separates easily from the pit. This plum variety is dried as prunes or eaten fresh. Plums are good for circulation, the heart and fluid retention. They have only a small amount of vitamins C and E, with a reasonable amount of vitamin A. Plums are a good source of potassium. The dessert variety has a higher sugar, lower acid content with useful medicinal values. Wild plums, which grow on the blackthorn bush, are known as sloe plums. The English use them to make the alcoholic drink, sloe-gin. The Asian use the plum for medicine and the Japanese Umebushi is used to help digestive disorders, but it tastes awful.

B. A. Smit

Tropical Fruits

These fruits are named for the climate in which they grow. There are many varieties of tropical fruits, with most now available in North America thanks to improved transportation options. Bananas are usually picked green and allowed to ripen in controlled storage areas. This is not a common practise with other tropical fruits which include figs, kiwis, mangos, pineapple, star fruit and passion fruit to name a few. There are many choices now available in the grocery stores, be adventurous and try something less common. When you are on a restricted diet, you can often eat the same foods out of ease. I am including some of the most common along with some less common fruits to help inform you of varieties of tropical fruits now available.

Bananas and Plantain - Bananas aid in stomach ulcers, are beneficial for chronic fatigue syndrome, glandular fever and exhaustion. Bananas are excellent for people who are convalescing and those who are very active. This fruit is at it's best flavor when the yellow peel is just beginning to turn brown. The starch in the banana can be hard to digest, so it is best to eat when ripe. This will ensure that it digests easier and along with soluble fiber, makes it a good fruit for the treatment of both diarrhea and constipation. This also helps the body eliminate cholesterol. Bananas have potassium, vitamin B6, folic acid and other vitamins and minerals needed to maintain a healthy body. Bananas are used in many dessert dishes, like banana cream pie. Plantain is becoming more popular for North Americans as it's availablity increases. It is from a large tropical tree-like herb. It is larger, starchier and less sweet than the banana. The flavor is best when the fruit is under ripe and cooked. The starch in plantain can cause discomfort if eaten raw. Cooking will help this. Plantain is often fried but can also be baked or broiled. This makes the fruit easy to digest. For stomach ulcers, there is a specific starch in plantain which can promote healing and aid in the prevention of further ulcers. Plantains have been a staple food in South America, East Africa, India and Southeast Asia for centuries. Plantain is as popular in the Tropics as potatoes are to North America.

Guavas - There are numerous varieties, usually oval in shape, ranging in size from a walnut to an apple. It has a thin skin with yellow to red fruit. Guava are sweet, juicy and very aromatic. These originated in Central America and are now grown in both tropics and subtropics. The large family, Myrtaceae, includes nutmeg, cinnamon, allspice, cloves and guava, the most important member of the family. This fruit is rich in vitamin C, calcium, phosphorus and nicotinic acid, plus soluble fiber. Guavas, when canned, are usually in a heavy, sweet syrup, so it is best to not use the syrup. Use caution when buying guava drinks, most are twenty five percent fruit nectar, ten percent sugar and sixty five percent water. For a healthy, refreshing start in the morning, try mixing guava purée with natural yogurt.

Kiwi - This tiny fruit in the fuzzy coat is loaded with nutrition. Originally from China, now it is a popular fruit from New Zealand. It is named after the Kiwi bird of New Zealand. The kiwi contains about twice the vitamin C as an orange and has more fiber than an apple. With most fruit, the vitamin C content is lessened by harvesting or processing, but at least ninety percent of the vitamin C content of the kiwi will remain. The kiwi has a rich amount of potassium, needed by the body to maintain normal blood pressure, fight fatigue and depression and help with digestion. To find ripe kiwi, choose fruit that is soft enough to yield to gentle pressure. Store kiwi in the fridge and peel just before eating.

Mangos - This tropical fruit is native to India and over the past four thousand years it has travelled to Africa, the Philippines, South China, the Mediterranean, Central and South America, the Caribbean, through to the United States and Canada. Mangos are helpful with skin problems, cancer protection and improving the immune system. They are best when eaten raw. Mangos are a part of the Anacardiaceae Family, with poison ivy also a member. Use care when handling the mango. The mango peel, especially before it's fully ripe, can be highly irritant. Even using the same knife for the flesh as for the peel can cause contamination. The mango has vitamin C, A and E, along with fiber, nicotinic acid, iron and potassium. This combination of antioxidants, and how easy they are to digest, makes the mango a popular fruit. To eat a mango, slice off the sides as close to the center pit as possible. Score the inside of the flesh in a crisscross pattern using a very sharp knife. Then turn the whole section inside out. You will have small mango cubes to either bite or cut off and enjoy. These can be added to salads or on top of yogurt, or eaten alone.

Papaya - This fruit is helpful for digestive ailments, good for the skin and helps improve the immune system. It is best eaten raw, and very ripe. Canned papaya is readily available, but it is not as nutritious as fresh. Papaya is native to Costa Rica and Southern Mexico, but is now grown throughout the tropics. The largest producer is the United States, where the crops grow in Hawaii. Papaya, like most orange colored fruit and vegetables, is a good source of beta carotene, which the body converts to vitamin A. Papayas also contain vitamin C, fiber, which helps lower cholesterol, and most importantly, an enzyme called papain. The unripe papaya has more papain than the ripe, which is commercially extracted as a white laytex, dried and used as a meat tenderizer. Papaya has also been used in herbal medicine.

Pineapple - This tropical fruit is almost always associated with Hawaii. Nutritionally, it has some vitamin C and it's fiber content helps break down blood clots. Pineapple is healthy for the heart, digestive ailments, sore throats and soft tissue injuries. The fruit contains an enzyme called bromelain. It can digest many times it's weight of protein, only breaking down food and dead tissue, leaving the intestines healthy. It is best eaten fresh, but is available canned or dried. Pineapple is a good fruit for many desserts and baking. The juice is popular for a wide range of drinks.

Quince - This oval to round shaped fruit varies in color, from greenish yellow to a bright yellow. The flesh is hard, with a strong smell. This fruit can be quite tart and should not be eaten raw. Quince is most common in jams, fruit pastes and syrups.

Tamarind - This fruit is often referred to as Indian Date. It is a large fruit pod grown on the tamarind tree. The flavor is somewhat sour, almost prune like. The pulp that surrounds the seeds is used in many Indian, Middle East and Indonesian dishes. It is available both dried and as a liquid.

B. A. Smit

Melons

This is a refreshing fruit related to the cucumber and squash families. There are many varieties and the size can vary from the size of an orange, to as large as a watermelon. They have been grown in Asia for centuries. The Romans, Greek and Egyptians all valued this fruit. Melons are divided into four main types. Cantaloupes, watermelons, muskmelons and the winter melons. Casaba, honeydew and crenshaw melons are included in the category of winter melons. To determine if a melon is ripe is as varied as the number of types, size, and when it was harvested. Cantaloupe can be judged by a "full slip". When the melon ripens on the vine, it will grow away from the stem, leaving a smooth edge. If it is taken before it "slips" from the stem, it will leave a rough edge. To add confusion, some ripened melons will have a soft stem end, but in other varieties, this can mean over ripe. Fresh aroma, and a good weight for the melon size, are good indications of ripeness for all melon varieties. Melons are nutritious and refreshing to eat during the hot summer days. For most melons, you will need a very sharp knife to cut the melon in half, then each half in half again. Remove the seeds if possible, cut off the skin or serve in wedges, eating the flesh and discarding the skin. It is believed that melons also help urinary infections and soothe the kidneys.

Cantaloupe - Though available year round, the summer is the best time to buy this fruit. They are larger than a grapefruit. The skin has a netting or vein like texture over the beige to yellow skin. The flesh is orange, firm, juicy and sweet. To prepare this fruit, use a sharp knife to cut the cantaloupe in half. Scoop out the seed mass in the center, cut each half into wedge size pieces and cut off the skin. This fruit can be cubed and added as a topping to ice cream or eaten alone.

Casaba - These melons have a green tinted, yellow skin and are best at the beginning of the fall. A ripe casaba melon has a firm, smooth skin with a fresh melon aroma.

Crenshaw - This melon has a salmon pink color with a very aromatic flesh. The peak season is early fall. A ripe crenshaw melon will be very fragrant with a slight softening at the stem.

Gallia - This is a melon that is similar in flavor and aroma to the cantaloupe. They have a green flesh. Though not as common to find at the market, this melon is a nutritious fruit to enjoy.

Honeydew - This is a familiar name in melons. They have a green flesh and a yellow skin that when ripe, will not have a green tint to it. The flesh is refreshingly juicy. Readily available during the summer months, a ripe honeydew melon will have a fuzzy, slightly sticky feeling to the skin.

Muskmelon - This variety has noticeable ridges with a yellow to tan colored skin. The flesh is a deep orange color with a fragrant scent. When ripe, it has a full slip, like the cantaloupe.

Persian - These melons have yellow markings on it's dark green skin. The flesh is an orange to yellow color. Summer is when these melons are most abundant. When ripe, the melon will have some yield when pressed and the weight will seem heavier than it's size.

Watermelon - This is a summer picnic standard. They vary in size, but are oblong, oval and large, usually three times the size of a cantaloupe. Some varieties are seedless. The skin is green, the flesh red (often with black seeds) or white. Peak season for watermelon is mid to late summer. Watermelon sit on the ground as they grow and ripen. A ripe watermelon will have some color on the area that rested on the ground. A white area is a sign that the watermelon is not yet ripe.

B. A. Smit

Grains and Flours

Grains Containing Gluten:

Barley

Oats

Malt

Rye

Wheat:

Atta	Graham
Bulgar	Kamut
Couscous	Matzoh Meal
Durum	Seitan
Einkorn and Emmer	Semolina
Farina	Spelt
Fu	Triticale

Hidden Gluten

About Grains and Helpful Tips

Tips for Cooking Grains

Gluten Free Grains and Flours:

Amaranth

Buckwheat

Corn:

Blue Corn	Corn Syrup	Hominy Grits
Corn Bran	Cornmeal	Popcorn
Corn Flour	Cornstarch	Sweet Corn
Corn Germ	Field Corn	Whole, Dried Corn
Corn Oil	Flint or Indian Corn	Whole Hominy

Flax

Gluten Free Flours

Grain Free Flours

Job's Tear

Kamut

Kasha

Kelp

Legume and Nut Flours

Mesquite Flour

Montina

Millet:

Millet Flour	Millet Puffed
Millet Meal	Millet Wholegrain

Potato Flour

Quinoa

Rice: Brown   Arborio
         Enriched   Basmati
         Long Grain/Short Grain   Jasmine White
         Parboiled   Thai Black
         Precooked   Wild Rice

Rice Bran	Rice Meal
Rice Bran Oil	Rice Noodles
Rice Crackers/Rice Cakes	Rice Paper
Rice Cream/Rice Milk	Rice Polish
Rice Flakes	Puffed Rice
Rice Flour	Rice Syrup
Rice Flour/Glutenous	Rice Wine

Sorghum
Spelt
Tapioca
Taro
Teff

Grains Containing Gluten

Barley - Ale, beer and lager drinks are made from barley, which is not gluten free. New varieties of these drinks are being processed that are made from buckwheat, rice or sorghum which are gluten free. Barley is available in several forms; flakes and flour are the most common. They all contain gluten.

Malt - This is an enzyme created from sprouted barley which may be used in various foods including malted milk, malt vinegar and malt flavoring. The malt flavoring is an extract and/or syrup which is used to show a concentrated liquid of barley malt has been used for flavoring.

Oats - Including bran, flour and oatmeal, oats are actually gluten free before they have been processed. Oats can be contaminated by the machines used for processing gluten grains. If a farm only grows and processes oats, they will be gluten free, but you do not know for sure if other grains are processed with the same equipment. For most people it is safer to avoid all oat products.

Rye - All forms of this grain contain gluten.

Wheat

All wheat contains gluten. There are many varieties of wheat and some varieties have less gluten than others. It is best to avoid all types of wheat. Some of the most common varieties are listed here. You should become familiar with these names to enable you to know what contains gluten and avoid them.

Atta - A fine wholemeal flour made from soft textured, low gluten wheat known as atta or chapatti flour. It is used to make Indian flatbread.

Bulgar - This is wheat that has been dried then cracked.

Couscous - This is wheat which has been coarsely ground. Many Middle Eastern dishes center around this versatile food.

Durum - This type of wheat is used mainly in pasta making.

Einkorn and Emmer - Both of these are varieties of wheat.

Farina - This is flour or meal made from wheat cereals.

Fu - A wheat gluten product that is packaged as round cakes or thin sheets. It is a protein supplement that is used in many Asian meals, soups or vegetable dishes.

Graham - This is found mainly as flour. It is made by adding wheat bran or wheat berry parts to wheat before grinding into flour.

Kamut - Some people who are sensitive to gluten can tolerate this grain. It has less gluten than other wheat varieties.

Matzoh Meal - This is made from a flour and water bread that is ground into this meal which is then made into dumplings.

Seitan - Also known as wheat meat, it is made from wheat gluten and is used in many vegetarian dishes.

Semolina - This is a coarsely ground wheat that is used mainly for making pasta.

Spelt - Also known as dinkel, farro or faro, this contains a small amount of gluten. Some people who can't tolerate gluten are able to digest spelt.

Triticale - This is a blend of rye and wheat that is made into wheat bran, germ, starch or flour.

There are several varieties of wheat free products made from the Einkorn, Spelt, Kamut or Emmer types of wheat. Though low in gluten, "wheat free" can not be mistaken for gluten free. Remember to read labels.

Hidden Gluten

Flour has a substance responsible for structure, texture and leavening called gluten. It is obvious in pastries, breads and cakes, it is less obvious in other products. Sauces, marinades, salad dressings, gravies, soups and even frozen french fries may contain gluten. Other foods, like prepared meats, candies, medicine and flavored teas and coffees could contain gluten. Read labels.

About Grains and Helpful Tips

- All come from cereal grasses whose seed is the grain we eat
- All grains are made up of several layers, each kernel has four sections
- The hull, which is not eaten, is removed when the grain is processed
- What is left after hulling is classified as the whole grain, and when eaten in this form, is the most nutritious
- The bran is full of vitamins, minerals and soluble fiber
- The germ is the embryo of the seed, used for sprouting, and is rich in enzymes, protein, minerals, vitamins and fat
- Last is the starchy center, called the endosperm, good only for carbohydrates and to produce white flour
- Processing takes away a lot of the nutritional values of the grain
- Grains, especially in recipes for baking, can come in a variety of forms
- Grits, groats, meal, flour, whole and cracked grains are the most common
- Buying in bulk can be economical, but make sure the bins are dry and clean, dampness in the air can cause mold to develop on the grain
- A busy store means a quick turnover of stock, a quiet store can mean stale grains
- Store properly to ensure freshness and nutritional value
- Read labels, natural and organic could also include sugars or salt
- Don't wash the grains before you store them, water can make some grains stick together or cause mold
- Clean grains by spreading on a pan with sides and visually find foreign matter; grass, pebbles or weeds and remove, this applies mainly to grains bought in bulk
- Stored properly, grains can have a long shelf life; because they look nice on a shelf, you can store in glass jars with tight rubber seals
- Some grains contain oils that, if stored improperly, can go rancid
- Keep your grain purchases in smaller amounts, don't buy a fifty pound sack because it is cheap, then take three years to use it up
- Keep grains in a cool dry place away from direct sunlight

Tips for Cooking Grains

- Try to use a nonstick pot for cooking grains, it will be easier for cleanup; soaking the pot after cooking if it is not a nonstick pot will help make clean up easier
- Make sure the pot has a secure lid so steam will not escape during cooking
- A deep pot will keep the grains covered in water with less need for visual checks to see if the level of liquid is o.k.
- A larger, wider pot will need to be checked more often
- Use medium high heat to bring the liquid to a hard boil, add the grains, stir, bring back to a hard boil, cover, lower heat to simmer, keep covered to cook until done, check recipe for proper time
- Depending on your preference, the grain is cooked when all the liquid has been absorbed
- If the recipe calls for less liquid and the grain, when cooked, is chewier than you prefer, increase the amount of liquid to allow a longer cooking time, this will result in a softer cooked grain
- Do not stir vigorously, grains may bruise or become sticky
- As with rice, no peeking, it lets the steam escape, which is how the grain is cooked, leave for the specified time then check to see if it is cooked to your preference
- With most grains, after you remove the pot from the heat, let it stand for 5 - 8 minutes with the lid still on, then fluff with a fork and serve
- When you are cooking corn pasta, it is best to omit the salt in the cooking water, use only water with about two tablespoons of oil, bring to a boil, add pasta, return to a boil, and cook to your taste
- When cooking rice pasta or noodles, use salt and oil in the water, bring to a boil, add the pasta or noodles, return to a boil, and cook to your liking

B. A. Smit

Gluten Free Grains and Flours

Amaranth - This is used as a grain, but is actually the tan colored seed from a broadleafed plant whose flowerettes hold the tiny seeds. It is a member of the Amaranthaceae Family. This grain has been used for centuries, dating to the Tehuacan cave dwellers, who discovered the amazing plant. The plant grows in Sri Lanka, India, Eastern Siberia, the Himalayas and China. It is still used in these areas and is often called Chinese Spinach. The nutritional value is more than most grains. It has more protein than beans or corn, more fiber than soybeans, rice or corn, and it has vitamins and the essential amino acid lysine. Amaranth can cook quickly, therefore holding it's shape without becoming mushy. It has a spicy, nutty flavor and is available as whole grain, flour, pasta (may be mixed with wheat, read labels carefully) and breakfast cereals.

Buckwheat - Simply put, you will either love it or hate it. Buckwheat is often missed because of it's name, you assume it is full of gluten, like wheat. Despite it's name, this is a wheat and gluten free grain. About half of the people with intolerance to gluten can eat buckwheat. It is actually a grass related to the rhubarb family. Buckwheat began in regions of Central Asia. It has the nutritional structure and characteristics of a grain. Buckwheat is quite gentle on the digestive system and can often be recommended for those who can't tolerate wheat. It contains protein, iron, calcium and B vitamin. It is available roasted, most often called kasha. This grain has a nutty flavor. Unroasted, it is called buckwheat. You can use it for baking, in soups or stews, as a breakfast cereal, and even some desserts. It is available as whole buckwheat groats, which is often used in stuffings or rice dishes, as grits that are used in cereal, or flour, dark or light, used for baking, or seeds, used for sprouting. The dark flour is made from the whole groat, including the hull. This makes it very nutritious, but can be heavy to bake with alone, so it is best to mix with other flours for baking. The light flour has few if any hulls, but still has many nutrients and can work well in many baking recipes. Buckwheat bran is from the outer layer of the groat. This is known as farinetta and is very nutritious, excellent in baking pancakes and muffins. Some buckwheat products can have wheat added, so make sure that you are buying one hundred percent pure buckwheat.

Corn

Corn has been around for centuries. Known as maize by the Indians, it is also found through out history in places like China, the Philippines and Europe. Some of the more popular, basic varieties are listed here.

Blue Corn - Originating with Southwest Native Americans, this corn was in danger of becoming extinct. People were not eager to try it's strong corn flavor because of it's color. Blue corn was most likely the first sweet corn harvested by settlers. It has a long growing season and therefore, most farmers of today aren't patient enough to grow it. The popularity of blue corn has dramatically increased over the past twenty years and is making a come back. You will find pancakes, cornmeal, bread and tortillas made from blue corn.

Corn Bran - This is an excellent source of soluble fiber. It is a layer within the corn kernel and can be used as an alternative for wheat, oat or rice bran. Corn bran is especially good in muffins.

Corn Flour - This is cornmeal that has been ground much finer, resulting in flour. Many brands of corn flour contain wheat and should be avoided in gluten/wheat free diets. If you want to use corn flour, make sure it is a fine ground, whole grain corn flour. It is available in blue, yellow or white corn, and is used mainly in baking. It also works well for breading meat or fish. You can find it as a pasta as well.

Corn Germ - This is the core of the kernel. It is the part used in new sprouts. Corn germ can be used the same as wheat germ, with a flavor similar to popcorn. You can sprinkle it on cereal, yogurt or salads. In baking, it can add both texture and flavor to muffins, breads and cakes.

Corn Oil - This is nonhydrogenated oil that after refining, has no odor or taste. Some of the many uses for corn oil include salad dressings, frying and as a shortening in baking. Corn oil and margarines made with corn oil are excellent for people who must watch their cholesterol levels.

Corn Syrup - There are two types of corn syrup, light and dark. Both are made from cornstarch. Read labels, some brands of corn syrup contain no corn product at all. Light corn syrup is decolorized and clarified. The dark syrup has a stronger flavor. Both types are used in baking, desserts and candy. It can also be used on pancakes, waffles and french toast. Corn syrup is used to give a smooth, creamy texture to frostings and frozen desserts.

Cornmeal - This is a whole grain product. The medium ground is best to use in baking recipes. All types of corn products can often be hard to digest for people with food sensitivities. Cornmeal is available as yellow, white or blue, with a medium fine consistency. The corn germ is often a part of cornmeal. Labeled either stoneground or waterground, this only refers to the power source used in the grinding process. Good quality cornmeal does not need to be mixed with other flours for baking, but remember that blue corn is denser and will be heavy if not mixed with other flour. Cornmeal is often used in breads, muffins, pancakes and polenta.

Cornstarch - Often confused with corn flour, cornstarch is made from indentata, a high starch type of corn. The endosperm layer of the kernel is milled into a fine powder which is used as a thickener for sweet and savory dishes. When cornstarch is mixed with cold liquids, it will settle to the bottom, so mix just before adding to the food. Cook just to the boiling point, stirring constantly, then cook for about one minute longer, continuing to stir. Overcooking may cause "weeping" (moisture on the top of the food) as the mixture cools. To prevent a skin from forming on puddings, lay plastic wrap on top of the pudding as it cools, removing the wrap before serving. Acid can also affect the thickening. When making citrus pies and puddings, add the lemon or

B. A. Smit

orange juice after you have thickened the food. Cornstarch will appear milky at the beginning of cooking, but will become translucent when thickened.

Field Corn - This is also known as dent corn. It is usually dried in the fields, and when dried, the kernel forms a dent at the top. Field corn is generally used for animal feed only.

Flint or Indian Corn - Multicolored, this variety is often used for fall decorations. The colors may include red, blue, orange, purple and yellow. When it is ground and used in recipes, it can be very tasty.

Hominy Grits - The brunt of so many jokes, grits were developed by Native American tribes. Originally it was nicknamed corn without skin, and was coarsely ground undergerminated white corn. Now it is available in yellow or white corn and you can choose from fine, medium or coarsely ground. Instant grits are also available. Hominy grits are cooked the same way as other hot cereals.

Popcorn - This corn has been grown for over five thousand years. Orville Redenbacher made it a household staple. Popcorn has a very hard hull with about fifteen percent moisture. This moisture turns to steam when the popcorn is heated, causing it to pop. Eaten plain, it is very nutritious.

Sweet Corn - This is often the "corn on the cob" corn. Known by at least one hundred names, if you buy corn on the cob, it will be sweet corn.

Whole, Dried Corn - Available as white, yellow or blue, dried corn is used in households by grinding it into meal or flour. It can be used in many recipes for meals and baking.

Whole Hominy - Various names are used for whole hominy, posole, samp, nixtamal and mate' are found using yellow or white corn. Chicos is from amber colored corn. The process uses whole corn and hydrated (saked) lime, or a combination of unsaked lime, calcium carbonate and wood ash. When water is added to the lime it loosens the hull and partially cooks the kernel. The corn is washed to remove the hulls, dried, then used in baking, mostly for soups and stews. When it is ground, it is called masa harina, the only cornmeal used to make authentic tortillas.

Flax
This is a dicot in the Linaceae Family. It is grown across the Canadian Prairies and Northern United States and is harvested for several flax products. Similar in shape and size as a sesame seed, flax is grown for both food and industry, which includes linen clothing and linoleum flooring. Milled or ground, flax seeds can be sprinkled over cereals, yogurt or other desserts. The light, nutty flavor is also tasty in baked goods. Ground flax seed can be used instead of rice bran, but the baked goods will brown quicker. Flax can also be used in place of eggs in some recipes. The most nutritional benefits are from ground seeds, not whole. Grinding the seeds will help the body to absorb the nutrients of the flax seeds. You can grind the seeds in a coffee grinder, preferably just

before using for optimum nutrient value. Whole flax seeds can be stored for up to one year at room temperature. Once ground, store the flax in an airtight container in the fridge and use as soon as possible. The natural fats in the seeds can turn rancid quickly if exposed to heat and air. Flax oil is good in cold foods, like salad dressings, but will break down if exposed to high heat, so it is not recommended for frying foods. Flax is a good source of both soluble and insoluble fiber, plant lignans and alpha-linolenic acid (an essential omega-3 fatty acid). Flax seeds are helpful in protecting against coronary heart disease, breast and colon cancers and has a positive effect on blood cholesterol levels, arthritis, lupus and auto-immune diseases. Flax is also beneficial in keeping the bowels regular. Flax is a good source of calcium, folate, vitamin B6, protein, zinc, potassium, phosphorus, iron and magnesium. Flax seeds have a subtle nut flavor that is more pronounced if roasted. They are very good when used in baking, fruit cobblers and burgers. Flax seeds, ground or whole, can be sprinkled on cold cereal, hot cereal, even salads, which makes these seeds very versatile. When baking with flax, remember to add extra liquid, one tablespoon for every three tablespoons of flax, and lower the oven temperature by about twenty five degrees because the flax will promote browning. As an egg replacer, soak one teaspoon of ground flax seed in one quarter cup boiled water for about five minutes. Cool before adding to the recipe. This egg replacer is best used in snack bar or cookie recipes. Flax oil is high in omega-3 fatty acids but contains no fiber. Whole flax seeds are high in fiber, protein, vitamins and minerals.

Gluten Free Flours - Buckwheat (also known as kasha), rice, millet, quinoa and corn are all grains that only contain minute amounts of gluten. These are considered safe for those who are sensitive to gluten products.

Grain Free Flours - For those who are unable to eat grains should use a substitute to add starch and bulk to their diet. Carob, amaranth, arrowroot, nut, tapioca, cassava and potato flours are good alternatives. Bean flours are also grain free. Soy, lentil and chickpea are a few examples of bean flours. Those with grain intolerance should try to use grain free flours and eat vegetables such as potato, squash, cauliflower, turnip and carrots to help add bulk to their diet.

Job's Tear - This grain is mistaken for pearl barley, but it is nothing like it. Job's Tear is not barley, it is the seed of an annual wild grass which looks like puffed brown rice. Some claim that Job's Tear will counteract the effect of eating animal proteins and fats. It may also be good for cancers, moles and warts. It is excellent in soups, stews or with brown rice.

Kamut - This is a Mediterranean unhybridized wheat pronounced "ka-moot". It has been ignored because of wheat named in it's definition. Some people who are intolerant to wheat can tolerate kamut. For those with severe intolerance, please talk to your doctor or dietitian before trying kamut. It contains forty percent more protein and sixty five percent more amino acids than wheat because it has not been over processed. It can be digested easily. Kamut has a nutty, sweet flavor.

Kasha - See buckwheat. Kasha is another name used for buckwheat.

B. A. Smit

Kelp - Usually ground, this seaweed powder is a healthy, flavorful addition to many foods. Main dishes, tomato and bean recipes are just some ideas for it's use.

Legume and Nut Flours - For centuries, peas and beans have been dried and ground into flour. Chickpea, fava, soy and lentil are some legume examples. Ground filberts, almonds and peanuts are nut flours. Legume and nut flours can be nutty in flavor and are often best if mixed with other flours, such as rice. Bean flours are high in soluble fiber, iron, protein, calcium, potassium and vitamins. Alone, they don't have all the amino acids to make a complete protein, but when you combine them with other grains, you have a more complete protein than in a fast food meal.

Mesquite Flour - There are over forty varieties of the mesquite tree that grows throughout South America, South Asia, Africa and North America. The pods from the tree are used in numerous applications, depending on the variety. Some pods are processed for syrup, coffee, jelly or jam. Other pods are ground into a coarse flour. This flour has an allspice, earthy aroma and is becoming popular in both Canada and the United States. The flour can be used in all types of baking, from muffins to pancakes. It is best to mix this flour with other flours when baking, it can be heavy and the resulting baked goodies may not be as light in texture and taste. The flour is very nutritious especially when the whole pod has been used. Calcium, iron, vitamins and fiber are some of the nutrients, as well as minerals and magnesium. And yes, this is the same tree that the bark is dried and used in grilling to add flavor to the food that is being barbequed.

Montina - Also known as Indian Rice Grass, it is named for the Native Americans who ground the black seeds into a flour that they would make into flatbread. Though it is a perennial native bunch grass, it is not related to rice. This is a gluten free, nutritious flour which is a light grayish brown in color. As with other grain flours, it has a nutty flavor and is best mixed with other flours when used in baking. Montina flour is high in fiber, iron and protein.

Millet

The first documented use of millet dates to about 2800 B.C. in China. It is the seeds found in grasses and has been used as a rice alternative for centuries throughout Asia. It is also popular in India and Africa. Actually, almost one third of the world's population use millet as a diet staple. Millet has many names. Panicum Milaceum is the true millet, also known as Broom-corn, Indian, Proso and Hog Millet. Echinochloa are also called Japanese Barnyard Millet, Deccan, Guinea, Barnyard Grass or Australian Millet. Setaria Italica, Foxtail Millet, is also known as Italian, German, Kursk, Turkestan and Hungarian Millet. Pennisetum Glaucum, Pearl Millet, is called Bajri in India and in the southern United States it is known as Cattail Millet. This type of millet is popular in Africa, Egypt and India. The flour made from this millet is used for making breads and cakes. Eleusine Coracana, African, Rage' or Finger Millet is grown from North Africa to Indonesia. This millet is also used in India for processing into flour that is used in cakes and breads. Millet is nutritious and easy to digest. It contains amino acids, phosphorus, iron and vitamin B. Millet has a nutty flavor and works well in stuffings, soups, vegetable and fish dishes, as well as stews. It is also used in baking and desserts. It is available in several forms and the most common are listed here.

Millet Flour - This is millet meal that has been ground finer. It is gluten free, so can be combined with rice or other flours for baking. Often heavy and a little bitter, this flour is best when mixed with other flours. When using in recipes, juice sweeteners, milk substitutes, cinnamon and allspice can help to balance the bitterness. This flour is best kept in the freezer.

Millet Meal - This is the whole grain that has been coarsely ground. It is most often used in cereals and baking.

Millet Puffed - The whole grain is puffed, making it a nutritious breakfast cereal. Added to breads, or puddings, it is a tasty, light addition that adds both nutrition as well as flavor.

Millet Wholegrain - This is not exactly a true whole grain. The grain is hulled because the outer shell is not digestable. You can cook this as a hot breakfast cereal, add to rice as a side dish, or use in dishes as a change from rice.

Potato Flour - This is not interchangeable with potato starch. With potato flour, the entire potato is used, including the skin. Potato starch only uses the starch. When potato flour is used in baking, remember that it is a heavy, more dense flour which expands so a dry, crumbly texture may result. Mix the flour with other flours when baking. It is gluten free. When it is used as a thickener, once boiled, it will thin out as it cools, so use immediately after cooking.

Quinoa - Excellent for allergy or intolerance diets, quinoa, pronounced "keen-wa" is gluten free, high in protein, and quick cooking. Though not a true grain, it is used in place of rice or millet, as a cereal, or in main dishes. Although quinoa has been around for centuries, the Inca's were the first known to use it. The taste is similar to rice, each person describes the taste differently, but all agree that it is worth trying. It was originally grown in Chile, Peru and Bolivia, but it is now grown worldwide. Quinoa is the fruit of a herb in the Goosefoot Family. It grows easily with little rain, in high altitudes, in cold or hot air. There are about eighteen hundred varieties with colors that also vary, white, black, red, green, orange, pink and even purple. Some Indians in Bolivia still use the entire plant, whole as rice, made into flour, or toasted then ground for tortillas. The leaves are eaten like a vegetable and the stalk is burned as fuel. Quinoa has protein, the amino acid lysine, iron and calcium. It is also rich in potassium, zinc, phosphorus and magnesium. Thiamin, niacin, riboflavin and dietary fiber are a part of the nutritional make-up. It is advised that you read the label to confirm it has been prewashed when you purchase whole grain quinoa. Saponin is the natural coating on the plant that acts as an insect repellant. It can be bitter tasting. Prewashing the quinoa takes away this bitterness. Quinoa can be expensive. This is because of it's size. The seed resembles sesame seeds, so many are used per pound. You can use the seeds in salads, in soups or stews, the flakes are a good hot cereal, or used in baking. Quinoa is also available as a flour and as a pasta, but it is usually mixed with corn. Versatile and nutritious, you should try this grain.

Rice

Rice is eaten three times a day by at least half of the world's population. People in parts of North America, Europe, Africa, Asia and South America eat rice as the main part of their meal. People of the Far East consume about four hundred pounds of rice per person per year. In North America, we consume about ten pounds per person per year. Rice was first grown in India about 3000 B.C., not in China as we would have thought. Rice needs to be submerged in water, between one to eight inches, during it's growing season. Where there is water, rice can grow, including in Italy, Indonesia and the Philippines. Rice is very nutritious. White rice is low in fat and sodium, high in fiber and has small amounts of protein, vitamin B, potassium and phosphorus. Brown rice is rich in vitamin B, thiamin, iron, niacin, riboflavin and calcium. There are over seven thousand types of rice grown worldwide. Up to about a decade ago, the majority of rice eaten, about ninety eight percent, was long grain white rice. Brown rice was only about two percent. In modern processing, rice goes to a drying plant where hot air is blown through it, curing it and reducing it's moisture content. The first milling process removes the husk. This leaves brown rice. The next process grinds away several layers leaving white rice. This also produces rice bran. Going a step farther, all the broken particles, seeds and defective grain is removed, leaving clean white rice. Years ago, it was then coated in talc or glucose. Old recipes will tell you to wash the rice until the water runs clean. This is no longer necessary. There are a number of forms of rice available, the basic are listed here.

Brown Rice - Described in the previous paragraph, this type of rice is nutritious because so little has been removed during milling. Brown rice has a nutty flavor which blends well in many dishes. This type of rice takes longer to cook than regular white rice.

Enriched Rice - As the name states, this rice has B vitamins and iron added to it. Long grain rice is the most common enriched rice.

Long Grain/Short Grain Rice - Most rice is short grain. Long grain rice will be specified on the label. Short grain rice is moister and more tender than long grain rice. This makes it a popular choice for dishes like risotto and croquettes. Long grain rice is fluffier, drier and cooks quicker than short grain rice. It is good in stuffings, pilaf and salads.

Parboiled Rice - This is long grain rice that has been partially cooked, steamed, then dried. This process helps it to retain a lot of the nutrients that would be lost in the milling. This type of rice takes longer to cook than regular rice.

Precooked Rice - This is a long grain rice that has been cooked, rinsed and then dried. It has a shorter cooking time, basically to reheat the rice.

There are so many types of rice. Each country seems to have a special style of rice which is used in their native dishes. We are becoming more in tune with how versatile rice can be. Jambalaya in the Carolina's of the United States, Picadillo of Cuba, Risottos of Italy, Paella of Spain, and of course, Sake from Japan.

For those who are on a gluten free diet, rice is a very valuable part of the diet. For a refreshing change from regular, plain rice, try some of these varieties.

Arborio - This is a short grain rice from Italy. The outer part of the grain is translucent, with an opaque center. It can absorb a lot of liquid, so this type of rice is very popular for risotto dishes.

Basmati - This long grain rice originates from the basmati blossom of Southeast Asia. It also grows in Iran, India and Pakistan. This rice is aged for about one year to let the flavors develop. Unhulled basmati rice is similar to wild rice in both texture and flavor. The most popular basmati type is hulled. In the United States, basmati rice is grown and has it's own names. Texmati from Texas and a reddish brown variety is grown in California known as Wahini. Another variety is milled to keep most of the bran, giving it a pecan like flavor, and it is named Wild Pecan Rice.

Jasmine White - This long grain rice is very white, soft and has a pleasing, subtle flavor. Thailand and the United States are the prominent producers of Jasmine White Rice. It can be substituted for basmati rice.

Thai Black - This black long grain rice has been grown in Thailand for many years. It has a shiny appearance and is somewhat sticky. Thailand uses it mostly for desserts. The coating on the bran is soluble so the dark color of the grain seeps into the cooking water, leaving the rice a purple color.

Wild Rice - This is actually a seed from an aquatic plant. It is found throughout the Great Lakes region of Canada and the United States. The seeds are picked by hand, making it more expensive than other types of rice. Many years ago, the Native Americans called it Mahnomen. Other varieties are grown in Korea, Japan, China and Burma. It is a good source of fiber, protein, vitamin B and minerals. Wild rice is sometimes mixed with other varieties of rice. You will be able to find these packages of wild rice blends at most grocers and they are a nice change from regular rice. There are three types of wild rice. Long, or giant, is the best quality as each grain is about one inch long. This also makes it the most expensive, usually saving this rice for very special dishes. Medium, or extra fancy, is the most common type. The grains are of uniform size and are unbroken. This variety is good in salads, stuffings and side dishes. The last variety is short, or select. This is whole or broken grains that are different sizes, making it ideal for baking.

Now that you have a knowledge of the basic types, here are some of the most popular rice products. Most of the products made from rice are gluten free and can be used in both sweet and savory baking and cooking. Remember to read labels for hidden ingredients,

B. A. Smit

such as wheat as a filler, in some of these products. Using rice products as a substitute for gluten products will enable you to expand the variety of foods you can enjoy.

Rice Bran - This is the rice outer brown layer, with a part of the germ included. It is high in fiber and can be used instead of wheat germ. Rice bran is a very nutritious addition to muffins, breads and cookies. It is best stored in a cool place, such as the fridge or freezer. Also, it is best to buy in smaller amounts so it can be used quicker to ensure freshness.

Rice Bran Oil - This is still being researched, but is known to possibly raise high density good liproprotein and lower the bad low density liproprotein, thus helping to lower cholesterol.

Rice Crackers/Rice Cakes - Rice crackers are made from rice flour and are available in a variety of flavors. Again, read labels as some rice crackers are made in the same place as wheat productions and cross contamination of gluten may occur. Rice cakes are made from puffed rice. More and more varieties are becoming available, even salted and unsalted. Read labels carefully, some varieties offer flavors such as multi grained that contain gluten. You can eat the crackers or cakes with a multitude of toppings from sweet to savory. Let your creativity guide you.

Rice Cream/Rice Milk - There are a number of rice milks available. I found that some types did not thicken for puddings. Some manufacturers use products that result in the rice milk not being gluten free. Barley malt is a common ingredient that can be added that is not gluten free. Read labels. This product is tasty by the glass, over cereal and in baking.

Rice Flakes - Rice flakes are made in a similar fashion as oat flakes. Heated, then pressed flat, rice flakes are thicker than oat flakes. They are good as a hot breakfast cereal and are cooked the same as oat flakes, commonly known as rolled oats. Rice flakes are also tasty in muffins, cookies and breads.

Rice Flour - This is a light, mild flour. There is no gluten in rice flour, so it is excellent for gluten free diets. Rice flour is great for thickening gravies, and works well in muffins, pancakes, breads and cakes. It has a finer texture than wheat flour. This means that rice flour does not bind well when used alone, so when baking, combining it with other flours, starches and eggs or other binder will produce a much better result. Rice flour is available as both brown rice or white rice flour. Brown rice flour is more nutritious and is preferred by most.

Rice Flour/Glutenous - This is the sweet, sticky or sushi rice flour that is gluten free despite it's name. This flour is made from the short grain rice that is higher in starch than white or brown rice grains, making it sticky.

Rice Meal - This is rice that has been ground. It is used mainly as a hot breakfast cereal.

Rice Noodles - Made from rice flour, rice noodles come in a vast array of shapes. Most are similar to wheat pasta, like macaroni, spiral or spaghetti pasta. There is also fine, thin angel hair pasta, broad or skinny noodles. Some varieties have dried vegetables added to the rice flour before the noodles are made. Read labels to ensure that the added ingredients are a part of your diet. You can create any number of dishes using rice noodles. They are cooked in boiling salted water like wheat pasta, but the cooking time is shorter.

Rice Paper - If you enjoy egg rolls and feel that you will miss them, rice paper is a gluten free option. Rice paper is very thin sheets of rice dough that have been dried. Usually they are round, triangle or square in shape. Soak in water to soften, about one to two minutes, fill with a sweet or savory filling then rolling as you would a tortilla or egg roll. Fry over medium heat in a small amount of oil.

Rice Polish - This is a flour that is collected during the processing of white rice. It contains small amounts of the bran and germ. Rice polish is high in fiber, vitamins and iron. It can be used in baking and can be a substitute for wheat germ.

Puffed Rice - As the name implies, this is rice that, under pressure, is filled with air, expanding or puffing the rice. It is used worldwide as a cold breakfast cereal. Puffed rice can also be used in candy, homemade granola or baking.

Rice Syrup - This is a sweet syrup made from brown rice. It can be poured on cereal or pancakes, used in baking as a sweetener and in beverages. Rice syrup can be used to replace maple syrup as a sweetener, but the maple flavor is not in rice syrup, something to remember when baking.

Rice Wine - Produced by both the Japanese and Chinese, the most popular type of rice wine is sake from Japan. It can be served hot, cold or at room temperature. Besides drinking sake, it is often used in Asian cooking.

There are many products available that are made from rice. These are just a few of the most common. With this knowledge, you will be able to find many substitutes for products that contain gluten.

Sorghum - This cereal grain thrives in hot, dry climates. It is grown worldwide, including the United States, Mexico, India, Africa and China. Sorghum is similar in composition and processing properties as corn. New varieties have been developed in the United States. They have a hard, white grain that is not bitter or dark like other sorghum grains. This makes these new varieties a popular choice for cereals, baked goods, snack foods and beer. Sorghum, like corn, can be milled into flour, grits and meal. The flour can be blended with other flours for baking, and with it's plain flavor, it will not alter the taste of baked goods. When using this flour, it is best to add about one tablespoon of cornstarch for every cup of flour used. This helps to maintain moisture. Wholegrain sorghum can be used instead of rice in soups and stews. Sorghum is rich in potassium, phosphorus, fiber and iron. It also has protein, niacin, thiamin and vitamin B6.

Spelt - Related to wheat, this is a European grain. It has a high gluten content, but a few people who can't tolerate wheat, can tolerate spelt. Check with your doctor first before using spelt. It contains more fiber, fats and protein than wheat, and is easy to digest. Be cautious with spelt, you may not be able to tolerate this grain. It is also known as Dinkel or Farro/Faro.

Tapioca - Sometimes called cassava, yucca or manioc, this flour is made from the root of the cassava plant. It is ideal for thickening sweet or savory dishes. When used with other flours for coating meat, vegetables or seafood for deep frying, it will produce a crispy coating. It is also used in baking, but use a small amount in ratio to other flours used. Tapioca flour, or starch, is pure white with no real nutrient value.

Taro - This is a large, starchy tuber from a tropical plant. The tuber is used as a vegetable in South Asian and tropical regions. It is also known as Dasheen or Eddo. It is gluten free.

Teff - This is an Ethiopian grain that is much lighter than wheat, but is gluten free. Teff is almost always sold as wholegrain, maintaining all the nutrients. Rich in protein, calcium, iron and magnesium, thiamin, niacin and riboflavin. It contains almost five times the iron, potassium and calcium than any other grain. Teff is also high in fiber. You can use it as a cereal, in baking, desserts, or as a part of main dishes. Teff is the smallest grain in the world, one hundred teff grains equal one kernel of wheat. It is available as brown or ivory colored seeds, has a light, almost earthy flavor and you can purchase it as wholegrain or as a flour. Teff is a major crop in Ethiopia and they make a porous, thin flatbread called injera from it. In North America, this flatbread can sometimes be made from a wheat and teff blend, so inquire before purchasing.

Herbs and Spices

Introduction

Introduction

Herbs are plants which add flavor to food. Flavoring is usually oils that are released into the food, adding a subtle enhancement of flavor. Herbs may be either the seeds or the foliage of a plant. The most popular herbs used are sage, thyme, parsley, dill, tarragon, basil, chives, oregano and savory. Though only seed plants that do not develop a woody persistent tissue are considered herbs, botanical plants are gaining popularity. Rose, marigold, violet and geraniums are a few. Herbs are used in teas, cooking, salads and some medicines.

When cooking with herbs, be selective with the types and amounts used. If the herb has a strong flavor, don't use too much as it will overpower the food's flavor. Use one half of a teaspoon dried herbs for every tablespoon of fresh herb called for in a recipe. Crumble dried herbs as you add them to the food or tear fresh herbs into the food to release the flavor.

Try to use fresh herbs whenever possible. Dried herbs are often stored close to the stove. The heat from the stove and keeping the herbs for too long are the two main reasons why these types of herbs lose their flavor. Dried herbs should be kept in a cool area away from heat and used within two to three months. If your herbs develop a musty or flat aroma, they should be thrown out. Try to purchase only enough dry herbs as needed for one month. Fresh herbs are best if you can grow your own and snip what you need when you need it. Store bought fresh herbs should be stored in the fridge and used within three to five days.

The most interesting herbs are included in this book to increase your knowledge for seasoning food.

The origin of spices is unknown, although a Chinese herb has been dated 2700 B.C. Spices and herbs are also spoken of in the Bible. Pepper is considered the most valuable spice as it has no smell to overpower food aromas. It enhances and adds zing to the food. Other popular spices include cinnamon, nutmeg, mace, cloves, curry, ginger and allspice.

We consume one hundred thousand pounds of spices worldwide per year. A profound amount when you consider how light the powder is and how little is used in each dish. Spices have been used for thousands of years, giving palate pleasing pleasures to all who dare to indulge.

Whole spices keep longer than ground spices. They should be stored in an airtight container away from direct light and heat. They will keep for about six months before they lose their potency. Grind only what you will use for each recipe or meal.

Although there are many spices, I have only included the most widely known and used in this book.

B. A. Smit

Herbs

Anise - This herb is grown in hot climates. Asia, Mexico, South America and India are some of the countries where anise grows. When dried, the seeds are brown with tan stripes. The leaves are sold fresh or dried, the flowers are powdered and the seeds are either whole or ground. Anise has a distinct licorice flavor. This herb is used in coffee cakes, cookies and other baked goodies. It also works well in meat, poultry and seafood dishes. Some salad and vegetable dishes can also be enhanced by this herb.

Basil - This herb has several varieties. Sweet, Dwarf, Italian and Lemon are the most common types of basil. Beginning in the Near East, it is now grown worldwide. The flavor is like cloves, only a bit spicier. The leaves and stems are sold as dried, ground or fresh. Basil is most popular in Italian or tomato based dishes, but is also good in meat, seafood, vegetable and poultry dishes. Herb butter, marinades and pesto are made with basil.

Bayleaf - This herb is also known as Sweet Bay or Laurel. It is grown in warmer climates like Portugal, Central America, Southern United States and the Mediterranean. The leaves are smooth and waxy, and when fresh, the underside is pale yellowish green, the top green. When dried, it is all yellowish green. It is available dried, whole leaves or ground. Bayleaf has a bitter aromatic aroma. This herb is used mainly in soup stocks, stews, chowders and tomato sauce. The leaf is placed in the food and simmered until the food is cooked then the leaf is removed before serving.

Capers - Native to the Mediterranean, it is now grown in North Africa, Southern Europe and the Southern United States. The caper plant is a straggly shrub with white flowers. Capers are the unopened flower buds. They must be picked in the very early morning before they have a chance to open. Usually, they are sold pickled, but dried capers are also available. They can be used instead of olives on appetizers, as a garnish for fish or in sauces. They are good in oil based sauces, dressings or in tartar sauce. Capers are a must for antipasta.

Caraway - This is grown in Europe, Asia, Japan and parts of both Canada and the United States. The dried fruit is the caraway seed. It can be used whole or dried. Caraway has a strong, sharp flavor, almost a cross between dill and anise. Use sparingly at first. The leaves and leaf stem can be found whole or dried. They are milder in flavor. The flavor of bean or cabbage soup is enhanced with the addition of caraway, either leaf or seed. Cheese, egg and cottage cheese are also foods that caraway blends well with. The most famous use is in rye breads, muffins and scones. The seeds add flavor to some cakes, cookies and fruit dishes as well.

Chervil - Though it began in Europe, chervil is now cultivated in the eastern part of the United States. The plant has bright green leaves that resemble a fern. This herb is often used like parsley because of how similar they look. Chervil has a very subtle licorice flavor. The leaves are available fresh or dried, as well as whole sprigs. The sprigs can be used in sauces, soups or as a garnish. With it's flavor similar to parsley and tarragon, it goes well in meat, poultry, fish, cheese and egg dishes. It enhances butter sauces, salads and some salad dressings.

Dill - This herb is native to Europe, but is now cultivated in North America. The plant grows to between two and three feet high, has fine, whispy green leaves, the flowers are yellow and grow in large umbrella shaped clusters. The tiny seeds are often dried before selling. The leaves and stem are available fresh or dried, though fresh is better. The taste can be powerful, bitter, with a bite resembling caraway. Dill's most popular use is in pickling, but adds zip to fish, meat, egg and poultry dishes. It is used in breads and muffins. Vegetables and salad dressings have more flavor when dill is added.

Fennel - There are three varieties, wild, sweet and carosella. Both wild and sweet are known for their bright green leaves. The stems are smooth and shiny. The sweet variety is shorter and the stems overlap with a base that is thick, similar to celery. The carosella is grown in gardens. It has a thick stalk, like celery, but is a shorter plant than the wild or sweet varieties. The leaves, stems and seeds are available fresh, dried or ground. The base (bulb) and roots of the sweet and carosella are edible. The flavor has a sweet, licorice tone to it. Fennel is used in Italian sausage, cabbage dishes, fish, eggs, some breads and is wonderful in many vegetable dishes.

Horseradish - This is native to Southeastern Europe. It is known for it's white root which is large, thick, wrinkled branches. The stem above the ground flowers and can reach three feet high. There are two kinds of leaves. The early, which are comb like, and the later, which are green, shiny and oblong with scalloped edges. Both the root and the leaves are used. The pungent sharp odor is released when the root is ground or grated. The early leaves are bitter with a sharp aftertaste. The root is available fresh or preserved in vinegar. As a vegetable dip, it is mixed with sour cream, horseradish often accompanies roast beef or lamb and is used in some dressings and stuffings. Fresh ground root is commonly mixed with tomato paste or sauce and used as a seafood sauce, known as cocktail sauce. Finely chopped leaves may be added to salads.

Lovage - Native to Southern Europe and the United States Atlantic Seaboard, wild Scotch Lovage grows and is used in herbal medicine. The lovage plant grows to about six feet high with dark green celery like leaves with clusters of yellow flowers. Sold fresh or dried, the leaves, stem base, leafstalks, root and seeds are all used. The leaves have a mild, celery like flavor, but the root's taste and smell are stronger. The leaves give a celery flavor to many foods, from cocktails to soups. The seeds, tied in a cheesecloth, are simmered in lamb, beef, venison or rabbit stew. The root can be blanched and served like celery. Rub the leaves onto the sides and bottom of your salad bowl or add the seeds to your salad dressing. The seeds can be used like caraway seeds to flavor or garnish foods.

Marjoram - Originally from the Mediterranean region, it also now grows in cooler climates like the United States. The plant grows to about one foot in height and has light green oval shaped leaves. The flowers are pink or lilac. This is an aromatic herb belonging to the mint family. It is similar to sage in flavor, though usually milder. The flowering tips are used in medicine and the leaves are used in cooking. It adds flavor to avocados, mushrooms, pate' and clam chowder. It blends wonderfully to flavor beef, pork, veal and stews. Sprinkle on fish or in cream sauces for fish. Marjoram is a perfect partner to season poultry. The flavor enhances salad ingredients as well.

Mint - There are at least thirty varieties of mint. About one dozen alone are grown in the United States and Canada. The plants differ in appearance, but all types have square, red tinged stems with purple flowers. The leaves are used to flavor all foods. Mint is available fresh, dried, as oil or powdered. Most species are interchangeable and can be used in juices, teas, soups, fish, cottage cheese or as a delicate flavoring for lamb. It is a subtle addition to salad dressings and vegetables like cabbage, carrots, beans, potatoes and in fruit desserts. The most popular varieties of mint are peppermint and spearmint.

Mustard - Native to Western Asia and Europe, mustard, black or white, can grow wild throughout the countryside. Black mustard is an annual plant that can grow to about four feet high. The leaves are smooth, yellow/green with bright yellow flowers. The white mustard is small, only twelve to eighteen inches high, with tender green leaves. Both mustard varieties are grown for the seeds which are often ground into a powder. This is used in prepared mustard or sold packaged as powdered mustard. The leaves of the white mustard can be eaten. The black mustard seeds are stronger in flavor than the white variety. Mustard powder is used to season roasts or creamed chicken. Eggs, cottage cheese and some fish dishes are enhanced by mustard. Mustard seeds are used in making pickles and can add flavor to salad dressings. And everyone knows that prepared mustard is a hot dog staple.

Oregano - Though oregano began in Eurasia, it is now grown across the Northwest United States and Canada. There are numerous varieties, each differing in appearance. Some varieties grow up to three feet high with hairy, branch like, purplish stems and oval shaped dark green leaves. The leaves can be used fresh or dried. Oregano has a subtle sweet flavor similar to marjoram or thyme, but is stronger in flavor so should be used carefully. It can be used as a light seasoning on beef, lamb, pork or poultry, including sausages. It gives a distinct flavor in cheese and egg dishes. Oregano is popular to flavor Mexican, Spanish and Italian dishes. It is great in spaghetti and pizza, but can also be added to salad dressings and vegetable dishes.

Parsley - There are about thirty varieties of the parsley plant, which is similar in looks to carrot tops. Named to describe the looks of the leaves or roots, some of the most known types are Doublecurled, Moss Leaved, Fern Leaved and Turnip Rooted. The parsley is a small plant with leaves and flowers that vary from plant to plant. The leaves have a refreshing flavor and aroma. It is used mainly as a garnish, but can be used in soups, stews, beef, pork or chicken dishes. It adds a perk to fish stuffings or sprinkled over egg or cheese dishes. As a herb, it is added to biscuits, muffins, breads and in butter and marinades. It is used as a seasoning for vegetables and in salads. Cilantro is very similar in looks and how it is used. The flavor though, is much stronger, with a pepper like tang. This herb is used in many Asian, South and Central American dishes. It will give a totally different flavor if used in place of parsley.

Rosemary - In Southern Europe it grows wild, but in the remaining Europe and the United States, it is now cultivated. A slow growing plant, it can grow to a height of three to four feet. It is an evergreen shrub with branching stems with one to one and a half inch long thin green leaves that resemble pine needles. The underside is slightly gray and fuzz like with blush colored flowers. The leaves are sold fresh or dried. They have a strong, spicy flavor. The rosemary flavor is good in chicken and vegetable soups. It blends well to the flavors of beef, lamb, game, pork, veal and poultry. It is often used in fish stuffings or salmon dishes. This herb is a sweet and subtle addition to herb breads, dumplings and biscuits. Rosemary is wonderful in marinades, salad dressings, vegetables and salads.

Sage - Beginning in Northern Mediterranean countries, sage now grows worldwide. Dalmation Sage, one of the best varieties, is grown in Yugoslavia. There are about five hundred species of sage including Garden, White, Cyprus, Meadow, Pineapple and Clary. Almost all varieties are perennial shrubs that grow to between twelve and twenty four inches high. They have grayish leaves and bluish purple flowers. Only the leaves are used and are available fresh, dried, chopped and powdered. It has an aromatically bitter flavor. A small amount added to dips, pates, chowders, soups, sausage and stews enhances flavor. It is especially good in poultry dishes, fish stuffings and seafood sauces. Sage also perks up herb breads, dressings and vegetables such as beans, carrots, eggplant and tomatoes.

Savory - There are two types of savory, Summer and Winter. Native to the Mediterranean area, it is now cultivated through out Europe and North America. The Summer Savory is bush like with many branches, growing to about eighteen inches high. The stem is weak, so the bush will often fall over. The leaves are dark green with a multitude of pink, blue or purplish flowers all over the bush. Winter Savory is similar, but the stem is stronger, woodier and spreads out more with stiffer leaves than the Summer Savory. The leaves are used fresh or dried. Winter Savory is stronger in flavor than the Summer variety, so use carefully. Both varieties are a great flavor boost to chowders, bean and lentil dishes, stuffings, poultry or fish, stews, dairy products like yogurt, herb breads, sauces and gravies. A wonderful addition with artichokes, beets, cabbage, green beans and salads.

Sorrel - This grows wild in Europe, Asia and North America. There are several varieties which differ in leaf shape and strength of flavor. All varieties have some acidic flavor. The mildest is Spinach Dock or Herb Patience Dock. Growing over five feet tall, it's foot long leaves are used in salads. French Sorrel has shield shaped leaves with a distinct sour taste. It is also used in salads. The most acidic is called Garden or Belleville Sorrel, also known as Sour Dock. The leaves are oblong, about four inches in length and green in color. The flavor is mild in spring, developing into a stronger flavor as summer turns to fall. Garden Sorrel is used in salads, cutlets, ham, lamb, omelettes, breads and vegetables. The most popular method uses a cream sauce for a soup or purée base.

Tarragon - Originating in Asia, tarragon now grows in cooler regions including the United States and Europe. This perennial shrub like plant grows to a height of about eighteen inches. The leaves are long, narrow, pointed in shape and dark green in color. The stems are stiff and woody. The leaves are available fresh or dried and have a light anise flavor. A pleasing addition to chicken livers, vegetable chowders, pheasant, sweetbreads, tongue, veal and poultry dishes. It is a delicious seasoning for seafood, especially lobster. Often it is sprinkled over eggs. Tarragon is added to flavor vinegar, butters and marinades. It is also in mustard, mayonnaise and tartar sauce and a staple herb for Sauce Bearnaise. Vegetables such as asparagus, beets, beans, broccoli, cabbage, tomato, including salads and dressings, work well with tarragon.

Thyme - There are two types, garden and wild, and each have a number of varieties. Garden Thyme grows in Europe, United States and Canada. Wild Thyme grows from South Eastern Canada to North Carolina. Garden Thyme is a small, bushy perennial about twelve inches high, with small gray/green leaves. English Thyme has wider leaves. There are many types of Wild Thyme, which usually creeps along the ground before rising into firmly matted small bushes. The leaves are many colors, depending on the variety. Some are striped, white or greenish yellow. The flowers range from blue to red. The leaves and flowering tops of both types are used as seasoning, either fresh or dried. It has a sweet aroma and sharp taste. Lemon Thyme has a lemony scent and flavor, like caraway. Thyme is added to cocktails, fish chowder and stews. Use sparingly on beef, game, lamb, pork or meatloaf. Seafood and egg dishes are enhanced by thyme. It is an important addition to stuffings, biscuits, herb breads and herb bouquets. Vegetables, particularly beans, beets, carrots, onions and potatoes are enhanced in flavor when thyme is used.

Watercress - Grown from Europe to North America, it is a small perennial with tiny, shiny, round dark green leaves. The stem is pale green and the flowers are small and white in color. The leaves and stem have a fresh, crisp, peppery flavor. They are used as a garnish, minced then added to meat sandwich fillings, chowders, soups, fish or cream cheese spreads. You can use watercress the same as sorrel in sauces, salads and vegetables. It is especially good with carrots, beans, potatoes, cauliflower and sweet potato.

Spices

Allspice - The berry of the allspice tree is used for this spice. It is either whole or ground. The flavor is a combination of cloves, nutmeg and cinnamon. It works well in many foods, from breads, cakes, fruit pies and puddings, to sausage, fish and eggs. Allspice is especially good when used in mincemeat and pickling.

Cardamon - This spice is native to Sri Lanka and South India. It is a vital spice used in Indian cooking. Cardamon is grown in pods, usually about twelve to fifteen seeds per pod. The spice can be purchased as whole pods, seeds or ground seeds. North Americans prefer using the ground seeds, though some use whole pods and remove them before serving.

Cayenne - Also known as Red, Whole or Chili Peppers, cayenne is used in many Mexican dishes. The flavor is hot and peppery with different strengths of heat. It is used in meat dishes, salad dressings, sauces, stews, egg and cheese dishes, as well as vegetable and chicken dishes. When using this spice, begin with a smaller amount and add more depending on your taste.

Cinnamon - The bark of the Cassia Cinnamon Tree is where this spice originates. It has a subtle sweet taste, and is found either ground or left in stick form. The stick form is used to add flavor to spiced drinks, or to enhance sauces, being removed before serving. Ground cinnamon is used in cakes, breads, pies, puddings and both sweet and savory sauces. Meat dishes, pickling and preserves also include cinnamon.

Cloves - These are small, spike shaped buds from the clove tree that are picked before they open. Left whole, cloves are used in ham roasts, spice bags for meats and stews, pickles, as well as scent sachets. Ground cloves are used in baked goodies, pies, fish and vegetable dishes. The warm, sweet pungent taste enhances all food that it is added to.

Coriander - This is the seed of a dried fruit from a small herb plant belonging to the Parsley Family. It has a light, pleasing flavor, similar to orange, anise and cumin. When ground, it is used in baking cookies, breads and soups. It also blends well in meats and salads. Many of the blended spices, such as curry, contain coriander. Remember way back to the jawbreaker candy, they contained a coriander seed in the center.

Cumin - The cumin plant is a member of the Parsley Family, like coriander. The plant grows to about six feet tall. The seed, which is used for the spice, is small, oval, with a strong, slightly bitter flavor. It resembles the caraway seed both in looks and flavor. The uses of both spices is the same, but cumin is stronger in flavor and you should use less than the caraway seed. The plant is native to North Africa, Western Asia, as well as the Mediterranean. The spice is used in pickling spices, curry and chili powders, as well as a seasoning in breads, cookies, cheese, egg and meat dishes. Cumin is available whole or ground. I find this spice is similar to curry, but not as strong in flavor and I use it in place of curry to give the food the flavor without the "bite".

B. A. Smit

Garlic - This bulb enhances so many dishes. Dried, ground, minced fresh, a little adds a lot of flavor. You can use garlic in stirfries, soups, stews, seafood, salads and pickles, to name just a few ideas. For fresh garlic, choose firm, white bulbs with fat cloves (sections) that are not discolored or shriveled. Store in a cool, well ventilated place for up to one month. There are several varieties of garlic available. Standard and Elephant are the most popular. The outer, paperlike skin may be streaked with a red/rose tint. When you use fresh garlic, remove the number of cloves needed from the bulb. Smashing the clove with the side of a knife will loosen the skin making it easier to remove. Slice, dice or mince the garlic as you want for your recipe.

Ginger - With many uses, this is a root spice that has a sharp, aromatic, lightly citrus flavor. When preserved or crystalized, it is a confection. Left whole or cracked, it is used in pickles, chutneys and fruits. Ground ginger is used in baking, fish, stew, meat, vegetable and fruit dishes. This spice is often used in Asian and Oriental dishes.

Mace - This is the light layer covering the nutmeg seeds. Stronger in flavor than nutmeg, mace is used in puddings, fruit dishes, candies and custards. When added to chocolate, it enhances the flavor. It is also used in sausage meats, poultry, fish, soups, vegetables, pickles, chutney and chowders.

Nutmeg - This spice is the seed of the nutmeg tree. It has a light, barely bitter hint of cinnamon flavor. When left whole, it can be freshly ground as needed, or it can be purchased already ground. It is used in many ways, from hot beverages, baked goodies, meat, poultry and fish to vegetable and fruit dishes.

Paprika - This is ground from the pods of a mild pepper. It has a dry, lightly sweet taste with a mild bitter after taste. It has a bright but deep red/orange color, which is why it's used as a garnish sprinkled over appetizers. Paprika is used in meat, vegetable and seafood dishes. Ketchup, chili sauce and pickles use paprika as a seasoning. Hungarian dishes are well known for their use of paprika.

Pepper, Black - This is the most widely used spice. The peppercorns are dried berries from the pepper vine. They are either freshly ground in a small, hand held mill, left whole or sold already ground. It has a strong odor with a biting pungent taste. If you breathe it in, you may sneeze. It is used as a seasoning for meats, fish, poultry, soups, vegetables and egg dishes. Black pepper is also used in chutneys, pickles and relish. It is used mainly in savory dishes, rarely for sweets or baked goodies.

Pepper, White - This is a variety of pepper. After the black hull of the berry is removed, the inside of the berry is used for white pepper. It is milder than the black pepper, so a little more is used. Since it is white and will blend in, it is valuable for it's use in white sauces, light meats and fish, not leaving black flecks like black pepper would. A note to remember is that sometimes white flour is added to white pepper as a filler, so not all brands are gluten free, read labels.

Saffron - This is taken from the stigma of a crocus flower. It is grown mainly in Southern Europe and parts of Asia. The cost is high for this spice. On average, it takes about two hundred and twenty five thousand stigmas to equal one pound of saffron. Because saffron is expensive, and often found only in specialty stores, turmeric is an affordable, easy to find substitute. Saffron has a subtle, bitter flavor and is used in teas, cakes, buns, breads, chicken and seafood dishes. It adds flavor to soups, sauces and rice as well.

Turmeric - Taken from the root of a plant in the Ginger Family, this spice has a slightly bitter taste, and is known for it's bright golden color. Turmeric is often used in place of saffron, and works well in curried dishes, eggs, sauces, salad dressings and rice. Most commonly found in the ground form, it is popular in curry powders, pickles, chutneys and prepared mustard.

Just a Note

Curry is a blend of spices, therefore, it is not classed as a true, pure spice. Curry powder is often a blend of turmeric, ginger, green and sometimes red chilies, fenugreek, cumin, nutmeg, cardamon, cinnamon and other herbs like lemon grass. In places like India, each family will have their own unique blend. When you purchase curry powder, you will find that there are different blends and levels of heat. You will have to find a brand or blend that you prefer.

Dried chilies are not the same as chili powder. Although they are both available ground, in bottles, dried chilies are whole chilies that have been dried then ground. Chili powder is a spice mixture.

B. A. Smit

Spice Blend Recipes
B.B.Q. Spice Mix

1 TBSP each:	Chili Powder	1 TSP each:	Garlic Powder
	Paprika		Dry Mustard
	Salt		Dried Oregano
	Ground Pepper		
2 TSP each:	Ground Cumin		
	Dry Sweetener		
1/4 TSP	Cayenne Pepper		

Mix well and store in an airtight container away from heat and direct light. Use amount called for in recipe.

Caribbean Spice Mix

1 TBSP Lime Juice		1 TSP each:	Cloves
1 TSP Minced Rind of 1 Lime			Cinnamon
2 TSP Oil			Cumin
1/2 TSP each:	Salt		Curry
	Pepper		

Combine all ingredients in a bowl. Marinate your chicken or turkey for at least two hours in this mixture. Discard marinade and cook your poultry. This recipe can be cut in half and mixed then added to two pounds of ground meat, chicken or turkey work best, and made into a meatloaf and baked. You can use lemon instead of lime in this recipe.

Chili Powder

3 TBSP Dried, Ground Chiles		1/2 TSP Garlic Powder	
1 TBSP Ground Cumin		1/4 TSP each:	Ground Oregano
1 TSP each:	Thyme		Cloves
	Cayenne Pepper		

Combine all ingredients, store and use as other spice mixes.

Chinese Five Spice

1 TBSP each:	Anise Seed, crushed
	Ground Cinnamon
	Ground Ginger
	Ground Cloves
	Ground Nutmeg

Combine, store and use as other spice mixes. This is good when rubbed onto pork, chicken or beef pieces then cooked. Rubbed on pork and roasted in a slow oven is also good.

Curry Powder

2 TBSP Cumin Seeds
1 TBSP Coriander Seeds
3 Dried Red Chilies
3/4 TSP Ground Turmeric

2 TSP each: Ground Cinnamon
Ground Cumin
Whole Mustard Seeds
Ground Ginger

Mix together the seeds and chilies. Roast on a baking sheet in a 350° oven for five minutes. Remove and cool. Split the chilies and remove the seeds. Grind all the spices together in a mortar and pestle, coffee grinder or spice mill. When blended evenly, put into a container, store and use like the other spice mixes.

Garam Masala for Indian Flavoring

3 TBSP Coriander Seeds
1 TBSP Green Cardamon Seeds
2 TSP Cinnamon
1 1/2 TSP Ground Nutmeg

2 TBSP each: Cumin Seeds
Black Peppercorns
1 TSP Ground Cloves

In a small pan over medium high heat, lightly toast the spices. Grind the spices in a mortar and pestle, coffee grinder or spice mill. Store and use as other spice mixes.

B. A. Smit

Legumes and Nuts

Legumes:
    Introduction
    Tips on Legumes
    List of Most Common Legumes

The Four Divisions of Legumes:

Unusual:
    Goober Peas   Yam Beans
    Winged Beans

Asian and African:
    Introduction   Cow Peas
    Adzuki Beans   Mung Beans
    Black Gram   Pigeon Peas
    Black-eyed Peas   Yard Long Beans

Old World Legumes:
    Introduction   Lentils: Introduction
    Chickpeas   Beluga
    Fava Beans   Brown
    Fresh Peas   French Green
    Garden Peas   Green
    Lipini Beans   Red
    Peas   Split White
    Snow Peas   Whole Red
    Split Peas
    Sugar Snap Peas

New World Legumes:
    Introduction   Kidney Beans
    Barlotti Beans   Lima Beans
    Black Beans   Navy and Great Northern Beans
    Black Runner Beans Pink Beans
    Cranberry Beans   Pinto Beans
    French Navy Beans Runner Beans
    Gigante Beans   Scarlet Runner Beans
    Green Beans   Small Lima Beans
    Green Romano Beans Small Red Beans
    Haricots Verts   Wax Beans
                        Peanuts

Heirloom True Bean Varieties:

Introduction	Rattlesnake Beans
Anasazi Beans	Red Valentine Beans
Appaloosa Beans	Rice Beans
Bolita Beans	Swedish Brown Beans
Calypso Beans	Zebra Beans
French Horticultural Beans	

Hemp
Carob

Soybeans:

Introduction	Soy Flour
Chinese Pastes	Soy Milk
Fermented Black Beans	Soybean Sprouts
Lecithin	Black Soy Sauce
Miso	Soy Sauce
Shoyu	Tamari

Tofu:

Introduction
Japanese Tofu: Kinu, Silken
                Momen or Regular
                Yakidotu

Tempah

Nuts:

Introduction	Macadamia Nuts
Almonds	Pecans
Brazil Nuts	Pine Nuts
Cashew Nuts	Pistachio Nuts
Chestnuts	Pumpkin Seeds
Coconuts	Sesame Seeds
Hazelnuts	Sunflower Seeds
Hickory Nuts	Walnuts

Homemade Legume or Nut Flour

Legumes
Introduction

Legumes are economical, nutritious and versatile. Nutritionally, legumes contain soluble fiber, which is good to lower cholesterol and stabilize blood sugar levels. Insoluble fiber, found in most legumes, can speed up the passage of food through the system, helping to keep you regular. It can also help to prevent some cancers. Legumes are a good source of potassium, which helps to regulate a steady heartbeat, stabilze water balance and blood pressure, as well as passing nutrients to cells. Legumes are also full of pantothenic acid, niacin, thiamin and pyridoxine, all that are needed for healthy nerve and brain cells. They also keep the digestive system and skin nerves functioning normally. Legumes are a good source of vegetable proteins that must be combined with complementary protein in order to become a complete protein that contains all the amino acids. Eating rice, nuts, seeds or grains with your legumes will make a complete protein.

Legumes are defined as plants that have pods which open along two seams when the seeds are ripe. It is usually the seed that is eaten. There are over eleven thousand varieties. The most common legumes are peas, beans, chickpeas, lima beans, peanuts, lentils and soybeans. In some countries, legumes are an essential part of their diet. Legumes can grow easily and then be dried, making storage easy.

Legumes have been used for centuries. Many countries have adopted native dishes from legumes. There is tamiya (bean cake) and ful mudamas (baked beans) from Egypt, hummus (chickpea) from the Middle East, India has dal (dried peas and lentils), France has cassoult and Asia has tofu (bean curds).

With so many varieties, there are almost as many variations in cooking. The flavors can also be vastly different from one legume to another. It is best to read directions, follow recipes and then experiment. Once you are familiar with the flavors and cooking of legumes, experimenting will be fun.

Legumes are available canned, frozen, dried or fresh. Canned, like kidney beans, chickpea and four bean are already cooked. They can be added to main dishes, salads and dips. Frozen legumes include lima beans and green beans. Quality is improving for frozen foods, so they can be quite tasty. Dried legumes are the most popular. These should be sorted and checked for dirt and stones before you store them and rinsed before cooking. Dried legumes store well and can be so versatile in their uses. Fresh legumes include green peas, string beans, sugar peas, snap peas, lima beans, snow peas, runner beans, red cranberry beans, yellow wax beans and black-eyed peas. Fresh legumes are the best for flavor, color and texture.

Beans have been given a bad name because they can cause gastric disturbance. If you suffer from gas, you could be lacking roughage in your diet. Begin by slowly adding legumes to your diet, small amounts at first. Include high roughage foods, grains, fresh fruit and vegetables in your diet at the same time.

Tips on Legumes

Remember to wash the legumes before cooking, and avoid using salt in the soaking water, it may toughen the beans. Some beans need to be presoaked over night, so read the instructions for each variety that you use. Here are some other tips.

- Generally, when soaked and cooked, small dried legumes like lentils will double in size. Medium to large sized legumes will usually triple in size.
- After buying, sort through your dried legumes and remove all foreign bits before storing. Only wash legumes just prior to cooking.
- Purchase your legumes from a good supplier who sells a lot of stock. A quick turnover of stock will ensure fresher legumes.
- Soaking helps to stop the bean's skin from cracking during cooking, or breaking before the bean is cooked tender enough to eat.
- Soaking helps speed up cooking. Soaking can reduce cooking time by up to one half.
- Soaking can break down the indigestable sugars that can lead to intestinal gas.
- If the beans float when you start the soaking process, discard these floaters. They are either too old or harvested before the bean matured. If you have too many floaters in one pot, it may be best to find a new supplier or company brand.
- Two exceptions to the soak all beans rule, split peas and lentils.
- Use one part beans, four parts water when soaking. (example: 1 cup beans to 4 cups water)
- Drain off and discard the water used for soaking.
- When soaking, do not salt the water. It can toughen the seed coating and prevent water from being absorbed.
- Beans that don't require soaking, lentils and split peas, rinse, check for any foreign matter and then cook according to the package directions.
- Do not add baking soda to the soaking water. It can alter the flavor, destroy nutrients and may also make the beans mushy in texture.
- Some canned beans use alkalines like baking soda in their processing, try to avoid these products.

List of Most Common Legumes

With over eleven thousand varieties of legumes, a person could get lost or confused trying to sort out what varieties they want to try. Through research, I have compiled a list of some of the more well known and used varieties. Following this, I have listed the four major sections. From these groups, I have included the description for the most common legumes and a few of the most unusual legumes.

Adzuki Bean (Red Mung Bean)
Appaloosa Bean
Baby White Lima Bean
Black Appaloosa Bean
Black Chickpea
Black-eyed Pea
Black Gram Bean (Black Mung Bean)
Black Soybean (Fermented)
Black Turtle Bean
Blue Shackamaxon Bean
Bolita Bean
Barlotti Bean
Brown Lentil
Calypso Bean
Chickpea
Christmas Lima Bean
Cowpea
Cranberry Bean
Cream Pea
Dark Green Chickpea
Dried Fava Bean
French Green Lentil
French Horticultural Bean
French Navy Bean
Giant White Coco Bean
Golden Split Chickpea
Goober Pea
Great Northern Bean
Green Bean
Green Fava Bean (Broad Bean)
Green Lima Bean
Green Mung Bean
Green Pea (Sweet, Garden or English)
Green Romano Bean
Green Soybean
Green Split Pea
Haricot Vert
Lady Pea
Large Brown Fava Bean
Lupini Bean

Marrowfat Pea
Monstoller Wild Goose Bean
Navy Bean
Peanuts (Spanish)
Peanuts (Virginia)
Pea Shoot
Petite Crimson Lentil
Pigeon Pea (Toor Dah, Yellow Lentil, Congo Pea)
Pink Bean
Pinto Bean
Purple Hyacinth Bean
Rattlesnake Bean
Red Chile Bean
Red Kidney Bean
Red Lima Bean
Rice Bean
Scarlet Runner Bean
Small Brown Fava Bean
Small Red Bean
Small White Fava Bean
Snow Pea
Spanish Pardina Lentil (Spanish Brown Lentil)
Split Fava Bean
Split Golden Fava Bean
Split Red Lentil (Egyptian Lentil)
Split White Lentil
Split Yellow Lentil
Sugar Snap Pea
Swedish Brown Bean
Tepary Bean
Trout Bean (Jacob's Cattle, Dalmation Bean)
Wax Bean (White Wax Bean)
White Emergo Bean (Sweet White Runner)
Winged Bean (Asparagus Bean)
Yard Long Bean (Long Bean)
Yam Bean
Yellow Split Mung Bean
Yellow Split Pea
Zebra Bean

Four Divisions of Legumes

Legumes are sorted into four divisions. Unusual, Asian and African, Old World and New World.

Unusual

These legumes are all tropical in origin.

Goober Peas - These legumes originated in West Africa and are related to the fava bean. Goober peas are also known as Bambarra, Congo Goober and Groundnut. The dried bean is often ground to make flour. In West Africa, the goober peas are boiled, mashed, patted into cakes and then fried. These legumes are similar to peanuts, but must be cooked before they are eaten. Their flavor is like the lima bean. Goober peas are not as popular now, since peanuts are often replacing these legumes.

Winged Beans - Other names for this legume are Asparagus Beans, Manila Beans, Goa Beans, Princess Peas and Four Angled Beans. They grow in Southeast Asia, where they originated, New Guinea and India. The plant, which includes leaves, flowers, shoots, pods, tubers and seeds are all edible. From the seeds, a cooking oil is produced. The pods can be purple, pink, red, or the most common, dark green in color. The pods are a little larger than green beans with four ruffled ridges that run the length of each pod. Winged beans can be prepared and cooked in the same manner as green beans. Cut off each end and slice diagonally. You can use them in a stirfry, boiled or steamed as a side dish. Their flavor is a little stronger than green beans.

Yam Beans - Native to South and Central America, the yam bean is a large tuber. It is also known as jicama (pronounced "hik-a-ma"). This brown skinned root must be peeled before it is eaten. It has a crisp, fresh taste, a cross between a potato and an apple. You can eat it raw or cooked. Asians often use yam beans as a replacement for water chestnuts in stirfries and salads. This plant's young pod can be eaten, but the pod and it's seeds become toxic once it matures and must not be eaten. Tubers from leguminous plants are more nutritious than other tubers such as potato. Yam beans are becoming popular worldwide.

B. A. Smit

Asian and African Legumes
Introduction

Asian beans are the Vigna Family. In China, it is known as Vigna Angularis, Mung. India has Vigna Radiata, the Black Gram or Urad Dal, the Vigna Mungo. There are about one thousand varieties of the soybean within this section. Asian beans are very small, oblong shaped with a distinctive eye. They are the small fruit of an annual plant. They originated in China. The adzuki bean can be popped like corn kernals are. In North America we know mung beans as bean sprouts, but in actual fact, in China they are known as pea sprouts. The soybean sprouts are called bean sprouts in China.

African beans are grown mainly in Southern America. They are a large group of peas with an eye. They were brought to the Caribbean and America by African slaves. African beans were first grown in Ethiopia about five thousand years ago. In Africa, the leaves, sprouts and seeds of the plant are eaten. Southern Peas are more commonly called Cow Peas. Other names include Crowder Peas, Field Peas and Cream Peas. Southern peas have an assortment of colors and many names for the numerous varieties, including Knucklehull Purple, Mississippi Silver and Zipper Cream. There are a few other common African beans. Cream peas are related to black-eyed peas. The peas are a cream color and are popular in the Southern United States. Black-eyed peas can be substituted for cream peas. Crowder peas are so named since the peas are crowded into the pod. These peas can be cooked like black-eyed peas. You can substitute black-eyed peas for crowder peas.

Adzuki Beans - These are small red beans. In Asia, they are simply called red beans. Azuki, Aduki and Asuki are all names used for the same bean. Soak or precook the beans then simmer until tender. This will take about one to one and a half hours. If you try to cook them in a pressure cooker, they will turn bitter. Adzuki beans can be added to soup or used with rice in main dishes. They have been a part of Chinese and Japanese diets for centuries, especially popular in dessert dishes. They are only about one quarter of an inch long, with a thin white line on the ridge of the bean. These beans grow on a bush, not the common vine, and have yellow flowers. The pod can grow to about five inches long. The adzuki bean has a mild, sweet, nutty flavor. It is available dried and as a flour.

Black Gram - These are a member of the Mung Bean Family. Black Gram Beans are also called Urd or Urad Beans. They are small oval beans with a black outer skin and a pale yellow center. In South India they are a common seasoning. The beans are placed in hot oil, which gives them a red color and a nutty flavor. In Northern India, the beans are combined with onions, ginger and butter to create a purée called kali dal. When the skin is removed and the bean split, the inside is white. This variety is called split white lentil. It is nutritious and easy to digest. Often it is added to stuffings, vegetable and curry dishes. When the black gram is toasted and ground, it is used as an Indian spice called urad dal.

Black-eyed Peas - These peas were brought to the United States by African slaves. They are an off white color, medium in size and oblong in shape. They have a small black round "eye" on the inner curved side. Black-eyed peas have a savory flavor with a crisp texture that blends well with garlic, chilies and smoked meats. The peas are available fresh, frozen or dried. To prepare fresh peas, break back the tips of the pod and pull down to remove the strings and show the peas. Remove the peas and cook in simmering water for about thirty minutes until plump and tender. Fresh black-eyed peas can be stored in a plastic bag in the fridge for about three days. Frozen peas can be cooked by the same method as fresh. Dried peas should be soaked overnight, rinsed and then cooked slightly before using in a recipe. The fresh peas are available all summer and into the fall. They can be cooked as a side dish, added to soups or stews, braised or puréed.

Cow Peas - The varieties of Southern Peas used mainly for cow fodder or soil fertilizer are called Cow Peas or Field Peas. Cow peas are the largest food crop in Haiti and are a member of the African black-eyed pea family. These beans need a hot climate to thrive, so they are found in Southern United States, India and Africa. Cow peas are divided into two crops. One is for the seeds, which are dried, and the young pods, which are eaten as a vegetable. The pods grow on tall climbers with the pod growing quite long. These are known as yard long beans. In parts of Africa, the dried peas are a staple food, while others eat the shoots and leaves as vegetables.

Mung Beans - These are more commonly referred to as bean sprouts and are used widely in Asian dishes. Other names include Green, Split, Golden or Black Gram. In India, where mung beans originated, the beans are available two ways. Sabat Moong is whole, Moong Dal is hulled. Whole, the bean is a green color, once hulled, it is a pale yellow. Mung beans are very small, about one quarter of an inch long. They are grown worldwide, including Africa, Asia and the West Indies. Mung beans are often sprouted before they are used. They have the same nutrients as lima beans. The sprouts can be used in salads and main dishes. The bean can be added to vegetables for both flavor and nutrition. In Asia, the bean is ground into a flour and used in a variety of dishes. The starch from the flour is made into a pasta called cellophane noodles. Mung beans are available as dried whole bean, fresh or sprouted. Some canned sprouts are available, though the flavor and texture is not as good as fresh.

Pigeon Peas - Originating in Africa, these peas are popular in India and the Caribbean. At least ninety percent of the world's pigeon pea crop is grown in India, where they are known as yellow lentils. Pigeon peas are a pale brown color with an "eye" on the inner ridge. Their flavor is somewhat earthy. In Jamaica, they are called Congo Peas or Googoo Beans. Puerto Rico knows them as Gandules. The unripe green seeds are eaten as peas and the young whole pod is cooked and eaten like green beans. In India, they split the pigeon peas and coat them in oil to preserve them. These must be rinsed in water before they are cooked. Pigeon peas are ideal in Caribbean dishes and soups.

Yard Long Beans - They are given this name because they can grow from one to three feet long. Yard long beans are related to the black-eyed pea and sometimes are nicknamed asparagus beans because the shape is similar to asparagus. The most common variety of yard long bean is a dark green color. Some varieties are purple. The beans have a starchy flavor. Choose thin, clean beans with small seeds. Cut the tips off before cooking. Blanch the beans before using in vegetable dishes or stirfries.

B. A. Smit

Old World Legumes
Introduction

There are three sections in this group. Beans, which include chickpeas and fava beans. Peas including sweet peas, starchy peas and lupini. Lentils are the last part of Old World Legumes, and includes all varieties of lentils.

Chickpeas - There are many names for chickpeas. In India, they are called Gram, which is the name used for legumes that remain whole, not split. Other names include Spanish Garbanzo, Portugese Grao-De-Bico, and the Italian Ceci. In any country and any name, chickpeas are all a tan color, turning golden when cooked. In India, the yellowy gold split chickpea is called Channa Dal. When unhulled, it is black skinned, skinned dark green whole chickpeas are also popular in Indian markets. Chickpeas have been a part of the Indian diet for centuries, using the nutty flavored pea for many dishes. It is used in soups, dips, salads and ground into flour. The flour is used to make fritters, breads and pancakes. It is best to keep the flour in the fridge to ensure freshness. When buying dried chickpeas, make sure that the store has a quick turnover of stock and the peas are not shriveled or stale. Chickpeas are the hardest pea and the most challenging to cook. Old, stale chickpeas will never soften. You must soak the dried peas overnight before cooking. Canned chickpeas are cooked, skinned and ready to use. Removing the skin will make digestion easier, but isn't necessary. To skin the chickpeas, place the cooked peas in a bowl of cold water. Rub the peas and the skins will float to the surface. Using a slotted spoon, remove the skins. Use the chickpeas in your favorite recipe.

Fava Beans - These beans are also known as Broad Beans, Faba, Horse Bean, Feve and Windsor Beans. Some varieties are purple, beige or tan in color. The most common variety is green in color, with the pod growing to about eight inches in length and about one inch in width. Fava beans grow worldwide. There is a bit of work involved before you can enjoy the fava beans. There is a string along one side of the pod, pull it and the pod will open where the green fava beans are next to a spongy white substance. This substance is to protect the beans. Each fava bean has a thick skin that must be removed before cooking. This skin can be tough and bitter in flavor. Bring a pot of water to a boil, add the skinned beans and cook only until the water returns to a boil. Drain and use in your recipe. These beans are good as a garnish, in soups, dips, sauces and mixed with rice or other vegetable dishes. The most common way to serve these beans is to cook then purée them. Some people like to cook the beans then serve them cold. Fava beans are also available dried. There are various shapes, colors and sizes available. The most common dried fava bean is the large brown variety that has the skin still on. There are also split fava beans with the skin removed. Dried fava beans are also ground into flour. Fava beans are available fresh spring into summer.

Fresh Peas - Known as English, French or Garden peas, they grow as pods, three to four inches long. When the pod is opened, there are about five to eight peas inside. The pod is usually not eaten. Sugar snap and snow peas have a delicate pod that is often eaten with the baby peas still inside. All of these peas have a fresh, sweet flavor. Lightly steamed and served as a side dish is the most common way to enjoy these peas.

Garden Peas - This variety grows in a slightly rounded, tapered green pod. When the pods are rubbed together they should "squeak". This ensures freshness and that the peas have grown large enough to eat. Garden peas can also be known as Petit Pois. The peas should be round and medium green in color, which intensifies when cooked. Peak season for garden peas is spring to summer. Versatile in their uses, these peas can be steamed, boiled, puréed or stewed. You can also use the peas as a side dish or in soups. The pod is not edible.

Lipini Beans - These are flat, round, brown to yellow colored beans with a small hole at one end.The most common way to eat lipini beans is to cook then pickle them, especially popular in Spain, Portugal, Italy and Lebanon. The pickled beans are drained and placed in a bowl. The guests suck the bean out and discard the skin. Lipini beans are a member of the pea family and are grown for their flowers. Certain varieties have toxic seeds or beans which must be treated before they can be eaten. Some of these beans are toasted or boiled instead of pickling. Even with the extra work to make these beans edible, they have been enjoyed by the Old World for centuries.

Peas - Dried peas are available in a number of varieties, differing in both color and taste. One common factor is that they are all nutritious. Vitamin A, riboflavin, thiamin, niacin, calcium, iron, phosphorus and potassium are found in all varieties of dried peas. Whole dried peas are about one quarter of an inch in size, round in shape and gray to green in color. Field peas are grown specifically for drying. These are sweet in flavor.

Snow Peas - These peas are often eaten whole, pod included. They have flat, medium green colored pods. Snow peas are popular in Asian dishes. Sautéed, stirfried or steamed, the green color brightens when cooked. Snow peas can be eaten raw, including the pod, which makes them an interesting addition to salads and side dishes.

Split Peas - These are available in two colors, green or yellow. The pea is peeled and split in two, leaving the pea smooth. When cooked they turn to mush. They both have a subtle, earthy flavor. These peas are often used in soups or mixed with rice. Black-eyed peas, also known as cow peas, are favored in the Southern United States. Chickpeas, also known as garbanzo beans, are used in salads and dips, especially well known as the main ingredient in hummus from the Middle East. The nut flavor blends well with many ingredients. Dried peas originated in the Middle East centuries ago.

Sugar Snap Peas - These are similar to snow peas, but are a deeper green color. They are used in the same methods as snow peas. The pod is also edible. Sugar snap and snow peas can be interchanged.

B. A. Smit

Lentils
Introduction

The origin of lentils is unknown, but they have been a staple of diets throughout the Middle East for centuries. They are often said to be the tastiest of all the beans. They do not need to be soaked or precooked. They will cook in only thirty minutes. Wash before cooking and discard any lentils that float in the water. Lentils have the same nutritional value as kidney beans. They can be combined with grains and vegetables to make complete protein. There are a number of varieties. Green, brown, red and french green are the most common and can be used as a side dish, in soups or stews.

Beluga - These lentils are small, black in color and very expensive. The lentils look like beluga caviar, hence the name.

Brown - These are also known as Persian Lentils or Small Chinese Lentils. They are more round and smaller than green lentils. They have a russet brown color.

French Green - These lentils are also known as Le Puy or Ponotes. They are only one sixteenth of an inch in size and are more rounded than flat. The color is an almost black olive green with a yellow inside. These lentils are expensive and are imported from France. They have a peppery flavor.

Green - Also known as Large Chilean or Laird Lentils, these lentils are about one quarter of an inch round and flat shaped. They are green to golden brown in color.

Red - These lentils are also known as Masur Daal. The lentils are only one sixteenth of an inch in size. They are peeled and split before packaging. Red lentils originated in India, Turkey and Egypt and are a bright red to orange in color. They are often used in soups.

Split White - These lentils are the legumes that are the seeds within the black gram bean. Split white lentils are skinless with a cream color. They are very popular in Indian dishes.

Whole Red - These lentils are also known as Chilka Masur and are only one eighth of an inch in size. They are a pinkish color.

New World Legumes
Introduction

This section has the Phasealus Family and peanuts. The Phasealus Family includes Common True Beans, of which there are over four thousand varieties. The best known are the white beans, kidney beans, black beans and pinto beans. Lima, runner beans, butter beans, tepary beans and scarlet runners are also in this section. Virginia and Spanish peanuts make up the peanut section.

Barlotti Beans - These beans are prevalant in the Tuscany region in Italy, so they are also known as Tuscan beans. In America, barlotti beans are often found in the dried form. The bean is solid, round in shape, with a flesh to tan colored skin with light maroon colored spots and lines. They are close in flavor and texture to the cranberry bean, and the two are interchangable. Throughout Italy, there are numerous members of this bean family. For each region where it grows, it is given the name of that region, such as Lamon, Seritti, Saluggia and Stregoni. All these varieties share the same robust, earthy flavor. They are available fresh from late spring through summer. These beans are often cooked and used the same as black-eyed peas.

Black Beans - These beans are about five eighths of an inch long, oval in shape with black skins and white or cream colored flesh. It has a white line on the ridge of the bean. They are also known as Spanish, Mexican or Turtle Beans. The skins can clog the vent on a pressure cooker, so it is not advised to use this cooking method. Black beans are nutritious, having vitamin C, vitamin B, riboflavin, potassium and phosphorus. They have a subtle mushroom, earthy flavor. Black beans blend well with tomatoes, green peppers and onions, so they are popular in Mexican, Latin, South American and Caribbean dishes. It is best to soak or precook the beans, then simmer until tender. They are available dried or canned.

Black Runner Beans - These beans are popular in both America and England because of their blossoms. The beans have a profoundly black skin, are large in size with a light, sweet flavor. When cooked, they hold their shape, making them popular in salads, side dishes or marinated.

Cranberry Beans - Medium in size, oval in shape and a soft white color with red streaks or spots, these beans are also known as Roma Beans. They are often found in Italian meals and soups. Cranberry beans were embraced by Europe and North Africa by farmers who took the American bean, bred them and began many new varieties. Italian immigrants brought the bean to America, where it grows on the coast of California, U.S.A. Cranberry beans have a mellow taste and can be cooked as a side dish, puréed or braised, but are best if cooked simply when fresh. Midsummer is the peak season. They will keep for about five to seven days in the fridge or frozen for use later.

French Navy Beans - These fine beans are rounded and smaller than the American Navy Bean. The color is a true white with a light green hue. French navy beans are smooth and tender, cook quickly and their small shape is a welcome addition to salads and soups.

B. A. Smit

Gigante Beans - A part of the White Runner Bean Family, these large, sweet tasting, off white colored beans are also known as Gigandes and Hija. This bean originated in Greece and Spain. They hold their shape well so are a good choice for marinating or adding to salads.

Green Beans - These are the most common and versatile of the bean family. They are long, slender, with a mid green color. You can find them year round fresh, frozen or canned, but for fresh, their peak season is mid to late summer. Green beans are also known as snap beans because when the pod is broken in half, it should be crisp enough to make a snap sound. Try to pick slender pods with even sized seeds. They should be a bright grass green in color and the end that was picked should not have turned dark in color. Green beans can be named string beans because originally, they all had a string down one side of the pod that needed to be removed before cooking. These beans can turn a drab olive in color if mixed with acidic foods like tomatoes, wine, lemon juice or vinegar. Always mix just before serving to retain the bright green color. Green beans can be cut or left whole, boiled, steamed or stirfried. They can also be pickled. Try to use fresh beans within three days of purchasing for maximum freshness. Wax or yellow beans are the same texture and flavor, but differ in color.

Green Romano Beans - At one time, this bean was only available frozen. Now this Italian bean is a special treat fresh. It is a wide, flat bean with a strong bean flavor. When young, these beans are very tender, but the larger, up to six inches with noticeable bean seeds, should be cooked longer until tender. Green romano beans hold their shape when cooked, and are especially good in strong flavored sauces like tomato and garlic. Try to choose small beans, slightly wider than green beans, with a bright green color. If the bean seeds are not that noticeable, the more tender the bean will be. Avoid pale yellow or pale green beans, they could be tough. Cut both ends off before cooking, for a visual effect, cut the beans diagonally into even lengths before cooking.

Haricots Verts - This means green beans in French. The pencil thin beans are a delicacy in France. Most are now grown in Central America, hand picked when just ripe. Other names include Haricots Filets (String Beans) and Haricots Aiguilles (Needle Beans). To cook these beans, trim the ends, and for the best color and flavor, steam instead of boiling.

Kidney Beans - These are a common, well known bean. There are a number of varieties, Cannellini Beans, White Kidney Beans or Red Kidney Beans are the best known. They are also known as Mexican Beans, Spanish Tolasanas and Raj Mah. About half an inch in size, often kidney shaped, with a tough outer skin and a smooth flesh, these beans originated in South America. Now they are also cultivated in Greece, Italy and France. They are a good source of vitamin A, riboflavin, niacin, thiamine, iron, calcium, potassium and phosphorus. Kidney beans can be found dried or canned. Salads, dips, soups and chilli are some examples of how versatile this bean is.

Lima Beans - These are also known as Rangoon, Burma and Madagascar. They are about three quarters of an inch long with a soft white to light green color. A heirloom variety known as Christmas Lima Bean is a little larger in size and has a blotchy maroon pattern on a cream colored background. The lima bean grows on a vine as well as a bush. The flavor is close to a subtle potato taste. Lima beans are rich in thiamine, riboflavin, protein, niacin, potassium and phosphorus. They are tasty in soups, salads or as a side dish. Succotash is a well known dish that includes lima beans, peas and corn.

Navy and Great Northern Beans - These two varieties of beans are often interchanged. You can sometimes have a mixture of both in one package of dried beans. They are both small, one quarter to one half of an inch in size. Navy beans are oval and white in color. Great northern beans are also white in color, but almost kidney shaped. Both varieties are rich in iron, vitamins, calcium, sodium, potassium, thiamine, phosphorus, riboflavin and niacin. They are a good source of protein as well. These beans should be presoaked and precooked before using. Read the directions on the package. These beans are most commonly used in baked beans and soups.

Pink Beans - These beans are oval in shape, with a pink colored skin. They are very popular in Puerto Rican dishes. Pink beans can be interchanged with pinto and cranberry beans.

Pinto Beans - Mexican Strawberries, Rattlesnake Beans and Appaloosa Beans are all types of Pinto Beans. Given the name Pinto, these beans originated in South America and were named after the Pinto horse because of the similar colors. Spotted pink and brown, these beans are common in Mexican dishes and chili. They taste like kidney beans but are a bit smaller in size. Pinto beans can be substituted for kidney beans and have all the same nutrients as other legumes.

Runner Beans - Over six thousand years ago, runner beans were found in caves in Mexico. They have been a part of both ceremonies and decoration in native cultures of Mexico and Southwest United States ever since. Runner beans can grow well in cooler climates, making them popular in England where many varieties have been cultivated. The beans grow on long runners that can develop pods one foot or longer in length. In England, they take advantage of the big blossoms and grow them as ornamental plants. Some varieties include White Dutch, popular for it's snow white flowers, Painted Lady Runners have white and red flowers and Scarlet Runners have bold red blossoms and lavender colored seeds streaked black. The blossoms of some runners are edible and are a bright addition to stirfries and salads.

Scarlet Runner Beans - Often grown for their bright red blossoms, these striking red beans are also called Stick Beans. In England, they are a favorite addition to decorative gardens.

B. A. Smit

Small Lima Beans - These are a different variety of the lima bean. They are about half the size and not as plump as the lima bean. Small lima beans are known by a variety of names, including Baby Limas, Butter Beans, Civet Beans, Sieva Beans and Calico Beans. These varieties also grow on a bush or vine. They have a similar flavor to lima beans. Both varieties, lima beans and small lima beans originated in Peru, being named after it's capital. Small lima beans are available fresh, frozen, canned or dried.

Small Red Beans - The name describes this bean, small, round and deep red in color. They cook quickly because they are so small. In the United States, small red beans are a popular addition to Hispanic dishes. They are also used in creole dishes and as a substitute for kidney beans.

Wax Beans - These are similar to green beans. One variety has a light green to almost white color and is known as Ice Beans. Other varieties include Heirloom, which have a string running down the pod that must be removed before cooking. Wax beans can be a little tougher than green beans. When young, wax beans can be a lemon yellow color and are tender. Wax beans can be found fresh, frozen or canned. Fresh wax beans can be cooked the same as green beans.

Peanuts

These were first grown in South America. Traders brought the peanut worldwide. African slaves introduced the Americas to the peanut, which is why some peanuts have African names such as Goober and Pinder. Different from other legumes, once the plant has flowered, it buries itself where the pod grows and matures. A common name that developed from this is called Groundnut. There are many varieties grown in the United States, with nearly half of them grown in Georgia. Depending on the variety, there could be as few as two kernels to as many as seven kernels in one pod. Most of the whole peanuts that we eat are the Virginia variety. Peanuts are healthy, high in energy and protein. They can be roasted and salted as a snack, added to sauces, as in Thai dishes, pressed into oil or ground into peanut butter. Spanish peanuts are small, round, red skinned and are most commonly eaten for a snack, ground into peanut butter or pressed into oil. Peanut oil is used in India, China, Africa and the Americas. It has fifty percent monounsaturated fats and thirty percent polyunsaturated fats, making the oil good for cholesterol lowering. Since the peanut is high in fat, it will turn rancid if not stored properly. Keep it in an airtight container in the fridge.

B. A. Smit

Heirloom True Bean Varieties
Introduction

Bean seeds are easy to save from your garden. If they are stored in a cool, dry place, they can be planted years from now and grow successfully. Most heirloom varieties are saved because of special characteristics or markings. These seeds help with genetic diversity within crops, which keeps the crops healthy. Beans are not cross pollinated by insects, they are self pollinating, which keeps the varieties true. I have included a few varieties in this section, some common, others not as well known.

Anasazi Beans - These deep red and white blotched beans are a close relative to the Appaloosa Bean, with a sweet flavor. Anasazi is a Navaho word that means ancient one, and represents the cliff dwelling Indians who lived in the areas now known as Utah, Colorado, Arizona and New Mexico in the United States. Settlers found the beans in the cliff ruins in the early 1900's. They are now grown exclusively by a milling company in Colorado. Anasazi beans grow at very high altitudes and are known to have about seventy five percent less of the gas causing carbohydrates than in pinto beans. These beans are excellent for baked bean recipes.

Appaloosa Beans - Sometimes confused with anasazi beans, these beans are different. Also known as Red Appaloosa Beans, they are a mottled deep burgundy to purple in color, similar to the markings of the appaloosa pony. The bean has an earthy flavor and holds it's shape throughout cooking. This makes it popular in baked bean recipes. They can also be substituted for the black-eyed peas or pinto beans which are a close relative to the appaloosa bean. Black Appaloosa Beans were found near caves in the Southwest United States, so they are sometimes called Cave Beans. They have a black and white marking which makes them appealing in salads or baked bean dishes.

Bolita Beans - These beans were grown throughout the Southwest United States by the Native Americans. When the Spanish settled in New Mexico, they developed the Bolita Bean. It has a stronger, richer flavor than the pinto bean, which is a close relative. These beans are used in many southwest style dishes.

Calypso Beans - These beans have a thin skin, are medium in size, white in color and have deep yellow "eyes". They have been around for about four hundred years and have numerous names, Steuben Yellow Eye, Butterscotch Calypso and Maine Yellow Eye, to name a few. These beans have a smooth texture, a subtle flavor and plump when cooked. The color may also change to an ivory or brown when cooked. The calypso bean is well liked for salads and baked dishes. The rumor is that these beans were used in the original Boston Baked Beans recipe. In Europe, a popular variety of calypso beans has black and white streaks.

French Horticultural Beans - This heirloom variety is from the Cranberry Family. It is also known as October Bean. These beans make a wonderful, tasty addition to stews, soups and salads. French Horticultural Beans have a nutty, sweet flavor with a solid texture.

Rattlesnake Beans - These are oval, tan and brown spotted, slender beans. While growing, the pod will twist, resembling a rattlesnake. They are a close kin of the pinto bean, with a more profound flavor, which makes them a favorite addition to casseroles and chili.

Red Valentine Beans - These beans grow in long pods, usually about six inches in length. The narrow pods are often a substitute for green beans. Red valentine beans have a pink pod with spots of dark red. They are called Turkish Date Beans in Germany. Once dried, they are called Purple Speckled Valentine, Refugee Bean or One Thousand For One Bean.

Rice Beans - Asian in origin, now popular in India, these small seeds are slightly larger than a grain of rice. They range in color, yellow, red, brown or black. Rice beans have a light flavor, almost sweet, and are very nutritious. They are often dried and eaten with rice. Rice beans are challenging to harvest. They grow on vines with the seed pod opening on it's own, spreading the seeds. The beans have a thin skin which makes them easy to digest.

Swedish Brown Beans - These toasty brown beans were brought to North America by Swedish settlers over one hundred years ago. They mature quickly, which makes them a popular bean. Light brown in color, the Swedish Brown Bean has a robust, lightly sweet flavor. They are the main ingredient in Swedish brown bean soup, as well as other soups, stews and casseroles.

Zebra Beans - Also known as Amethyst Beans, these heirloom beans are white with dark markings, which resemble a zebra. They are well known for their fine, light texture and rich flavor. Zebra beans are popular in Spain and in Spanish dishes brought to North America.

Hemp

Hemp has been around for centuries, mainly in textiles and rope. Now it is the base for many products, including energy bars, breads, salad dressings and snack foods.

Marijuana, or for some, B.C. Bud, is not the same as industrial hemp. Hemp is related to marijuana, but is grown specifically for food and textiles. Hemp contains almost no T.H.C., the mind altering chemical in marijuana. Industrial hemp is sown from specially bred cannabis seeds, regulated by government health agencies, that contain undetectable levels of T.H.C., the psychoactive ingredient in marijuana.

For a number of years, people have been switching to soy products. Soy is not good for all people. It can interfere with prescription medications and for some, their body does not react well to soy. Mad cow disease, Avian bird flu, PCB's in fish and genetically altered soy are just a few reasons that people are trying hemp as a safe alternative protein source.

The edible part of hemp, the shelled seed, is an excellent source of protein. The protein content, 34.6 grams/100 grams, is similar to soybeans and better than most nuts, seeds and dairy products. Hemp oil, hemp nuts and hemp flour are ideal choices for baking and adding to foods. The hulled hemp seeds have a nutty, crunchy flavor, making them a nutritious topping on yogurts and cereal.

Hemp has a superior protein than soy. It contains all essential amino acids in a balance that meets the body's needs. It contains no "antinutrients" like trypsin in soy, that can interfere with proper protein absorption, or cause bloating or gas. Hemp protein is also a good source of chlorophyll. This is important as an alkalizing element in the body. If your body has more alkaline, you strengthen the immune system. With a balanced pH, the muscle tissue is increased and retained, and fat is lessoned. Hemp protein is made from whole seeds that are pressed to extract the oil. The remaining cake is ground using a special technique to remove the fiber from the shell. One serving of hemp protein powder is equal to six ounces of cheese or two medium sized eggs.

Hemp seeds are rich in Omega 6 and Omega 3 fatty acids. These fats are essential since the body can't produce them and they must be obtained through foods. Hemp contains fifty six percent Omega 6, nineteen percent Omega 3 and between seven and nine percent Omega 9. Since most people include too much processed foods that include safflower, soybean or corn oils in their diets, we often get too much Omega 6's and too few Omega 3's. Skin disorders, arthritis and heart problems can be attributed by this imbalance. Hemp food and hemp oil contain about eighty percent essential fatty acids (EFA), putting them at the top of the list of good fat, having an optimal three to one balance that no other food has. Hemp seeds are also an excellent source for Gamma Linolenic Acid (GLA), which is a metabolite proven to be helpful in allergies and rheumatoid arthritis. Hemp also contains calcium, magnesium, B vitamins, vitamin D and E as well as potassium carotene.

Hemp is environmentally friendly. It needs very little water and is a natural insect repellant. Though it is legal to grow and distribute hemp in Canada, it is restricted within the United States. This leaves Canada as a principle supplier of hemp seed and hemp seed products.

Carob

Most often, carob is used as a chocolate substitute. It contains less fat and calories than cocoa powder. The fruit of an evergreen tree, grown on the shores of the Mediterranean, carob buds are dark, flat and about six inches long, by one to two inches wide. Roasted, dried pods have a pleasant, almost malt flavor. They are crunchy, but don't eat the seeds. Carob is available in powder and chip form (as like chocolate chips for baking), the same as cocoa, but carob contains no caffine.

B. A. Smit

Soybeans
Introduction

    Soybeans originated in China. There are over one thousand varieties with colors like green, red, black, yellow, white and spotted. They range in size from a pea to a cherry and grow in gray fuzzy pods. Soybeans are extremely nutritious and high in protein. Generally, soybeans are plain tasting, but fresh green soybeans have a light, pleasing flavor with a smooth texture. The soybean has been cultivated for several thousand years throughout Asia. It has many forms and uses. The fresh young sprouts are eaten much the same as bean sprouts. Soybeans are soaked in water to create soy milk, as well as tofu. The beans are fermented to make soy sauce, miso and tamari. The bean is dried and ground into flour or a sweet paste for desserts. It can be made into textured vegetable protein, known as tempah or seitan. Soybean products are also used as a filler in ground meats. Close to seventy five percent of the world's supply of soybeans are grown in the western hemisphere. The United States can produce fifty five million tons of soybeans per year. Half of this amount is exported. Soybeans are used in nonedible products also. Linoleums, soaps and plastics are a few examples. Imitation cheese and butter can be made with soybeans. Soy cheese is a nondairy product available in several flavors. Most contain casein, a protein dairy derivative, so could be unsuitable for those who are lactose intolerant. Soybeans contain valuable antioxidants which protect the body from damage that can develop into heart or circulatory problems. The actual bean is not often eaten in it's natural state, but is most commonly mixed with or made into other products. Read labels as some brands may contain wheat. I have included descriptions for some of the more popular soybean products.

Chinese Pastes - Bean pastes are a group that are used as condiments for many Asian dishes. Bean pastes are made from fermented soybeans. One type is hot bean paste, a lumpy, spicy hot paste that is mixed with sauces. Sweet bean paste is a smooth, sweet paste used in sauces and marinades.

Fermented Black Beans - The Chinese have these beans as a specialty. They are small soybeans that are preserved in salt before packing. They have a very strong, salty flavor. Some people prefer to rinse the beans before using. They are used in many Asian dishes.

Lecithin - This soy product is used as a binder or natural preservative. The granules can be added to food being cooked and the liquid can be put into energy drinks or baked foods. Note that the liquid is very sticky and should be handled carefully. It is easier to "eye" (guess) the amount instead of using a measuring cup. The lecithin can also be used as a margarine substitute. Some people can tolerate the oily taste, but others prefer to mix it into food to blend the taste.

Miso - This has been a vital part of Japanese dishes for hundreds of years. All varieties are made the same way. Soybeans are boiled, then crushed and rice, wheat or barley is added. The mixture is then infused with a yeast style mold. It then matures for six months to three years. Yellow miso is made from rice mold and is a sweet addition to

A New Kind of Normal

dressings. Barley produces red miso, a savory addition to soups. A thick brown miso is made primarily from soybeans, it is rich and salty and can be cut with a knife. Miso will keep for up to one year in the fridge. *This is NOT for gluten free diets.*

Shoyu - This is a naturally fermented and aged soybean product. It has a mellow flavor compared to soy sauce.

Soy Flour - The soybeans are dried then ground to make flour. It is used in baking and as a thickener. It contains no gluten. Soy flour is rich in protein and low in carbohydrates. It is often mixed with other gluten free flours for making cakes, breads and muffins. This flour is a safe alternative in gluten free diets.

Soy Milk - This is a nondairy substitute for those who can't tolerate cow's milk. It has more protein than cow's milk, is cholesterol free, has iron, sodium and is low in fat. Because soy milk usually lacks sufficient amounts of calcium, it is often added. Soy milk is curdled to make tofu. It is also used to make soy cheese.

Soybean Sprouts - The Chinese use these sprouts more often than mung bean sprouts. Soybean sprouts must be blanched or cooked before eating to help in digestion. They make a tasty addition to salads, stirfries and other Asian dishes.

Black Soy Sauce - This is a concentrated soy sauce with molasses. It is good when you want a lot of flavor and color, without a lot of liquid. This type of soy sauce is good when tossed with noodles. Mushroom soy sauce has dried chinese mushrooms added to it. The sauce has a smooth, earthy flavor. Both black and regular soy sauces are used to marinate, in stirfries and most Asian dishes. *This is NOT gluten free.*

Soy Sauce - Available light or dark in color, this is a salty sauce made from fermented soybeans. A roasted grain, usually wheat or barley, along with hydrochloric acid to break down the soybean, is added. It is combined with corn syrup, caramel coloring and salt. This mixture is then diluted with water. It is used to flavor many Chinese and Japanese dishes. Japan and China each manufacture a number of varieties of soy sauce, light, dark, thin, thick, black soy and mushroom soy. The sauce is fermented for up to one year. The Japanese use more wheat, so their sauce tends to be sweeter, less salty than the Chinese. The Japanese sauces are thinner and lighter than the Chinese. Read labels to ensure that the soy sauce your buying is naturally fermented. *All soy sauce will not be gluten free.* Cheap versions of soy sauce are chemically fermented in three to four days, not the year that natural fermentation takes. Artificially brewed will list the ingredients as water, salt, hydrolyzed soy protein, corn syrup, caramel color and potassium sorbate as a preservative. Naturally brewed will list water, wheat, soybeans then salt with less than one tenth percent sodium benzoate as a preservative. Again, *all soy sauce is NOT gluten free.*

Tamari - This is a Japanese product, a thick, very dark liquid. It is a cousin of the Japanese soy sauce. Tamari is stronger in flavor than soy sauce. It is made primarily from soybeans, cultured and fermented in a similar way as miso. This sauce is used for dipping or basting. Tamari sauce is wheat free.

B. A. Smit

Tofu
Introduction

Bean curd, the true name for tofu, has been used for centuries. The Japanese name for bean curd is tofu. Japanese tofu has a lighter flavor and is softer in texture than the Chinese style. Bean curd is made the same way as cheese, liquid that has curdled. Bean curd is high in protein, inexpensive to purchase, but is very perishable, lasting only a few days in the fridge. Bean curd is made by soaking dry soybeans in water until soft, crushing, then boiling them. A coagulant is added to cause the milk to separate into curds and whey. The curds are placed in molds and left to settle. The curds are soaked in water to firm, keep cool and keep fresh. Chinese bean curds often have excess water pressed out of them. It is not advisable to freeze tofu as it will change the texture and become chewy. Tofu is very plain tasting and will absorb other flavors well, taking the flavor of what it is cooked with. Tofu is rich in protein, iron and sodium.

Japanese Tofu
There are three types of Japanese tofu.

Kinu, Silken - This is the soft tofu that hasn't been drained. It is somewhat fragile and shouldn't be pressed.

Momen or Regular - This tofu has been drained in cloth giving it a course texture.

Yakidotu - This is lightly broiled tofu. It has a toasted appearance with a solid texture. These forms of tofu are packed in water.

The last item in this section is a product that is also made from soybeans.

Tempah - This is much firmer than tofu. It can be used in many cooking techniques. Originally from Indonesia and used for centuries, it is a fermented food made with split, cooked soybeans and a fungus style starter to help the fermentation. Tempah has at least fifty percent more protein than ground beef, so it is a superior substitute for meat by vegetarians.

Nuts
Introduction

   Nuts and seeds have become known as the high in salt, high in fat snack food. Commercially manufactured nut products contain saturated and/or hydrogenated fats. Try to avoid these types of nut products. Nuts can be an abundant source of energy and nutrients. They can be an indispensable addition to a balanced, healthy diet. The total fat content in nuts is usually more than fatty meats. Coconuts being the exception, a mixture of mostly unsaturated fats is in all nuts. Peanuts have the most protein and all other nuts follow close behind as good sources of protein. Peanuts have the equivalent protein as the same weight of cheese. Walnuts, almonds and Brazil nuts have as much protein as the same weight of eggs. The protein found in nuts is not complete, some amino acids are missing. You are able to complete the protein with a balanced diet. Nuts do not have the B 12 vitamin, but the rest of the B complex is as complete as meat. Minerals are in all nuts, including phytic acid, which makes it difficult for your body to absorb the minerals. Peanuts contain oxalic acid as well. Using the nuts in cooking or roasting them will help break down these acids. Foods with a good source of vitamin C can be eaten at the same time as nuts to enhance the absorption of iron. A note of caution, nuts and nut oils may turn rancid or stale rather quickly. As well as possibly making you sick, rancid oils can be harmful to your digestive system. It interferes with the activity of vitamin E, which may lead to blood clots. Also, research has shown a link between a high consumption of rancid oily foods and stomach cancer. Most nuts include linoleic acid, which research believe counteracts cholesterol deposits, helping to protect against heart disease. Pine nuts and coconuts are the exception, they do not contain linoleic acid.

Almonds - The most common variety of almond is the sweet variety. Bitter almonds, the other variety, contains a toxic prussic acid. These almonds should not be eaten raw, the poison is only destroyed through heat. These almonds are used mainly for almond oil. Almonds are high in protein, fat and minerals. Potassium, iron, zinc and magnesium, with a few B vitamins, are all included in almonds. Phytic acid and oxalic acid are both found in almonds, so you should eat foods high in vitamin C with the almonds to help your body to absorb the minerals found in the almonds. The almond has more calcium than other nuts. Almonds are about twenty percent protein, and the same weight of almonds and eggs, the almonds have one third more protein than the eggs. Almonds can be found whole, shaved, slivered, chopped and ground. They are good in baking, on cereal or yogurt and in granola mixes. Almond oil can also be used in cooking and baking. Almonds are used for nonedible products as well. Soaps, body oils and lotions are all soothing.

Brazil Nuts - These nuts grow primarily in the tropical climate of South America. The rainforest in Brazil can grow trees that are over two hundred feet tall. These rainforests made this nut famous. Brazil nuts are high in fat and can turn rancid quickly. Try to purchase Brazil nuts from a good supplier and only the amount you will need. Large in size, these nuts are often roasted and salted then packaged with other nuts. Chopped, they can be used in granola, trail mixes or baking. Brazil nuts are one of the best sources for the essential mineral, selenium. Eating a few Brazil nuts each day will help to protect you from heart disease and cancer.

B. A. Smit

Cashew Nuts - In Brazil, the cashew tree grows in the rainforest, where the Brazilians prefer the fruit, not the nut which hangs beneath the fruit. Cashews are always shelled and roasted before selling. The roasting is necessary to destroy the very caustic oil between the two layers of the shell. Cashews can be found both salted and unsalted. The salted cashew, just one hundred grams, will give you more than half of your daily required amount of salt. This is not good for high blood pressure or heart disease. Unsalted cashews are loaded with monounsaturated fats, good for protecting the heart. Cashews are also high in nicotinic acid, folate and potassium. Cashew nut butter is a nutritious alternative to peanut butter. Cashews are often in nut mixtures for snacking, some main dishes and baking.

Chestnuts - Best known for the roasting variety, chestnuts are available whole or shelled. You will find chestnuts fresh, dried, frozen, canned and also ground into meal. Chestnuts originated in southern Europe, but can be found in North Africa, Asia and the United States. Britain is known to produce poor crops and must not be mistaken for the poisonous horse chestnut, used in herbal medicine. Chestnuts must be cooked before eating. They blend well in both sweet and savory dishes. One, perhaps most familiar recipe, is chestnuts in turkey stuffing. They can also be added to vegetables, soups or stews. Dried chestnuts ground into flour can be used in baking. Chestnuts have less fat than most nuts, making them lower in calories. There is also less protein in chestnuts but they are a source for vitamin B6, potassium and vitamin E.

Coconuts - These palm trees are abundant throughout the tropics. Coconuts are a main part of many native dishes. When eaten fresh, the coconut is very tasty. The milk found inside the coconut can be refreshing, though it has little nutrients. Coconut is often dried and shredded. It can be sweetened or left natural. Try to avoid the sweetened coconut as it contains a large amount of sweetener. Coconut can be compacted into solid slabs of coconut cream. This cream is sold in cans and is a major ingredient for curry dishes. Fiber and other nutrients are found in coconut, but it has a large amount of saturated fats and should be eaten in moderation. Coconut, shredded, can be used in baking. To use fresh coconut, choose one that feels heavy and "sloshes" when shaken. Pierce the eye on top with an ice pick or screwdriver. Drain the milk and crack open with a hammer. Remove the meat, grate, then spread on a cookie sheet to dry before using. Popular sweets include coconut cream pie and macaroons.

Hazelnuts - A small county in England, Kent, has had great success growing these nuts. They also grow throughout the Mediterranean area. Hazelnuts are rich in magnesium, fiber and protein. They also have zinc, iron and vitamin E. One hundred grams of hazelnuts would give you about seven days worth of vitamin E. Hazelnuts are low in salt, making them a nutritious snack. These nuts are eaten alone or in a trail mix. They can be ground and used in baking. Chopped hazelnuts are delicious in salads, cereal or made into hazelnut butter, a nice change from peanut butter.

Hickory Nuts - Pecans and pignut trees are members of this family. These nuts have thin shells compared to the hickory nut. The hickory nut shell is so hard, a hammer is often used to crack them open. The nuts are used in cakes, cookies, breads and candy. They can be used as a substitute for pecans.

Macadamia Nuts - These nuts were originally from Australia. The plant found it's way to Hawaii, where today it is a major crop. Often roasted and salted before packaging, it is rare to find fresh nuts. They are packaged alone or added to trail mixes. Some are found roasted and unsalted, and these are used in baking, such as muffins, loaves and cookies. Macadamia nuts are rich in fats, so can turn rancid quickly. These nuts have protein, fiber, zinc and iron so they are nutritious, which makes the macadamia nut a healthy choice when eaten in moderation.

Pecans - The native North Americans were thought to be the first to include pecans as part of their diet. Pecans are nutritious and versatile. They can be used in both sweet and savory dishes. Pecans can be used in granola, cereals or roasted and salted to eat with other nuts or alone. They are plentiful in protein, unsaturated fats and contain some fiber. Calcium, zinc, iron and magnesium are also found in pecans. There is a small amount of vitamin A and one hundred grams of pecans will provide more than the daily amount of vitamin E.

Pine Nuts - Several varieties of pine trees yield what the Mediterranean consider a delicacy, pine nuts. The Italians developed their traditional pesto with pine nuts which are ground and mixed with olive oil, garlic and basil. Pine nuts add texture and flavor to salads. The Middle East combine rice and pine nuts. The nuts are high in protein, zinc, iron and magnesium. There is a small amount of fiber, but has rich quantities of vitamin E and potassium. Pine nuts are used in trail mixes, cereal, baking and are a tasty addition to main dishes.

Pistachio Nuts - Like potato chips, it's hard to have just one. Often salted, we tend to eat too many at one time, giving us more sodium than we need. Pistachio nuts can be found with or without their shell. Some shells are dyed, most are salted. They can be shelled and ready to add to baking, cereal, cookies or cheesecake. Most often they are added to nut mixtures or eaten alone. Pistachios are high in protein, have a good amount of fiber, zinc, iron and vitamin A. As with pine nuts, pistachios are an excellent source for potassium and vitamin E.

Pumpkin Seeds - Although high in calories, pumpkin seeds are also high in nutrition. Nearly one quarter of it's weight is protein. Pumpkin seeds are lower in fats than other nuts or seeds. They are rich in potassium, magnesium and fiber. Pumpkin seeds are high in zinc, phosphorus and iron. There is a small amount of vitamin A in these seeds. Men can benefit by eating pumpkin seeds. The zinc is vital for fertile sperm as well as providing a protective substance for the prostate gland. Pumpkin seeds can be found roasted and salted. Unsalted, they can be added to baking, cereal, granola or trail mixes.

Sesame Seeds - For many centuries, sesame seeds have been a vital part of cuisine in the Far East and Middle East. Their content of vitamin E and iron led many to believe sesame seeds were an aphrodisiac. These tiny seeds are an excellent source for protein, magnesium and calcium. Sesame seeds are also high in niacin, folate and B vitamins. The sesame seeds are ground to a smooth paste called tahini. This paste is popular in the Middle East. It is similar to peanut butter in texture. It is a good source of protein and calcium for those who are replacing dairy in their diet. Sesame butter is made from unhulled seeds that are ground. Compared to tahini, it has a stronger flavor and can be hard to digest. Sesame seeds are added to breads, cakes and muffins. Often you will find sesame seeds sprinkled on top of breads and buns. They are an important part of Asian dishes, used in stirfries or sprinkled on foods, both sweet and savory. Sesame oil is used in salad dressings and cooking. It has a strong flavor and not used for deep frying. Sesame milk is a good source of calcium and makes an excellent dairy substitute.

Sunflower Seeds - The sunflower is grown worldwide, but warm climates such as the Mediterranean, are the best areas for growing. Sunflowers are large, tall plants with bright yellow flowers. They have been around for centuries. The Inca worshipped this stately plant. Each tiny seed is encased in a hard shell. Often roasted and salted, the seeds with their shell, are then packaged and sold. The seeds are available shelled as well. There is a lot of nutrition in these tiny seeds. They have protein, potassium, selenium, iron, zinc and B vitamins. Sunflower seeds are an excellent source of vitamin E as well. The sunflower seeds can be found packaged alone, included in both trail mixes and granola, and can be used in cereals and baking.

Walnuts - Grown in North America, the Middle East and Europe, walnuts have been eaten for centuries. When walnuts are eaten fresh, before the shell has dried, they are considered a delicacy. Walnuts are popular and versatile. Eaten fresh, dried and salted, chopped and used in baking, or pressed into a light, delicate oil for salads, walnuts are also nutritious. They are low in saturated fats, high in monounsaturated and polyunsaturated fats and have protein, folate, zinc and vitamin E. Walnuts have only trace levels of sodium. You can add walnuts to cookies, cakes, breads, cereal and trail mixes.

Homemade Legume or Nut Flour
2 - 3 cups legumes - brown or red lentiils or green or yellow split peas
> OR

2 - 3 cups nuts or seeds - almonds, cashews, hazelnuts, walnuts, pecans, pumpkin seeds or sunflower seeds

Sort the legumes or nuts to remove any foreign matter or bad legumes or nuts. Use a blender and grind 1/4 cup at a time, until it becomes a powder. For a food processor, you can grind 1/2 to 3/4 cup at a time. Grind as fine as possible. Sift through a sieve. What is left, process again. Repeat until all the legumes or nuts are ground. Try to only grind what you will need for your recipe. Store any remaining in an airtight container in the fridge and use within a few days.

Stores now carry a good selection of legume and nut flours if you don't want to grind your own.

Meats and Poultry

Introduction

Meats are available in many different forms, from raw to cooked. Remember that the more processed the meat, the more ingredients are used. When you have food sensitivities, it is better to buy raw meat and cook it to your own preference, thus controlling exactly what ingredients are used.

When purchasing meats, check for freshness and color. When you purchase from a butcher, the meat should smell fresh, and when buying from a store, ensure that the package has no punctures and it is sealed completely. Read the label for the date it was packaged and for an inspection stamp. The government is responsible for the inspection of all meats. The inspections occur on the farm, the slaughter house and again at the butcher or store. This is strictly enforced to ensure that the meat is not contaminated, diseased and is suitable for human consumption.

Grading meats is not done by the government and is not considered as mandatory. It is a system designed by the Department of Agriculture to grade meat for it's quality. This is something that packers are paying for, not taxpayers. The grader considers the type of meat, ratio of lean to fat, color, marbling (fat within the flesh, resembling a marbled design) and how much meat versus bone. A few are chosen as prime, the best. Most are select or choice. Anything less is used for processed meats such as cold cuts and wieners.

Once you purchase your meats, you must store them properly and cook them correctly to ensure that no bacteria can develop. To prevent cross contamination, always store each type of meat separately. Beef with beef, chicken with chicken. Wrap the meat and store in the fridge. Use a tray or plate to sit the meat on so it doesn't drip onto other foods within the fridge. Storing the meat in air tight containers is not advised as it can promote bacteria growth. Meats should be used within several days or frozen. Remember to date and label the package before you place in the freezer.

B. A. Smit

Kosher Meats

There are some religions that have strict dietary laws. The meat must be slaughtered then prepared following very specific guidelines. In North America, beef and veal forequarters, game and poultry are mainly used for kosher meats. The legs and loin of veal and beef are not often used in kosher meats because the method to create kosher would ravage the meat beyond pleasant presentation. The meat is slaughtered by a shohet, a rabbi who has been specially educated and then qualified. He must use only one stroke of a knife to kill the animal, then the blood is drained completely. Then all the arteries and veins must be removed. This is why some types of meat are not recommended for kosher use.

Beef
Introduction

Throughout the world, there are numerous types of beef available. In North America, there is Certified Angus, natural, aged and organic beef. In France, there is Limousin beef and the popular Kobe beef is from Japan.

In North America, organic and natural are based on no chemicals or pesticides within the land used. There are several groups who all have their opinion of how many years of the land being chemical free deems it organic. So you may want to research your own area for organic options.

Though less popular now, aging meats such as venison, game birds, as well as beef is still done using temperature and humidity controlled areas, often meat lockers. The meat is hung uncovered, and the natural enzymes begin to break down the meat fibers, leaving the meat with more flavor and tenderness.

For people who have digestive problems or food sensitivities, beef is one of the meats that can be hard to digest. If you do use beef, keep this in mind, as you may have to limit or eliminate your consumption of beef.

Other cuts of beef that are not used by many are the liver, heart and tongue. Oxtail is very strong in flavor and is often braised or used in stews and soups. The heart is best when braised or simmered slowly. Beef liver is either loved or loathed. The most common method to cook beef liver is pan frying with onion then making a gravy to serve with it. Tongue is found fresh, cured or smoked. Asian countries profoundly prize tongue, which makes it a little harder to find in North America. The tongue is usually simmered in a broth and made into sandwiches that are a delicacy in deli's. Tripe is the lining of the first two stomachs of a cow. It is commonly referred to as honeycomb tripe. True sweetbread is from young beef, the thymus gland. As the cow grows, the gland disappears, so most beef sweetbread can be the pancreas gland, a larger, but softer organ. Veal sweetbread is the most desired and common variety. Fresh sweetbread must be washed to remove any blood. Simmer for about twenty to thirty minutes, drain, cool, remove the membrane and use in your recipe.

B. A. Smit

Brisket - This is suited for one method of cooking, simmering. It is found fresh or corned. Fresh brisket is known for pot roasts, which are slow cooked, often in liquid. Corned beef is mainly used in sandwiches or served hot with root type vegetables such as potato, turnip and carrot. It is made by curing the meat with brine and seasonings.

Chuck - This beef is from the very active shoulder muscles. Slow cooking improves the flavor and tenderizes the meat. Ground beef, stew meat and beef cuts for braising are the most common varieties made from chuck.

Flank - Also known as skirt, these steaks are located on the edge of the loin and rib area. The design of the steak has made them popular, especially for barbeques. The fibers are long, but even in length, with fat evenly distributed between the fibers to keep the steak tender. Flank and skirt steaks should not be overcooked.

Loin - Another very tender area of beef, known as the tender loin, it is cut to create medallions, fillet mignon, chateaubriand and tenderloin tips. Steaks and roasts are also available, known as strip loin or New York strips.

Ribs - This area is tender and therefore one of the best quality of beef comes from this area. Often presented as roasts or steaks, this beef is usually broiled, grilled, roasted or sautéed. Prime rib dinners are popular in many fine dining restaurants.

Round - Based on the area of the cow that this beef comes from, these cuts are often stewed, simmered or braised. Round is often less tender than the rib or loin area. Top or bottom round can be roasted with great results as long as a little care is given. This can be an economical choice since the leftovers can make great sandwiches. Round is often used to make ground beef.

Shank - This cut is most commonly used in stews or braised to maximize tenderness.

Veal

This is revered by some as the most superior meat available. There is a lot of contraversy regarding the method involved in obtaining veal. The calves are separated from the mother and raised until a certain age, when they are slaughtered.

The highest quality of veal is known as nature or milk fed. These calves never eat grass, grain or feed, which results in a pale pink colored meat. Because the calves do not reach maturity, their size limits the amount of veal available per calf. This is why veal is so expensive and only available in a limited number of cuts.

Chuck, shank, rib, loin and leg are the cuts available. They are cooked the same as beef. Cutlets are very popular, taken from the leg. They are often pounded flat (scallopini) and breaded then fried. Veal also has the same types of organ meats as beef.

B. A. Smit

Pork

This is known as the "other white meat" and comes from pigs. It is very popular throughout North America. The pigs have been raised specifically for food for many years, which has resulted in leaner cuts of meat. Handling pork is a little stricter than beef. It is butchered in buildings used only for pork and no other meats are processed there. Food borne illness and the disease trichinosis mean that more care is needed when using pork at home. The area used for prep must be cleaned both before and after, the meat should be refridgerated to thaw, and the pork cooked completely before consuming.

Pork is available as ribs, chops, roasts, ground and cutlets, to name the most common. The butt or shoulder is used for stew meat, ground or roasts. The loin is usually cut longer in pork than beef, lamb or veal. The loin can be found bone in or boneless and is often roasted. The crown roast, often served at catered events, is from the rib end of the loin. Pork chops can vary in thickness. The thickest chops can be stuffed with traditional bread or rice stuffing and baked. Other chops can be broiled, fried or baked. The tenderloin is the most expensive cut because of it's tenderness. It is often sliced and grilled. Boneless smoked loin is often called Canadian Back Bacon.

The leg is usually referred to as the ham, even if it is not smoked or cured. Fresh pork hams have a completely different flavor than cured hams. Ham steaks are popular for breakfasts and are often fried. Smoked or cured hams are available ready to eat, but roasting will bring out more flavor and tenderness.

Spareribs are extremely popular, especially in Asian cooking, but are more bone than meat. Country style and babyback ribs are the most common for barbequing.

In North America, we prefer to use the common cuts, such as roasts, chops, ribs, but almost every part of the pig can be eaten. For some ethnic dishes and snacks, the snout, knuckles, feet and ham hocks are used. They are cured, smoked or fresh. The most famous breakfast food is bacon. This is the belly of the pig that is cured then sometimes smoked. It is sold in slices, as a slab and with or without the rind. Different countries produce their own varieties, like the Italian pancetta.

The clear fat from the pig's back is used to line pate molds. The belly fat is often called streak of lean because of it's streaks that are similar to bacon. Jowl bacon is best used to flavor soups or in cooking, not sliced and cooked like regular bacon.

The heart, liver and kidneys are rarely eaten in North America. Availability and acceptance by the buyer limits it's sales.

Lamb

For many years lamb was not often eaten by most consumers. The popularity has grown as improvements in breeding, feeding and raising of the lambs has improved the flavor. Changes in breeding techniques ensures availability year round instead of the traditional spring season.

Like veal, lamb is slaughtered while young, keeping the meat tender. This enables lamb to be cooked in many ways yet still remain tender. Both hothouse and spring lamb are never fed grains or grass. Once they begin eating grass, the flesh becomes less tender. As the lamb gets older, the flesh becomes tougher, the color darkens and the flavor becomes stronger. Sheep that are slaughtered before one year old are called lamb, those over one year are called mutton.

Lamb cuts are similar to veal. There are hindsaddle and foresaddle, sides, leg, shoulder, breast, shank, loin and rack or rib. As mentioned, lamb can be fried, braised, baked and roasted the same as veal. Mint jelly is often served with lamb.

B. A. Smit

Poultry
Introduction

Poultry farming has changed over the past few decades, leading to more people including poultry in their daily meals. Science has led to superior breeding and care by poultry farmers enabling them to provide a consistently better tasting bird. Whether you grill, roast, fry or poach, the poultry will always remain tender and tasty.

Poultry is graded and inspected. The bird's shape, meat to bone ratio, number of pin feathers, hair and tears, all contribute to it's grade. Poultry is available whole or precut into parts, but remember, the younger the bird, the more tender the meat.

There are various birds included in the domestic section. Though the chicken and turkey are the most common, I have included other less common poultry as well. Chicken can be found as a broiler, fryer or roaster. Included also is the stewing hen and capon. Tom turkey, yearling turkey, young hen, duck (boiler, fryer and roaster), young goose, guinea hen and the squab (a domestic pigeon that has not flown) are all considered poultry. Cornish and Rock Cornish hens are also in this category. They have increased in demand for home cooking, but once were only a delicacy in fine restaurants.

Natural   Free Range   Organic

Poultry is divided into three basic catagories. Natural, free range and organic. Though all have a specific guideline, the methods used while raising the poultry may vary in each category.

Natural are raised in cages with a specific formula for the feed. To ensure that the poultry is safe for public sale, antibiotics and immunizations, steroids and/or growth enhancers could be included.

Free Range birds can have time in an exercise area where they get some food on their own, but still rely on the feed formula for the majority of their food intake.

Organic birds have no steroids or growth enhancers, but it is still best to ask about the source of your poultry purchase when possible.

Chicken

Chickens are often sold according to their size, as roasters, fryers or broilers. Poussins are very young, small chickens. Capon is a larger, unsexed male, often six pounds or more in size.

Chicken is sold whole, or in parts, legs, wings, breast or thighs. There are many ways to cook chicken. It can be fried, roasted, baked or sautéed. The more mature the stewing fowl or hen can be tougher, so it is best stewed, braised or simmered. This is why this type is used in stews and soups.

Less common are the chicken gizzards, heart, liver and backs, but they are still used by some cooks. Rendered chicken fat is known as schmaltz, which is very important for kosher cooking.

Crossbreeding resulted in the Rock Cornish hen or Cornish hen. These have the greatest ratio of dark and light meat, but are plump, small birds excellent for stuffing and roasting.

Chicken Roasting Guide

	Weight (lbs.)	Temperature (F)	Minutes per Pound	Time
Chicken	2 1/2 - 3 1/2	325°	35	1 1/2 - 2 1/2 hr
	3 1/2 - 5	325°	35	3 - 3 1/2 hr
Capon	5 1/2 - 6 1/2	325°	35	4 hr

This guide refers to stuffed birds, allow about ten minutes less per pound for an unstuffed bird. This is only a guide. Baste and check the chicken about every thirty minutes.

To Roast

Rinse the chicken under cold water after removing any parts in cavity, (giblets etc.). Pat dry then stuff. When stuffing a bird, remember to stuff loosely, try not to pack stuffing into the cavity. It will plump while cooking and if stuffed too tightly it will result in soggy stuffing.

Place in a roaster, rub skin with margarine or butter, or place seasoned margarine under the skin. * see turkey roasting guide * Place breast down in pan. Do not cover or add any water. Roast using the timetable as a guide.

When done, the leg will easily break away from the body and the thickest part of the thigh will be tender when pierced with a knife. Allow the bird to rest, covered, for twenty minutes after it is removed from the oven. This is the time to make the gravy if you want.

B. A. Smit

Turkey

This is a larger bird than the chicken. Once only cooked at special occasions, it is used year round in a variety of ways. There are two grades, young or mature hens and toms. The best meat to bone ratio is in birds over twelve pounds. Turkey is available whole, breast, which is either boneless or with the neck and back attached, legs, thighs and wings. Thin slices of meat are sold as scallopini or thicker slices are cutlets. As with chicken, it can be fried, baked, roasted or sautéed. Turkey club sandwiches and hot turkey sandwiches are popular menu items in most restaurants.

Turkey Talk
- Frozen turkey should be thawed completely before you stuff it
- Do not refreeze turkey unless it is cooked first
- It is best to thaw in the original wrapping in the fridge
- Cook the turkey within twenty four hours after thawing, keep in fridge until ready to cook
- Allow one pound per person, one and a half pounds to ensure leftovers

Approximate Thawing Times

Weight (lb.)	Fridge	Cold Water*
4 - 12	1 - 2 days	4 - 6 hours
12 - 30	2 - 3 days	6 - 8 hours
20 - 24	3 - 4 days	8 -12 hours

*Until recently, most turkeys were put either in a sink of cold water, or in a sink with cold water running on the turkey to thaw. This is no longer thought of as a safe method because of bacteria. To safely thaw your turkey, please read the instructions on your turkey package or ask your butcher when buying.

Turkey Roasting Guide
- Preheat oven to 325ºF.
- Remove bag of giblets, wash turkey, inside and out, under cold running water
- Season* and stuff turkey and insert thermometer**
- Brush with margarine (can use lactose free or butter)
- Cover just the turkey with tin foil (shiny side on the turkey) don't seal tight, leave foil "sitting" on the bird
- Roast turkey using the roasting timetable as a guide, baste every thirty to forty minutes

*To season, I blend a mixture of rosemary, thyme and sage, about one teaspoon of each, with margarine (or lactose free or butter) and place under as much skin as I can.

** If using a thermometer, push it into the thickest part of the thigh muscle, do not touch the bone, when the proper temperature is reached the bird is done.

Turkey Roasting Timetable

Weight (Lb.)	Uncovered (with tin foil)	Covered (with lid)
6 - 8	4 - 4 1/2 hrs	3 - 3 1/2 hrs
8 - 10	4 - 4 1/2 hrs	3 1/2 - 4 hrs
10 - 13	5 1/2 - 6 1/4 hrs	4 1/2 - 5 hrs
13 - 16	6 1/4 - 6 3/4 hrs	5 - 5 3/4 hrs
16 - 20	6 3/4 - 7 1/4 hrs	6 - 6 1/4 hrs

- If your time is limited, you won't be able to baste, or if the turkey is not tender, usually larger birds, cover with a lid during part of the cooking then uncover for the last hour.
- Is it cooked ? Pinch the thickest part of the thigh, protecting your fingers with a cloth, if done, the meat will feel soft, you will be able to move the drumstick up and down easily.
- If using a thermometer, it should read 185° and the turkey will have a uniform browned skin.
- Test the turkey about thirty minutes before the timetable guide's suggested time indicates the turkey will be cooked.
- An unstuffed bird will cook faster, so adjust your cooking time, about ten minutes less per pound, remember that this is only a guide.
- Let the turkey rest on a platter, covered, for about twenty minutes before carving.

B. A. Smit

Ducks

Ducks who are under one year old are called ducklings. They are most commonly roasted. Ducks which are full grown can be braised, roasted or stewed. Confit is duck which has been cooked and preserved in it's own fat.

The most common breeds of duck, in North America, are the Long Island, Muscovy, Pekin and Moulard. The Moulard is the breed of duck used to make foie gras, which is fattened liver. Now produced in North America, it has become easier to purchase the foie gras fresh. Foie gras is also used in sausages and other meats. Remember to cook with care as it will shrink when cooked. Sauté slowly is recommended for the best results.

It is possible to purchase duck as parts, such as liver, legs or breast. Though the breast is more commonly seared or grilled, the leg is generally slow roasted.

Geese

When less than a year old, geese are called goslings, and like duck, should be roasted. Geese are generally packaged and cooked the same as duck.

Game Birds

Game birds are available, but for most people, are not common in the kitchen. I am including a quick summary of the most readily available. For people with digestive problems and sensitivities to food, it is best to use caution when you are trying new meats and poultry. Keep the cooking method simple and without too many seasonings, at least until your body adjusts to the new food.

Pheasant

These are domestically raised and have a less gamey flavor than wild. The pheasant is meatier than most game birds. It is most commonly roasted or braised.

Quail

Quail are the smallest breed of the duck family. They are mainly roasted. Quail eggs are often sold in specialty markets and are cooked the same as chicken eggs, but are often served in more elegant meals.

Snipe

This bird is thought of as the finest quality game bird to many gourmets. It is available as small, common or large in size. Snipe is generally roasted.

Wild Duck

This bird is cooked in the same manner as domestic ducks. As the wild duck ages, it's flesh can become oily or fishy in flavor. Teal is a small duck that is considered a delicacy by most chefs.

B. A. Smit

Oils and Fats

Introduction

The terms fat and oil are often interchangeable. Fats applies to solids at room temperature, oils are liquid at room temperature. Food oils are made from olives, corn, cottonseed, peanuts, coconuts, palm nuts, soybeans, rapeseed, poppy, sesame, sunflower and safflower seeds. Other oils are made from walnuts, hickory nuts, almonds and beechnuts, to name a few of the most common.

Corn and cottonseed oil are most widely used in cooking, salad and vegetable oils. The three main categories for oil are:

1. To give flavor and richness like mayonnaise and dressings. Olive oil is the preferred oil because of how it's flavor enhances the foods.
2. Sauté, panfry or deep fry - when choosing a fat, the physical and chemical qualities are as important as the flavor. Oils are best since most have high smoking points (the amount of heat needed before it's too hot and begins to smoke), and a pleasant flavor. Olive oil is an exception because it can splatter.
3. Shortening - used in biscuits, muffins and pie crusts. Oil can be used in baking when shortening is called for, but recipes that call for oil need oil as a liquid ingredient.

Natural oils are best because they are made without chemicals. Try to choose ones that are light in color and flavor. Sunflower, safflower, sesame and nut oils are best for breads and desserts. For salads and general use, try safflower or sunflower oil. Sesame oil can be strong, only a small amount is needed. It is excellent when used in stirfries. Corn oil gives foods a buttery flavor. Olive oil is light and has a fruity flavor that works well in salad dressings, or drizzled over food before serving. Peanut and soybean oils are stronger in flavor and work well for frying foods. Remember that some of these oils may turn rancid, so read labels and follow the recommended storage instructions.

Butter - When used in moderation, butter is better than nearly all margarines. Unfortunately, butter contains a lot of fat, nearly sixty percent of it is saturated fats. Butter has vitamins D, E and A, and some brands have more salt than others. Dairy is a good source of calcium, except butter, it has very little calcium and almost no vitamin B's. Butter can be used on toast, potatoes and vegetables, but for baking, butter should be used in moderation.

Canola Oil - This is also known as rapeseed oil. Golden in color, canola oil is similar to safflower oil. This oil is extracted from the seeds of several varieties of turnip, which is also known as broccoli rabe. Canola oil is low in saturated fats.

Coconut Oil - This oil is virtually colorless, but heavy. It is made from fresh coconuts and is often used in shortenings, blended oils and processed packaged foods.

Corn Oil - A nonhydrogenated oil obtained from the kernel of the corn. It has no taste or smell. Corn oil is commonly used in cooking and salad dressings. Corn oil is low in cholesterol.

B. A. Smit

Cottonseed Oil - This is extracted from the cotton plant and is a pale yellow in color. It is used in salad dressings and some frying.

Grapeseed Oil - A light oil with a medium yellow color. It is a by product of wine making.

Lard - This is solid pork fat that may be treated to neutralize the flavor. Lard can be used in frying, baking and pastry crusts.

Margarine - This is a multi chemical product, blending flavoring, oils, fats and coloring. Most margarine is a combination of animal or fish oils and vegetable oils, which hydrogenation changes from liquid to solid or soft margarine. It is this process that creates trans fats, which is now considered unhealthy and the process is changing to eliminate the trans fats. The low fat margarines are lower in calories and fats and are cholesterol free. Margarines contain more vitamin E than butter. Margarine can be used in baking.

Nut Oil - This oil is pressed from nuts, walnuts, almonds and hazelnuts being the most well known. With a nutty flavor, they are often used in salads and dressings. Hazelnut oil can be expensive, with the majority coming from France. It can be cost effective to mix this oil with soy or corn oil without losing the sweet, nutty flavor. The nut oils are cold pressed, making them more perishable than other oils. They should be used as soon as possible after opening.

Olive Oil - This oil is made by crushing ripe olives and extracting the liquid. The crude oil is obtained by letting the liquid settle. Refining produces a clear oil. Olive oil is used both for cooking and salad dressings. The best quality of olive oil is golden yellow. Oil that has a green tinge is a poorer quality. The olive oil should not be exposed to extremes of light or temperature. Light will fade the oil and cold will cause the oil to congeal. The oil has a distinctive fruity flavor that is preferred by most for cooking. High heat will cause the oil to splatter, so it is best to cook over medium heat. Try to use extra virgin olive oil. The vital antioxidants are saved during processing, keeping it's nutritional value.

Omega-3 Fats - Fatty acids are polyunsaturated fats. Polyunsaturation means that these fats are missing numerous hydrogen atoms, which makes them the kind of fats that won't clog arteries, raise blood cholesterol or pose a risk of heart attack. This is why omega-3 fats are a vital part of a diet for healthy and balanced nutrition. There are three common omega-3 fats. Two of these are found in fish, EPA - eicosapentae acid, and DHA - docosahexaeonic acid. The third is alpha - linolenic, ALA, found in plants and flax seed. Fish with the highest content of omega-3 include salmon, tuna, mackerel, herring and sardines. Plant products include canola oil, soybeans, walnuts and flax seeds. It is advised to try and have two servings of fish per week. Those with implantable defribrillators should not increase their intake of omega-3 fats.

Peanut Oil - This oil has a pronounced nutty flavor, with a high smoke point. Peanut oil is low in saturated fats and high in monounsaturated fats. It also contains a good source of polyunsaturated fats. Peanut oil is a good general use oil.

Safflower Oil - This is from an old world herb that resembles a thistle with a large, bright red to orange colored flower. The flowers are used in Asia for dyeing silks. When the blossoms fade, the remaining white seeds are cold pressed into oil. It is light, colorless and has no flavor. It will not solidify in the fridge like some oils, so it is ideal to use in salad dressings and marinades. Safflower oil works well for frying and baking. Margarine that is made from the oil has a butter like flavor and is low in cholesterol.

Sesame Seed Oil - This oil is available in two basic types. A light, mild sesame oil is the Middle Eastern type and a darker kind, produced from toasted sesame seeds, is the Asian variety. This type is available in a light or dark brown color. The darker oil has a stronger flavor. Asian sesame oil is used mainly as flavoring because it has a low smoking point.

Soybean Oil - The soybean is about thirty four percent oil. This makes the process to create oil and margarine much simpler. Soybean oil is often blended into vegetable oils. Soybean oil is good for stirfries and salad dressings.

Sunflower Oil - This oil is pale yellow, odorless and with almost no flavor, is very versatile in cooking and salad dressings. It is pressed from sunflower seeds.

Vegetable Oil - With all fats, there are a lot of calories. There is a small amount of saturated fat and a good supply of vitamin E in vegetable oils. The exceptions are coconut oil and palm oil which both contain large amounts of saturated fat and coconut oil has almost no vitamin E. Try to avoid products that are simply labeled vegetable oil. When the label reads vegetable oil, most often it is coconut or palm oil, so buy only oil that is identified on the label. It is best to store oil in a cool, dark place, heat and sunlight can deteriorate oil quickly. Vegetable oils contain polyunsaturated fats which are vital since they contain essential fatty acids that our body can't produce. Oils can retain most of their nutrients when used in baking, but frying will reduce the percentage of polyunsaturated fats by up to twenty percent. Olive oil is usually the best for flavor, but safflower, sunflower and corn oils all work well for salad dressings and cooking. Walnut, soybean, sesame seed and the specialty oils all have gained popularity in recent years. The almond oil is a tasty oil for salad dressings and canola (rapeseed) oil has no real flavor, so it is good for cooking. The distinct, nutty flavor of hazelnut oil is good in sauces and dressings, but the low smoke point makes it a bad choice for frying. When deep frying, it is a health risk to overheat or repeatedly use the same oil, toxic chemicals may be produced. If your oil has "smoked", discard when cool and start fresh with new oil the next time you deep fry. The delicate flavor of extra virgin olive oil is lost when it is used for deep frying.

B. A. Smit

Sweeteners

Introduction
Sugars:

Beet	Fructose
Brown	Granulated White
Cane	Muscovado
Coarse White	Raw
Confectioner	Sucrose
Date	Superfine
Demerara	Turbinado

Fruit Concentrate
Fruit Juice
Saccharin
Splenda
Stevia

Syrups:

Agave
Corn
Glucose
High Fructose Corn Syrup
Honey
Maple
Molasses
Rice
Sorghum

Introduction

The amount of sweetener used in a recipe can be adjusted to suit your taste. Maple syrup can be substituted for honey. Less maple syrup is needed as it is sweeter than honey, and it will change the flavor slightly. Fruit juice can be used as a sweetener in some baking recipes. Remember to balance your wet and dry ingredients. Changing the recipe from a dry sweetener to a liquid, you would need to decrease your wet ingredients to balance the recipe.

Research is showing that an excess of sugar can be unhealthy. Breakfast cereal may contain up to sixty percent sugar, hidden as molasses, honey, corn syrup, sucrose or dextrose. Honey, though natural, only has trace amounts of nutrients and may contain up to twenty percent water. Corn, maple and glucose syrups, maltose and fructose are simply names for sugar. When the body digests sugar, it is converted into fructose and glucose. They enter the bloodstream, where they travel to the liver. If you consume large amounts of sugar, your body does not handle the fructose in the normal fashion. It can raise the levels of blood lipids, a form of fat, which increases the danger of cholesterol deposits in the arteries. If your diet includes healthy polyunsaturated fatty acids and is low in saturated fats, you have some protection, but most diets, high in fat, high in sugar, are a risk to good health.

Artificial sweeteners, acesulfame-k, aspartame and saccarin contain no calories, but they are still chemicals. You are better to reduce the amount of sugar instead of using sweeteners. Bulk sweeteners like sorbitol, xylitol and mannitol are used in processed foods. They do not contain sucrose, so won't promote tooth decay, but they are still chemicals that the body doesn't need.

The manufacturers rarely disclose the true amount of sweetener in their product. Sugar is for taste. A healthy person does not need extra sugar, especially the chemical sweeteners. If you want to lose weight, eat healthier. Always read the labels on food packages to find hidden sugars.

I am including descriptions of the most common sweeteners, so you can decide which is best for you.

B. A. Smit

Sugars

Beet - This is the sugar that is extracted from sugar beets. It can be used the same as refined sugar.

Brown - This type of sugar is often used in baking. It is refined sugar that has either some impurities left in after processing, or molasses has been added. It can be found in granular form.

Cane - Made from the sugar cane, this sugar is not processed like refined sugar. It is filtered using natural extracts and vegetable purifiers. This natural, often organic sugar can be used the same as refined sugar. There are several varieties available, depending on the process used. It is found as granular sugar and is similar in color to brown sugar.

Coarse White - Known as preserving sugar, this is a large crystal sugar. It can dissolve slowly so it is not recommended for baking.

Confectioner - Often used in baking and for frostings, this sugar is a fine, white powder made from refined sugar. It may have cornstarch added to help prevent clumping.

Date - Pleasing and lightly sweet, date sugar is made from dried dates that are ground into a coarse sugar. It can be used in baking for cakes, cookies and can be substituted for granulated sugar.

Demerara - Dissolves easily, with the same sweetness as brown sugar. Demerara is partially refined golden brown sugar. The granular size is much larger than brown sugar, it resembles large crystals. It can be used in place of brown sugar on hot cereals like porridge and in many baking recipes.

Fructose - This is a natural monosaccharide that is much sweeter than refined sugar. Simply put, fructose is the natural sugar found in many fruits and vegetables. It is very popular as a sweetener in many processed foods. Since it is natural and contains calories, you may find it easy to overeat because it won't trigger the insulin response or give you a feeling of being full. So as a result you may eat more, increasing your calorie intake and causing unwanted weight gain. Be sure to read labels to know that the fructose is natural and not chemically altered. Fructose can be used instead of refined sugar.

Granulated White - This is the most common form of refined sugar. It has uniform, small crystals and can be found loose or as cubes.

Muscovado - A soft, moist, granular brown sugar that is not processed as much as brown sugar. It has a distinct, but subtle molasses flavor. A nice choice for baking.

Raw - For a long time, the original raw sugar was only manufactured in Europe. In North America, we can often find raw sugar as Sucanat, (SUgar CAne NATural). This is the true raw sugar. Most other "raw" types can actually be white sugar that molasses and color additives have been combined with, then crystalized. Sucanat is not as sweet as regular refined sugar.

Sucrose - This is often made from cane sugar and beets. It is classed as a disaccharide, which means that it is made from equal amounts of fructose and glucose. Refined, granulated sugar is sucrose.

Superfine - Also known as bar sugar, it is white refined sugar that is very tiny crystals that dissolve quickly. This makes it popular for baking.

Turbinado - A coarse granular type of sugar that is similar to demerara, but is more refined. It is good on cereals and for baking sweet desserts.

B. A. Smit

Fruit Concentrate - This is a manufactured sweetener made from highly concentrated fruit product. This fruit concentrate is not the same as fruit juice concentrate found in grocery stores. It equals maple syrup and honey when used to sweeten cakes, cookies or desserts. Frozen or bottled fruit juice concentrates bought at the grocery store can be used in some recipes, but for sweetness, the true fruit concentrate is the best choice.

Fruit Juice - Pure juice or juice from concentrate is healthier than juice with artificial flavors, colors and sweeteners. Fruit juice can be used in baking for flavor and a little sweetness.

Saccharin - This is about four hundred times sweeter than sugar, so tiny amounts can go a long way, but it can leave a metallic after taste. Use care in the amount you use in baking.

Splenda - Sucralose is a synthetic compound used in the Splenda sweetener products. It has no nutrition value because it has no calories. To create sucralose, scientists took sugar through several steps which replaced three hydrogen-oxygen groups on the sugar molecule with chlorine atoms. This process ensures a heat stable, very sweet product that, because of it's make up, has no calories therefore can't be turned into energy, therefore your body will not turn it to fat. Splenda products add dextrose and/or maltodextrin, which do have calories. Read labels and use this product in moderation. It can be used in baking, beverages and anywhere refined sugar is used. Diabetics often use Splenda products, but again, read labels.

Stevia - Known as honeyleaf, sweetleaf or sweetherb, this strong herbal sweetener is a native of South America. It can be found as a liquid or a powder. Stevia leaves can be processed into a fine beige powder that is about two hundred times sweeter than refined sugar. You only need a small amount, about two drops of liquid stevia are equal to two tablespoons of honey. Through some experimenting, it can be ideal for baking. Because of the small amount needed, you may have to alter your recipes. When using stevia in place of sugar, the texture and browning of baked goods could be affected. Try using fruit juice, extra flour or applesauce to balance the recipe. The liquid stevia is often a concentrated liquid with alcohol and water as a base. Other brands of liquid stevia may contain glycerin. Stevia blends can include maltodextrin or starch to make the stevia appear more like sugar crystals. Some stevia products use fillers from the plant that could leave a bitter after taste. Read labels.

Syrups

Agave - This is a part of the tequila plant family. It is a syrup that is sweeter than refined sugar with a flavor that is similar to maple syrup and honey. Though excellent in baking, remember to adjust the amount used, less is needed than refined sugar.

Corn - Natural corn syrup is the liquid sugars that are extracted from corn. It is not as sweet as maple syrup or honey. Corn syrup is used in baking and desserts. It is available light or dark colored. The light corn syrup is pale yellow, almost clear, and the dark is a deep amber color, usually from a longer cooking time than the light syrup. Some corn syrup is artificial, made of numerous ingredients, none are from corn. Read labels.

Glucose - This syrup is widely used for sweetening, moisture control and adding shelf life for various foods. It can be made from the starches of corn, potato, tapioca, rice or wheat. Corn is the most common. These syrups are purified and processed to separate, then remove, the protein from the starch. Fungal or bacteria enzymes are then used to break down the starch into glucose syrup. This process will render wheat starch gluten free.

High Fructose Corn Syrup (HFCS) - This is a heavily refined sweetener that begins with corn. There are two types of this version of corn syrup. HFCS 55 which is fifty five per cent fructose and forty two percent glucose. The second type is HFCS 42 which has forty two percent fructose and fifty three percent glucose. This product is used in many commercially packaged foods, including many baked goodies. Researchers believe that this type of sweetener, used in so many products including soft drinks, can lead to obesity. Glucose is known as a monosaccharide, it is used by the body to break down carbohydrates into glucose used for energy. Glucose can prompt the body's insulin response causing the body to begin storing energy as fat.

Honey - The most popular form of honey that is used is liquid. Creamed honey is also available. Read labels carefully and choose a good quality honey. With raw honey, there is a risk of contaminants and bacteria, so people with allergies and sensitivities and especially babies, should only use this honey for cooking. It would be ideal to choose other honeys instead of raw. Pasteurizing honey destroys bacteria, enzymes and nutrients, but is much safer to use. Honey is used to sweeten beverages, on toast and muffins and is suitable for all types of baking.

Maple - Harvested from maple trees, this boiled, sweet sap is often used instead of honey, or poured over pancakes. Maple syrup is sweeter than honey. When a recipe calls for half a cup of honey, it is suggested to use one quarter of a cup of maple syrup and one quarter of a cup of fruit juice to keep the wet/dry balance of the recipe. It is best when you use the pure, one hundred percent maple syrup type. There are many artificial syrups, but they are mostly sugar and other additives, so they are not as healthy.

B. A. Smit

Molasses - Simply, you will either love it or hate it. There are three main varieties of molasses, cooking, unsulphered and table. Unsulphered is mainly used for cooking. Table is the best variety for everyday use, it is also called fancy. Cooking molasses is a mixture of blackstrap and fancy and is a good balance of sweet and bitter, making it ideal for cooking. Blackstrap molasses is a good source of iron and nutrients, but is too strong for most people. There are some varieties that contain wheat, so read labels carefully. Molasses is the by product of refined sugar. It is made by pressing the liquid from sugar beets or cane sugar. It is then cooked down to extract the sugar crystals. The brown liquid that remains is molasses. Light molasses is from the first cooking and dark molasses is from a second cooking. Blackstrap is the thickest, darkest molasses available. It is from the last processing of the sugar. It can be bitter and is not used in most recipes, but gingerbread cookies are often made from this molasses.

Rice - This syrup is used the same as glucose syrup, also known as corn syrup, though not the same as pure, natural corn syrup, for sweetening and enhancing the flavor of foods. Most syrups are gluten free, but a few use a barley malt enzyme in the processing, which can leave low levels of gluten in the product, read labels. Rice syrup can be purchased in most markets, but is not as sweet as honey or maple syrup. It can be used in baking.

Sorghum - This is used primarily in the Southern United States. It is a syrup made from a grain similar to Indian corn. Gluten free and as an unrefined sweetener, it can be used in baking and daily use.

Vegetables

Introduction

Brassicas: Introduction   Cabbage: Introduction

Bok Choy	Kale	Green
Broccoli	Kohlrabi	Napa
Broccoli Rabe	Okra	Red
Brussel Sprouts	Pakchoi	Savoy
Cauliflower	Spinach	

Cooking and Salad Greens: Introduction

Cooking Greens:

Beet Greens	Mustard Greens
Collard Greens	Spinach Greens
Dandelion Greens	Swiss Chard
Kale	Turnip Greens

Salad Greens:

Asparagus
Celeriac and Celery
Chicory Root, Chicory and Endive
Watercress

Lettuce:

Introduction	Iceberg Lettuce
Arugula	Leaf Lettuce
Belgian Endive	Mache
Boston Lettuce	Oakleaf Lettuce
Curly Endive	Radicchio
Escarole	Romaine Lettuce

Edible Seaweed:

Introduction	Kombu
Arame	Laver
Dulse	Nori
Hiziki	Wakame

Gourds: Introduction   Squash:

Cucumber:	Squash	
English	Acorn	Pattypan
Kirby	Butternut	Pumpkin
Seedless, Burpless	Chayoto	Spaghetti
Slicing	Crookneck	Yellow
	Hubbard	Zucchini

Eggplant:

Introduction
Japanese
Purple
White

Mediterranean Vegetables: Introduction

Tomatoes:			
	Introduction	Mushrooms:	Introduction
	Beefsteak		Boletus
	Cherry		Chanterelles
	Cranberry or Currant		Cremini
	Pear		Morels
	Roma or Plum		Oysters
	Slicing		Portabello
	Tomatillos		Shitake
			Truffles

Onions, Garlic and Leeks:

Onions:			
	Introduction		
	Boiling	Red	Sweet
	Cippolini	Scallions	White
	Pearl	Shallots	Yellow
	Ramps	Spanish	

Garlic

Leeks

Peppers and Chilies:

Peppers

Chilies:			
	Introduction	Chipotles	Poblanos
	Anaheims	Habaneros	Scotch Bonnet
	Banana	Jalapenos	Serranos

Pod and Seed Vegetables

Roots and Tubers: Introduction	Potatoes: Introduction
Artichokes	Bliss
Beets	Chef's
Carrots	Heirloom
Florence Fennel	Idaho or Russet
Jerusalem Artichoke	Irish
Jicama	Red
Parsnip	Salt
Radishes	Sweet
Salsify	Yams
Taro	Yellow or New
Turnips and Rutabagas	Yukon Gold

Soft Vegetables:	Avocado
	Corn

B. A. Smit

Introduction

Vegetables are a vital component of the nutrition we need daily. In this chapter, I have written about some of the vast varieties of vegetables, some are common and others are less known, but still should be tried. Using this information, try to choose a variety that are within your diet. There are some points to keep in mind when choosing vegetables.

People who suffer from allergies or sensitivities often find lettuce varieties hard to digest. Spinach is a good substitute. Other suggestions may be helpful when you want to keep salads in your diet. Zucchini is easier to digest than cucumber, and red pepper can digest easier than green pepper. Members of the nightshade family, such as tomato, potato and eggplant, can be slightly toxic and hard to digest, either raw or cooked. You may want to avoid these foods. Organic vegetables are a better choice as they are free of chemicals and pesticides that may irritate allergies. Today, there are many varieties of organic vegetables available. It would be an idea to explore your local farmer's markets to find fresh, local produce. You will be able to ask questions and learn more about what is available within your area.

Brassicas
Introduction

   All members of the brassica family, cauliflower to watercress, and all other members should be eaten in moderation by those taking thyroid medication. The brassica family contain the factor goitrogenic, which can interfere with the thyroid's ability to absorb iron. You would need large amounts to be at risk of illness, but it is best to limit your consumption of vegetables from this family.

   Brussel sprouts, cauliflower and cabbage are the best known of the brassica family. They are good sources for vitamin C, beta carotene and are helpful protectors against cancer.

Bok Choy - This is best known as an Asian vegetable, but has become popular in North America. It is a loose head cabbage, shaped long, similar to a bunch of celery, not the traditional round shaped cabbage. The leaves are a dark, shiny green color with the stems a very pale green, almost white in color. Bok choy is available year round, but is best during late summer to early fall. It is often used in stirfries and many Asian dishes. Baby bok choy is a more delicate flavored, smaller version of regular bok choy and can be eaten raw. When choosing bok choy, ensure that the leaves are not withered and the stems are firm.

Broccoli - Given the nickname little trees, this vegetable grows in clusters on a stem, resembling little trees. Dark green in color, broccoli is a member of the Cruciferous Family. It is helpful for skin problems, chronic fatigue, anemia and a good protector against cancer. Studies have shown that broccoli and other family members (kale, cabbage, turnip, cauliflower, horseradish and brussel sprouts) are vital for protection against cancer. Eating good amounts of this vegetable helps to lower the risk of cancer. Broccoli has ample carotenoids, including beta carotene, which the body converts to vitamin A. There is also iron, vitamin C and folate found in broccoli. It can be eaten raw in salads or lightly steamed, and is a good choice for veggie and dip platters. When purchasing broccoli, it is best if the flowerettes (clusters) are tight and the stem solid, firm with no splits. When preparing broccoli to eat, you can use just the tops, opting to discard the stem, or you can lightly peel then chop the stem into small chunks, about one inch in size, and cook with the tops.

Broccoli Rabe - Also known as rapini, it is green, leafy, with small florets and stems. Their peak season is a little later in summer than broccoli. The signs of a good broccoli rabe is no yellow flowers, firm leaves and the stem should be a light green, almost white in color. It can be used the same as broccoli.

Brussel Sprouts - These look and taste like miniature cabbage, and are often called baby cabbages. They are a medium to light green in color. The peak season is late fall to winter. Brussel sprouts are best if the leaves are firmly attached to the sprout and rounded into small, solid, ball shapes. They are a member of the cabbage family, with the same healthy nutrients. Brussel sprouts are full of glucosinolates, a strong anticancer chemical. This makes them a good protector against cancer. They also improve overall resistance to illness, help skin problems and constipation. If possible,

B. A. Smit

it is best to steam these vegetables to keep the vitamin C and folate contents. The vitamin C is helpful to improve the natural resistance to disease. Brussel sprouts are a good source of beta carotene and fiber. When cooking, it is advised to cut some of the stem and remove a few of the outer leaves. To ensure even cooking of the sprouts, most cooks will cut an "x" shape at the end of the stem, then steam or boil in water until nearly tender. They are tasty alone or mixed with other vegetables.

Cauliflower - This is a creamy, almost white colored flowering head with dark to medium green colored leaves at the base of the stem. It looks much like broccoli, but cauliflower is round shaped, not on stalks like broccoli. Although it is a part of the brassica family, cauliflower has lower amounts of folic acid, riboflavin and beta carotene than cabbage. Cauliflower contains vitamin C, is also a cancer protector and helpful in general immunity. To prepare the vegetable, remove the cluster from the stem as you would broccoli, and cook in the same way, steam, boil or stirfry. Cauliflower can be eaten raw as well. It is best to lightly steam this vegetable, essential nutrients can be lost if it is overcooked. Choose cauliflower that is firm, the clusters solid with no flowering, no wilted leaves or browning. Cauliflower should be stored in the fridge. Remember to place the vegetable stem down, it will keep moisture that is in the cauliflower from seeping into the clusters causing them to spoil faster. Cauliflower is another good vegetable for veggie and dip platters. A popular sauce to serve over cooked cauliflower is a cheese sauce.

Kale - Originating within Europe and the Mediterranean, kale is now distributed worldwide. It is a member of the Cruciferae Family. Kale is, like other members within it's family, rich in anticancer properties and beta carotene. Kale is a very hardy plant, surviving both extreme cold and heat. It has round ruffled leaves, often a dark green to purple in color. Kale is often used as a filler to decorate salad bars. It is best eaten raw, chopped into salad, or cooked, like the Danish dish stampot, which is mashed potato mixed with steamed, chopped kale. The leaves can be braised, steamed or sautéed. Adding garlic will enhance the flavor.

Kohlrabi - Known as a cabbage turnip, it is close in flavor to others in the cabbage family. Kohlrabi is a round bulb that is shaped like a turnip, with a stem and leaves attached to the bulb. It is a descendant of the wild cabbage and is a cruciferous vegetable. The kohlrabi and the cabbage are nearly identical in their nutrients. The kohlrabi contains vitamin C, folic acid and potassium. However, it has no beta carotene. Choose firm bulbs that are not cracked or turning yellow and have firm fresh leaves. The best time for fresh kohlrabi is early summer.

Okra - This is a pod which tastes best when it is tender. Often referred to as gumbo, because it is used in gumbo, a type of soup, it can also be added to other main dishes and stews. A popular vegetable in the Southern United States.

Pakchoi - This is one of the more famous oriental brassicas, a general name used for a number of members. The Chinese have grown pakchoi for food and medicine for centuries. It is very nutritious, containing vitamin C, beta carotene, potassium, folic acid and some of the B vitamins. Pakchoi is often eaten raw or added to stirfries.

Spinach - This small, leafy vegetable is high in some nutrients and lacking in others. Spinach is a good protector against vision impairment and cancer. There are generous amounts of iron and vitamin C in spinach, but high levels of oxalic acid combines with the minerals in spinach and are expelled by the body as insoluble salts. This makes spinach a bad choice for those with arthritis and gout. For people suffering from stress, fatigue or anemia, spinach has ample chlorophyll, which is beneficial for those ailments. Spinach has folic acid and beta carotene, along with lutein and zeaxanthin, which are a helpful protector against age-related macular degeneration (AMD) a common vision impairment of the elderly. Spinach has deep green, flat leaves that vary in size and shape, depending on the varieties. To prepare spinach, wash the leaves well and trim off the stems, if you prefer, though not necessary. Spinach leaves are available year round, fresh, frozen or canned. It is best when eaten raw, in salads, or very lightly steamed. Cooking quickly, a light steaming is the most common method used to cook spinach, but it can also be braised, sautéed, or baked within other foods such as lasagna or chicken dishes.

Cabbage
Introduction

All types of cabbage are good cancer protectors and are beneficial for the treatment of stomach ulcers, acne, anemia and respiratory ailments. Cabbage is known as a "heading" vegetable, meaning it grows in a round head shape and is best raw, as in coleslaw salad, lightly steamed or boiled. Cabbage is a good source of vitamin C, iron and beta carotene. For maximum nutrients, do not overcook the cabbage.

Green - This is a very solid, round heading cabbage. Like the Napa variety, green cabbage should feel heavy and solid. The color ranges in the medium green tones. Fresh cabbage should not be withered, browning or have bore holes from insects. The peak season is late summer and can continue into early fall. Cabbage that is stored through the winter before selling is more solid and tight than the freshly picked then sold types. Cabbage rolls are often made from green cabbage.

Napa - This is a heading cabbage, long in shape, pale green to yellow in color, and is available late summer into fall. To ensure freshness, it should feel heavy and have no withering or brown tinged leaves. International cookbooks will have recipes for this type of cabbage.

Red - Sometimes called purple cabbage, red cabbage is very similar in appearance of weight, size and solidness as green cabbage. The color will vary from maroon to deep purple and when cut, the veins will be a cream color. Red cabbage is used in many dishes, including salads. When purchasing, look for cabbage heads that are glossy and shiny. You can use this cabbage the same as the green variety.

Savoy - A heading cabbage with leaves that are not as tight as other varieties. The leaves are rippled, with a waffle type texture. The color is a medium green shade and should look crisp and fresh with tight leaves to ensure it is fresh.

Cooking and Salad Greens
Introduction

This type of vegetable includes both salad and cooking greens. Watercress, endive and spinach are examples of leafy vegetables known as salad or cooking greens. They are often used raw in salads or steamed as a vegetable side dish. Lettuce, which has many varieties, is often the base for salads. Today, many varieties of salad mixtures are prepackaged for convenience. These mixtures can include herbs and edible flowers like pansies or nasturtiums. Most of these leafy vegetables are highly perishable, so you will have to find the variety that suits you best and can stay fresh in your fridge. Typically, four to seven days is the average time that salad will remain fresh in the fridge. Some of the most widely available varieties are described in this section. Cooking greens are very versatile. They can vary in both flavor and cooking methods. Most are stirfried or steamed. Both cooking and salad greens have a lot of healthy nutrients, so it is important to include them in your diet.

Cooking Greens

Beet Greens - This vegetable is found during the summer and fall as fresh, but is available year round in most areas. The leaves are dark green, flat, with prominent red ribbing. The most common cooking methods include steaming, braising and sautéed.

Collard Greens - These have rounded, large flat leaves and the fall is the peak season. Like beet greens, these greens are steamed, braised or sautéed. Garlic adds flavor to any greens.

Dandelion Greens - Most abundant in the spring, they have narrow leaves with an uneven rough edge. Dandelion leaves are mainly sautéed, but can be steamed or stirfried as well.

Kale - This vegetable has two food group identities. It is a brassica but can also be a part of the cooking greens section. I have described this vegetable in the brassica section. As a cooking green, kale is often steamed.

Mustard Greens - These have narrow leaves that are prominently scalloped. Mustard greens are most abundant in the summer and are cooked the same as kale and dandelion leaves. Both mustard and collard greens are popular in Southern United States cooking.

Spinach Greens - Like kale, spinach can be found in both brassica and cooking greens sections. You will find spinach in the brassica section.

Swiss Chard - A type of beet plant, swiss chard and beet greens are often thought to be the same, but they are not. Swiss chard is similar in looks to the beet greens, shiny, deep green leaves, but the ribs and stems vary from deep red to white or varigated in color. It is most abundant in the fall and is cooked by the same methods as other cooking greens.

Turnip Greens - These have flat, green colored broad leaves with a rough texture. They are available mainly in the summer months into the fall. The turnip greens are cooked by the same methods as other cooking greens.

Salad Greens

Asparagus - This vegetable, once thought of as a gourmet food, is now widely used by many. It is good for fluid retention, arthritis, rheumatism and constipation. It is not a good choice for those with gout, as it contains purines, which can irritate gout. Asparagus is best when it is lightly steamed, grilled or sautéed. The woody stem is usually not eaten. To prepare, place a hand on each end of the sprig, bend until it snaps. Discard the stem end or use to flavor soups, lightly peel any stem remaining near the tip, then cook as desired. Best known as a diuretic, asparagus also contains fiber.

Celeriac and Celery - Both of these are beneficial for arthritis, gout and rheumatism, reducing blood pressure and reducing fluid retention. Celery and celeriac are both helpful in calming nerves and are good antistress foods. Celeriac is a variety of celery with a turnip like root, the bulbous round stem is eaten and not the stalks. It has a smell similar to celery, but the flavor is milder. Celeriac can be grated and added raw to many salads. Both celery and celeriac are alike in nutrition and chemical make up, but the white bulb of celeriac and the blanched white celery stalks do not contain beta carotene. The dark green stalks of celery do contain beta carotene. Celeriac is a very good source for folate. Both celery and celeriac have fiber, potassium and vitamin C. Research has shown that the oils drawn from celery seeds are beneficial as a calming effect on the central nervous system. They also lower high blood pressure. Celery is used to help gout, arthritis and rheumatism. When making tea or cooking with the seeds, only use the culinary variety. Traditional seeds used for planting may contain toxic chemicals. Celeriac is crisp in texture and is often cooked the same ways as potato. When purchasing celeriac, it should be firm, heavy in weight, with no deep dents, cuts or soft spots. The stems and leaves should be green and fresh looking, not wilted. Celery is similar, look for blemish free, firm stalks of a medium green color. Both of these vegetables are good raw as in salads, or cooked into stirfries, soups or main dishes.

Chicory Root, Chicory and Endive - All of these vegetables are members of the plant family, Cichorium. They are good for detoxifying and cleansing the digestive system, are a good diuretic and a stimulant for the liver. The slightly bitter taste of chicory works well in salads and endive, also called curly endive, also has a bitter taste and often is only used in salads. The chicory root can be dried and ground then used as a coffee substitute. Wild chicory is also known as wild succory and for centuries has been used both as food and in medicine. Chicory and endive are good sources of vitamin A (if eaten raw), vitamin C and some B vitamins. They also contain bitter terpenoids, which stimulate the liver and gall bladder. For people who have trouble digesting milk and milk products, the dried chicory can be beneficial. It stimulates the functions of the glands in the digestive tract, helping to break down the milk into tiny particles that are then digested easier. As an efficient eliminator of toxic wastes, chicory is helpful in arthritis, gout, rheumatism and skin problems. Chicory and endive are good both raw and cooked.

B. A. Smit

Watercress - A light, delicate vegetable with rounded leaves and a pepper like taste. It is a member of the Cruciferae Family, and like broccoli, cabbage, kale and other family members, should be eaten often by those who are at risk of cancer. Watercress is good as a cancer protector, helps with food poisoning, anemia and stomach infections. It is best well washed and eaten raw. Watercress is an ideal source of vitamins A, C and E, the strong antioxidants which help to protect against cardiovascular disease and cancer. Watercress is closely related to the nasturtium and both contain benzyl mustard oil. A similar ingredient (which researchers have shown to be a strong antibiotic) puts the bite in radish and horseradish. This ingredient is harmless to our intestines, but very helpful for the health of our intestines. Eating watercress will help your natural resistance. Watercress also contains iodine, which is needed for the thyroid gland to function properly.

Lettuce
Introduction

Similar to cucumber in it's high water content, but unlike cucumber, lettuce does have many nutrients. Lettuce is about ninety five percent water and in one average serving, there are only about seven calories. Lettuce is either loved or loathed by dieters. There are many varieties, the nutritional value changes with each variety, the season it is grown in, or whether you eat the dark outer leaves or the pale inner heart. To some degree, they all contain folic acid, vitamin C, beta carotene, potassium, calcium, iodine and small amounts of iron. The darker the leaf, the higher the content of beta carotene. The ancient Romans named wild lettuce, of which our modern lettuce is a descendant, Lactuca Verosa, the verosa meaning slimy or rank. They are referring to the milky juice from the broken stem. In large amounts, this substance is poisonous. The lettuce grown today is less potent. There are numerous phytochemicals in lettuce including flavinoids, lactucin and coumarins, which makes it popular for herbal medicines. Lettuce is used mainly in salads and sandwiches.

Arugula - This has tender leaves that are rounded and uneven on the edge. The flavor is a distinct peppery taste that intensifies as it ages. Baby arugula is popular because of this, it has a lighter peppery taste.

Belgian Endive - This grows in a similar shape as romaine lettuce, but is more compactly layered. It is oblong in shape, mainly white with the tips varying from green to yellow. Belgian endive is slightly bitter in flavor and is used mainly in salads, but sometimes it is braised and served as a vegetable dish.

Boston Lettuce - Also known as butterhead, this is a heading lettuce, meaning it grows into a round head shape with the leaves growing from the base center, like the cabbage. The leaves are tender, mild in flavor and like the belgian endive, can be braised as well as served raw.

Curly Endive - This is a heading lettuce with sharp uneven edges on curly leaves, hence the name. It is also known as frisee. The center leaves are a pale yellow color. Curly endive has a light bitter taste, and in some cases, very bitter taste. It can be interchanged with escarole.

Escarole - This is also a heading lettuce that, besides using in salad dishes, can be added to soups and stews. The leaves are scalloped at the edge and like endive varieties, can have a peppery or bitter taste.

Iceberg Lettuce - A compactly grown heading lettuce popular in salads. It has a pale green color with a mild taste. It can also be used in sandwiches.

Leaf Lettuce - This is a head lettuce that has loose instead of compact leaves. The leaves vary from all green to red tipped green in color. When young, this is a tender,

B. A. Smit

mild flavored lettuce, but as it ages, it can become bitter. It is another good choice for salads and sandwiches.

Mache - It is also known as corn salad or lamb's lettuce. This is a very tender, very delicate flavored variety with rounded leaves.

Oakleaf Lettuce - A nutty flavored variety with tender, scalloped edges. A good choice for salads.

Radicchio - Considered to be a type of endive, this is a heading lettuce. It has purple to deep maroon red leaves, with white veining. Radicchio is a very bitter, but popular lettuce for salads.

Romaine Lettuce - A long, oblong shaped variety of lettuce with the outer leaves being the most thickly ribbed. Green in color, the inner leaves are paler in color and are considered the heart. Romaine hearts are mild, tender and lightly sweet in flavor. These are often used in many types of salads, especially the popular caesar salad.

Edible Seaweed
Introduction

Seaweed has been used both as food and as medicine for centuries. Most edible seaweed consists of the brown, red or green varieties. It is often referred to as kelp, which is really a member of the fucus species that normally only grows in the northern seas. There are some slight nutritional differences in the numerous varieties, but seaweed should be included in the diet, especially for vegetarians, because of the amount of B12 vitamins that it contains. Seaweed is also a good source for protein, magnesium, calcium, potassium, beta carotene and soluble fiber. It is a rich source of zinc, iron and iodine. As popularity of Japanese and Chinese cooking increases, so does the availability of various types of seaweed.

Arame - This is suitable for beginner's, arame has a sweet flavor. It is best in soup or salads.

Dulse - Most popular in both Britain and the U.S.A., this seaweed is not suggested for the beginner. Dulse grows along the seaboard of North America, Canada, Ireland and Iceland. The Irish make a dulse soup, which needs an aquired taste to enjoy. The seaweed is tough, and has a very salty taste.

Hiziki - This seaweed is usually sun dried and then shredded. Hiziki has a light, sweet flavor. It is a good source of both calcium and iron.

Kombu - This is a strong flavored seaweed, used to enhance soups and savory dishes. It is a good source of calcium and vitamins C and A. Kombu contains a large amount of sodium, so it is not a good choice for low salt diets or for people with high blood pressure. One strip is enough to flavor two cups of soup stock.

Laver - This has been popular in Wales for hundreds of years. It grows off the coastline of South Wales and Ireland. Laver is a red seaweed that is often gathered off the beach. It has a strong flavor and the Welsh often roll it in oatmeal, fry it and serve it with bacon and eggs for breakfast. Like dulse, the flavor is strong and often needs aquiring a taste for it.

Nori - This variety is rich in minerals and proteins. In Japanese cooking, nori is used to wrap tasty bites of savory foods. It is also used as a garnish, sprinkled on vegetables or savory dishes before serving.

Wakame - This is a good seaweed for beginner's. It is full of proteins, calcium and iron, and it's flavor resembles that of green vegetables. The Japanese use wakame in their miso soup.

B. A. Smit

Gourds
Introduction

Cucumber, squash and eggplant may not seem to be related, but they all belong to the gourd family. All three vegetables have similar tough skins (rinds), flat, oval shaped seeds and the flesh is thick and firm. Cucumbers are a common ingredient in salad dishes and uncooked sauces. Although some recipes do include cooking cucumbers, it is not a common practice. Pickles, of numerous varieties, are made from cucumbers and cooked brine. Most pickles will sit to cure (enhance the flavor) for several months before eating. Crookneck, yellow, zucchini and pattypan are all summer squash. These vegetables are almost always picked before they are fully mature. This will enable you to enjoy the light flavor, tender seeds and thin rind before they mature and become thick skinned with a heavier flesh. The light flavor makes summer squash ideal for baking, soups and stews. Winter squash include butternut, pumpkin, acorn, hubbard and spaghetti. These varieties are best known for their solid rind and hard seeds.

Cucumber

English - This variety is very popular in the summer months. A long, tube shape, the skin is slightly ridged and thin. This makes it ideal to slice and use without peeling. Often used in salads and on canapes and crackers, it's uses are many. Also known as Long English Cucumbers.

Kirby - These are short, pudgy, bullet shaped cucumbers. Kirby varieties are green in color, often with pronounced ridges and wart like bumps. This cucumber is eaten fresh, in salads and sandwiches, and can be used in pickle recipes.

Seedless, Burpless - Very similar to English cucumbers, these are also long, tube shaped with very few or no seeds. They are used the same as the English variety of cucumber.

Slicing - Long, lean and medium green in color, this variety is often used in pickle and relish recipes. They can also be used in salads and sandwiches.

Eggplant
Introduction

These are a member of the Solanaceae Family, so people with rheumatoid arthritis should eat them with caution. Eggplant originated in Southeast Asia and India. For thousands of years, they have been grown for both food and medicine. This deep purple skinned vegetable contains protease inhibitors which are known as anticancer chemicals. Eggplant can help to lower cholesterol levels and high blood pressure. It is available in a variety of shapes and sizes, but the larger sized vegetable can be bitter in taste. The smaller sized eggplant is ideal for grilling, pan frying or baking with seasonings and a little oil. The larger size are best for baked dishes like ratatouille. There are many dishes that include eggplant, most are Middle Eastern in origin.

Japanese - This is a long, narrow, tube shaped vegetable with the same purple to black colored skin as the purple eggplant. It can be used the same as other varieties, grilled, baked or stewed.

Purple - Also known as standard, it is the most common variety. It is usually a rounded, long pear shaped vegetable averaging eight to twelve inches in length. It has a very dark purple, almost black skin with green leaves at it's stem. This eggplant is often sliced, then grilled, braised or stewed.

White - This variety can be either oval or cylinder in shape. The skin can be streaked with purple. White eggplant can be braised, grilled or baked.

Squash

Acorn - Gaining popularity, this squash often is a deep green color, but some have an orange tint or are completely orange. The shape is similar to an acorn, hence the name. Acorn squash also have deep ridges. It can be baked, often with maple syrup, fried or made into soup.

Butternut - This squash has several colors on it's skin. It can range from orange to tan to brown. The shape resembles a stretched pear. As with other winter squash, it is usually baked or fried. Butternut squash also makes a nice soup.

Chayoto - A pear shaped, soft green colored squash with deep ridges between the halves. This squash is also known as Mirliton. It has a large seed that is edible. This type of squash can be cooked in the same methods as other varieties, stuffed and baked, stirfried or grilled.

Crookneck - Yellow in color and as the name implies, the neck is thin and slightly bent. Usually this squash is pan fried, sautéed or steamed.

Hubbard - This is a sage green colored squash, with many wart like bumps over the entire skin. It is used in the same ways as acorn squash.

Pattypan - This variety has a flattened ball shape with streaked green and yellow skin. It can be pan fried, sautéed or steamed.

Pumpkin - These are often oval to round in shape, a deep orange color with noticeable ridges. At Halloween, they are carved into lanterns, but there are many nutritious elements to pumpkin as well. As with most orange to yellow colored vegetables, they are full of beta carotene. This is the vitamin A precurser that helps to protect against heart and respiratory disease, as well as cancer. Pumpkin are also rich in zinc and protein. This makes it a wise choice for vegetarians. Available in the fall, they are often baked into pies for Thanksgiving dinners. Pumpkin is available fresh, frozen or canned. It is used in many baking recipes, main dishes and breads. The seeds can be dried, seasoned and eaten as a snack. One variety, sugar pumpkin, is used for

B. A. Smit

baking. To prepare the pumpkin, cut the vegetable in half then into smaller wedges. Cut off the rind and cut the pumpkin into chunks about one inch in size. Place in a pot with enough water to just cover the pumpkin. Bring to a boil, reduce heat to medium and simmer until just tender. Drain, mash and use in your favorite recipe.

Spaghetti - This squash is yellow in color with a cylinder shape. It is named for how the flesh resembles pasta spaghetti when it is cooked. The flesh is scraped with a fork to remove it from the skin resulting in long, thin strands that can be topped with pasta sauce and eaten like pasta spaghetti. It can also be baked, steamed or roasted.

Yellow - This is shaped like a lengthened pear and is yellow in color. It is used the same as the crookneck squash.

Zucchini - A green colored vegetable from the squash family, it is not a baby squash, as some think, but a specific variety of it's own. It is one of the most versatile and popular variety of squash. The shape is similar to the English cucumber, but are often bigger and less uniform in shape and length. Zucchini has been popular in Italy for centuries, which is why there are so many Italian recipes available. The zucchini is healthy and nutritious. Good for our skin, it contains vitamin A, potassium and folic acid. The zucchini skin is rich in beta carotene. It is best when eaten raw, as in salads, but can also be cooked into savory dishes or muffins, quick breads or cookies, ideally with the skin left on. The best flavor is found in zucchini that are four to eight inches in length. The larger sized zucchini can be less flavorful. Zucchini can be stirfried, stuffed and baked, pan fried or sautéed. You can use it in jams and relishes as well. Low in calories, zucchini is liked by dieters.

Mediterranean Vegetables
Introduction

I have put tomatoes and mushrooms into this section because they are considered Mediterranean vegetables. There are many varieties of both tomatoes and mushrooms worldwide. Described here are the most common.

Tomatoes
Introduction

Often referred to as a vegetable, tomatoes are really a fruit. They are useful for skin problems and help as a cancer protector. Tomatoes are one of the world's most important crops, yielding tens of millions of tons worldwide each year. Available fresh, juiced and canned, the tomato is very versatile. The tomato originated in South America and is a member of the Solanaceae Family, which also includes the deadly nightshade. Tomatoes may aggravate the pain of rheumatoid arthritis, cause allergic reactions, recurring mouth ulcers or eczema. If you have a reaction, you should avoid tomatoes. All in the Solanaceae Family contain alkaloids, tomatoes contain tomatine. This is generally not toxic and is only in small amounts in ripe tomatoes. However, green tomatoes have nearly double the amount as ripe red tomatoes. Carotenoids like lycopene and beta carotene are present in tomatoes. They are also a good source for antioxidants, vitamin E and C, which makes tomatoes good protectors against some cancer and the cardiovascular system. Tomatoes are low in sodium and high in potassium. Canned tomatoes may contain added salt, so try to choose a low salt variety. All tomatoes have a smooth skin, juicy flesh and small edible seeds. Tomatoes that are grown commercially are always picked early and allowed to ripen in transit. Of all the varieties now available, most are red, but some are green or yellow in color. Vine grown tomatoes are preferred by many because they are rich in flavor. The most common varieties also include roma, beefsteak and cherry. They can range in size from small, oblong or round, to large and round, as in the beefsteak variety. Growers are now developing specific varieties including low acid that are available in cherry tomatoes and the slicing variety. Heirloom species are also becoming more common. Since there are no hard rules restricting the uses of any varieties, you can choose the varieties that you enjoy most and use them in any of your recipes. In general though, slicing, beefsteak and other deep ridged, solid tomatoes are used raw in salads, sandwiches and on burgers. Smaller, drier flesh types like roma and plum are best cooked, as in sauces, purées and casseroles. The most common tomato varieties are described here.

Beefsteak - Available year round, these tomatoes are easy to recognize. Large, round and firm, their peak season is late summer. This variety is best eaten raw, their firmness makes them ideal for slicing. Use in salads, salsa or other dips, they are especially good for topping burgers and sandwiches.

Cherry - Opposite to beefsteak, these small, round tomatoes are named for their size. Cherry sized, often red or yellow, these tomatoes grow in clusters. The yellow variety is often low acid. Peak season is mid to late summer. Cherry tomatoes are often put into salads or served with salad platters.

Cranberry or Currant - These tomatoes are very similar to cherry tomatoes except smaller. Like cherry tomatoes, these are also low acid in the yellow variety and are eaten the same as cherry, mainly in salads.

Pear - Named because of their shape, they are smaller than beefsteak tomatoes, but have the same firmness in the flesh. Pear tomatoes are red or yellow in color and their peak season is also mid to late summer. The pear tomato is used the same as the beefsteak variety, raw in salads, sandwiches or with salad platters.

Roma or Plum - These are oval in shape and about the size of a large egg. Both of these tomatoes are often used in cooking, mainly sauces, because they have more flesh with less seeds than other tomato varieties. Late summer is their peak season.

Slicing - Yellow in color and low in acid, these tomatoes are large, round and smooth skinned. They are available mid to late summer. Slicing tomatoes are often eaten raw, in salads or sandwiches.

Tomatillos - This variety differs from other tomatoes. They are small, round green berries that grow within a brown to light green, paper like husk. This husk is removed before using. The taste is similar to green tomatoes and are best cooked into sauces.

Mushrooms
Introduction

Mushrooms can be delicious or deadly. Know exactly what you are buying and who you are buying from, like a known grocery chain. The mushroom is the edible part of fungi, with many varieties. Some are edible, but a few are toxic and can cause severe cramps, headaches and in some cases, even death. Mushrooms are now cultivated in controlled environments. They range from the basic white to the more elite, such as oyster and shitake. Some varieties are still grown wild. With any variety, the mushroom should be fresh and if the stem is tough or damaged, it should be discarded. Today, many more varieties are available dried, which add an intense flavor to the food. Woodears, morels and shitake are the most common dried mushrooms. Vegans and vegetarians should include mushrooms in their diet because of the B12 vitamin. Mushrooms can also help with anxiety and depression. Mushrooms can be eaten raw, in salads, lightly sautéed or added to casseroles, stews or soups. To prepare mushrooms, you must realize that they have a lot of moisture content. This will cause them to "weep" when cooked as the moisture is drawn out. It is best to wipe or brush the mushrooms clean, not wash with water, then use in your recipe. For most recipes that call for fried or sautéed mushrooms, it is best to cook slowly over medium heat. Like spinach, most varieties of mushrooms will shrink down as they cook, so what may look like a lot, will lessen in volume when cooked. They are a good source of protein, phosphorus, some of the B vitamins and potassium, plus vitamin E. There are many varieties of mushrooms, shitake, button, oyster, reishi, maitake and portabello to name a few. The most common mushrooms are listed here. Testing for flavor and texture difference will give you your own favorites. Those with food sensitivities may find mushrooms hard on the digestive system, so be careful when testing, using only small tastes to begin.

Boletus - These have rounded, yellow to brown caps with round white stems. The flesh is pale, tender and doesn't change color when cooked. They have an earthy, nutty flavor. The caps may be peeled, as some can be sticky. Other names for boletus mushrooms are Boletes Caps or Porcini. Remember that these mushrooms are perishable and should be bought the day you want to use them. These mushrooms are also available dried.

Chanterelles - These are a trumpet shaped mushroom. The stem is a pale yellow and the cap is brown in color and delicately ruffled. They have a fruity, not dirt aroma. Chanterelles must be washed diligently as their shape can hold and hide the dirt. Dry well before cooking, which can be longer than other mushrooms. Other names include Cantarello, Gallinaccio and Finferlo.

Cremini - These mushrooms are a solid, deep brown variety of the basic white mushroom. They have a richer flavor than the white, but can be used in the same recipes as the white variety. Common names include the Roman or Brown mushroom.

B. A. Smit

Morels - A nutty, earthy flavored mushroom with a deeply pitted, cone shaped cap that, along with the stem, is hollow. The flesh has a light, airy texture. The morel mushroom is a tan to dark shade of brown. These mushrooms often hold dirt or bugs, so must be washed carefully, generally using a vegetable brush. Morels are also known as Spugnole or Morille.

Oysters - These mushrooms are named for their fan shape that resembles an oyster shell. The caps are a smooth off white to gray in color, with the short stem and underside, or gill, being white in color. Oyster mushrooms are found growing on tree trunks and can range in size from a thumbnail to three inches across. These mushrooms require a longer time to cook and are also known as Oak mushrooms.

Portabello - This mushroom is actually a fully grown cremini mushroom. The caps are very large, usually between four and six inches across and when cooked, have a solid texture with an earthy flavor. The stems are often tough or "woody". This is why they are used to flavor soups, sauces or stocks. The caps are often used in place of meat patties for burgers or made into a vegetarian version of meatloaf.

Shitake - These mushrooms have a cap that resembles an umbrella, in a dark brown color. The stem and gills (underside) are a cream color. The flavor is similar to portabello mushrooms, earthy and slightly meaty. The stems are very tough and are rarely used.

Truffles - These grow underground and specially trained pigs or dogs sniff them out. They are knobby and rounded with a rough skin. Truffles have a distinct earthy flavor. Black truffles are always cooked. France claims to have the best quality of black truffles. White truffles from Italy are the finest and are often served raw, mainly shaved over pasta dishes or rice. Truffles are truly a special mushroom and therefore, very expensive. You can find truffles as an essence or oil, fresh or canned.

Onions, Garlic and Leeks
Onions
Introduction

The onion family is a part of the Lily Family. They belong to the same family as leeks, shallots, chives, scallions and garlic. There are many varieties, shapes and sizes, but they all share the same sharp aroma and flavor. Onions contain a specific enzyme, allinase, which is activated when you slice the bulb. The allinase reacts with sulphur compounds to create the chemicals that make you cry as you cut the onion, but also gives it's distinct flavor. Onions and garlic are considered to be kitchen staples. For those who cannot tolerate these flavor staples, using celery, zucchini and herbs can enhance flavors, though not in the same distinct taste as onion and garlic. Onions are low in calories and contain trace minerals, vitamin C and some B vitamins. Onions are also a strong diuretic, eliminating urea, which make onions helpful in the treatment of gout, rheumatism and arthritis. Research is showing how effective onions can be to your health. It has shown that, among other traits, onion has powerful antibacteria properties which help fight infections. The onion has been shown to reduce cholesterol, reduce the chance of blood clots and is beneficial for respiratory ailments and asthma. Originating in the northern hemisphere, onions are now grown worldwide. There are two types of onion, dried and fresh. The dried should be stored in a dry, cool area in jars or bags that are airtight. Fresh onions should be stored in the fridge. Chives are considered a herb, but are a member of the onion family. Onions are used in every type of cooking, from soups to sauces, main dishes and battered then deep fried and eaten as a snack. Some of the most common are listed here.

Boiling - These are small, round onions that are less than two inches in size. The skin is white in color. To prepare, remove the skin and chop or slice then add to your recipe. These onions can be used in soups, stews or casseroles.

Cippolini - A flattened round onion with a yellow skin. As with boiling and other onion varieties, remove the skin before using. These are best grilled or baked.

Pearl - Popular for pickling, these onions are small, round, or more often, oval in shape. Pearl onions vary in color from white to red or yellow. Used in stews and other main dishes, vegetable dishes, but the most common use is for pickles. They can be boiled or baked into casseroles as well.

Ramps - A type of leek, they can grow wild and are smaller than leeks. The root end is small and white in color. The tops are green and flat shaped. The ramps are often sautéed or stewed.

Red - These are a flattened round shape with paper like skin. The flesh is a varied red and white color. These onions are popular sliced or diced raw in salads, sliced and grilled then added to burgers or added to main dishes.

B. A. Smit

Scallions - Also known as green onions, they resemble the shape of the leek, but are much smaller. They are often chopped and added to Asian dishes. The plant has a white slightly bulb shaped end that turns green at the top, which resemble blades of grass. The root end is cut off, but the remaining bulb and green tops can be used. Common uses include chopping and adding to salads, over stews or rice dishes and in some Mexican dishes. These onions are very versatile and colorful when added to many foods.

Shallots - These are a small onion, often milder and sweeter than other onions. Some varieties are clusters of cloves (like garlic cloves) while other varieties grow as a single shallot. They have a paper like, tan colored skin with a purple tinged white flesh. Shallots are often minced and added to salads, dressings and main dishes. As with other onions, the skin is removed before using.

Spanish - These onions are not as sharp in flavor as yellow onions. They are large, round in shape with a yellow to brown toned skin. The flesh is yellow to white in color and can be used in a variety of recipes. Spanish onions can add a subtle flavor to the food without over powering the flavor with a strong onion bite. This makes them good in soups, stews or on burgers or sandwiches. Remove the skin before using.

Sweet - These onions are ideal for burgers, hot dogs and salads. There are several types of sweet onions including Maui, Walla Walla and Vidalia. Sweet onions are generally a slightly flattened round shape with white to beige colored skin. The flesh is very sweet and grilling or sautéeing will enhance the sweet flavor. Remove the skin before using.

White - Basically, white onions are the same size, shape and flavor as yellow onions. The difference is that the skin and flesh are white. They are used the same as yellow onions, removing the skin before using.

Yellow - Slightly smaller than the Spanish onion, this variety has the same paper like yellow to brown toned skin. The flesh is very strong tasting but is used in many main dishes. Again, remove the skin before using.

Garlic

The two main types of garlic are standard and elephant. It is available year round. They grow in a bulb shape covered in a paper like skin that is streaked red or white in color. Inside is a cluster of cloves, each also covered in a skin. Remove the skin and crush, slice or mince the clove to use in a recipe. The whole bulb can be roasted before using in your recipe. To roast, place the bulb, drizzled in oil, onto a pan and roast in a 350° oven for thirty to forty minutes. When cool, squeeze the cloves out of the bulb and use in your favorite recipes. The cloves can be added to salads or dressings, or used to flavor a multitude of main dishes, dips or soups. Garlic is beneficial for lowering your cholesterol levels, improving circulation, lowering blood pressure, fungal infections, coughs and is a good cancer protector. Civilizations of ancient Egypt through to Greece, Rome, England to the Middle Ages, garlic was used as a medicinal plant. Allicin, the sulphur compound found in most of the Allium Family, is released when the bulb is cut, encouraging the elimination of cholesterol from the body and reducing the amount of unhealthy fats produced by the liver. Asthma, bronchitis, sore throats, constipation, diarrhea and athlete's foot can be improved by eating garlic. Like onions, if you find that you can't tolerate the garlic, using celery, herbs or zucchini will help to enhance flavor, but not the same sharp flavor of garlic.

Leeks

Leeks are similar in shape as the green onion (scallion). They are larger, about one inch wide and often about ten to twelve inches in length. Leeks have a white root end with dark green, flat leaves. Gaining popularity, leeks are a delicious addition to salads, soups and main dishes. They help with voice and chest ailments, is a cancer protector, is beneficial for reducing cholesterol levels and high blood pressure, gout and arthritis. Leeks have been used for over four thousand years. A member of the Allium Family, with onions, chives, garlic and shallots, leeks have the anticarcinogenic chemicals which are vital in the detoxification process. The plant family name is Lily for all these vegetables, but the chemical make-up puts them into the Allium Family. Leeks are also antibacterial, which is beneficial as a cancer protector, destroying the bacteria that can change harmless nitrates into cancer causing nitrates. Most people only eat the white part, but the dark green leaves of the top are a good source of beta carotene, which the body converts to vitamin A. Leeks contain small amounts of minerals and vitamins, fiber, folic acid and potassium. Like onions, leeks are a diuretic with the ability to eliminate uric acid, making leeks a healthy choice for those who suffer from arthritis and gout. To use leeks, cut off the green tops and root end. Wash carefully as dirt can hide within the many layers. Slice, dice or leave whole. They can be fried, sautéed, baked, grilled or served raw in salads. They add flavor to many types of dishes.

B. A. Smit

Peppers and Chilies
Peppers

There are two types of peppers. Sweet, also known as bell peppers because of their shape and chilies, which are smaller. The sweet or bell pepper can come in several colors, though the flavor is basically the same. Red, green, yellow and orange are common, with white and purple colors available, but not often found. Sweet peppers all begin green and change color as they ripen based on the variety. Red and yellow peppers tend to be slightly sweeter than green peppers, but you can use any color in any recipe without radically altering the flavor. Using a variety of colors will enhance the food's appearance. Sweet peppers are somewhat square, tapering smaller at the bottom, hence the name, bell. The center is hollow except for a core of seed clusters. The core, seeds and the white ribs are removed before using. Peppers are popular in Mexican and Italian cooking. When purchasing, find peppers that are firm, free of blemishes and have a glossy shine. They will keep in the fridge for up to one week, but try to use as soon as possible before they begin to soften.

Chilies
Introduction

Chilies are hot, spicy and some varieties contain oils that can irritate the skin if not prepared properly. They are available fresh, canned or dried and many varieties with as many levels of heat are easy to find in local markets. Often, the dried chilies are given a different name than the fresh chilie. The hotter chilies need to be handled with care because of their oils. Habaneros and Banana chilies for example, can irritate the skin, so when preparing them, wear gloves, clean the cutting surface and knife immediately afterward and don't rub your eyes until you have removed the gloves and washed your hands. Once cooked, the oils aren't as irritating. Chilies are small, but very hot. A small amount can produce a lot of flavor, so use less than called for in the recipe unless you are familiar with the flavor and degree of heat in the chilies. Heat is the term used for the degree of how hot the flavor of the chilie is.

Anaheims - These are tapered, tube shaped chilies with a glossy, dark green color. The red variety of this chilie is called the Colorado chilie. Anaheims are available fresh or dried.

Banana - These are similar in shape to the Anaheim, but are yellow or a yellow to green color. Sometimes these chilies are called Hungarian Wax Peppers. Used in stews, sauces and soups, Banana chilies are thought to be the hottest variety of chilie. Banana chilies are popular for pickling.

Chipotles - These are Jalapenos that have been dried and smoked. Chipotles can be found dried or canned, often in a sauce called adobo.

Habaneros - A common chilie that is only the size of a cherry tomato. The skin is wrinkled and the flavor very hot. These are used in many dishes.

Jalapenos - Pronounced "hala-pea-nose", these can vary from medium to very hot. They are common worldwide. These chilies are small, tapered and dark green to red in color. Popular in many dishes from Mexican to Canadian, they are available fresh, dried, pickled or canned. The canned variety can be whole or sliced.

Poblanos - These are deep green to black in color. Slightly flattened and tapered in shape, they are a mildly hot chilie. The most popular dish, Chilies Rellenos, is made from poblano chilies. They can be stuffed, battered then deep fried and served as a snack. Some poblanos that are left to get very ripe, then dried, are called Anchos.

Scotch Bonnet - These chilies are close in size and shape as Habaneros. The color can range from yellow to red to green. The heat is similar to the Habaneros. This variety of chilie is used in condiments and sauces and is the main chilie used in Jamaican jerk seasonings.

Serranos - These are very small, but very hot. They are dark green in color and can be interchanged with Jalapenos.

Pod and Seed Vegetables

Examples of these vegetables include beans, peas, corn, bean sprouts and legumes. These types of vegetables are most tender and sweetest when still young and freshly harvested. Once these vegetables begin to age, their natural sugars convert to starch, changing the flavor from sweet to almost a mealy taste. This can occur in as little as thirty six hours from harvest, especially in corn and peas. Pod and seed vegetables are therefore best if bought from the markets of farmers. Supermarkets may have older vegetables considering the time to travel from farm to store. Some fresh beans and peas are eaten whole. Snow, snap and sugar snap peas, as well as wax and green beans are examples. When freshly picked, the pod is still sweet and tender. Other pods are not edible, lima beans, black-eyed peas and scarlet runners are the most common. The beans or peas are removed and eaten and the pod discarded. Many of the pod vegetables are found in the legume section of this book.

Roots and Tubers
Introduction

The roots or tubers store the nutrients for the plant above ground. This means that they are very rich in starches, vitamins, minerals and sugars. The most common root vegetables include beets, carrots, parsnips, potatoes, radishes, rutabagas and turnip. These last two are often mistaken as the same, but they are two different vegetables. A less known root is salsify, which can be either white or black. Tubers are slightly different from roots. They are bulbous, enlarged roots which are able to generate a new plant. In this section is the Jerusalem artichoke, which despite it's name, is not originated in Jerusalem, or really an artichoke. Tubers and roots are best stored in a dry area. They should not be peeled or washed until ready to use. If purchased fresh with greens attached, these should be discarded as soon as possible before storing. They could cause the vegetable to rot or take nutrients from the vegetable. Most roots and tubers will keep for several weeks when stored properly.

B. A. Smit

Artichokes - The global artichoke has a bitter chemical, cynarine, which is a boost for digestion and a strong stimulant of the liver and gall bladder. Artichokes also lower the cholesterol, have a good diuretic effect and are useful for rheumatism, arthritis and gout. They are best raw, if very small, but larger globe artichokes should be boiled, and hot or cold, are ideal when drizzled with olive oil and lemon. Traditionally, when serving highly rich meals, artichokes are served as a first course since they stimulate the production of bile, which makes the digestion of fats easier. Herbalists use artichokes to treat high blood pressure. The globe artichoke originated around the Mediterranean. It is a good source of potassium, but has no other real nutrients. Starch is not found in artichokes, a chemical called inulin is it's replacement. This, like fiber, does not get broken down during digestion and is fermented by bacteria in the colon. It may cause gas. The artichoke is known as a detoxifier and cleanser.

Beets - The three most common varieties are baby, red and golden. Baby, as the name implies, are small, round, young beets. Often these beets are slightly sweet in flavor. Red beets are usually used for pickling or borscht. Golden beets are small, round, golden yellow to orange tinged in color. For many years, the beet was revered for it's medicinal properties. The list of what beets are helpful for is long, including being beneficial for leukemia, chronic fatigue syndrome, anemia and women of child bearing age. The beet tops, (leaves) which are cooked like spinach, are good for osteoporosis. Beets contain iron, vitamin C, folate and potassium. The leaves are equally nutritious with beta carotene and other carotenoids as well, making both the root and the leaves especially good for women planning pregnancy. Do not be alarmed if your urine or stool look like they have blood in them, it's the beet color that has gone through your system. All beets can be glazed, boiled, roasted or used in salads after they are cooked. The most common uses for beets are to pickle them, grate cooked beets over salad or make into a soup called borscht. Beets are harvested in the late summer into the fall. To prepare beets, wash well, cut off the green top, boil in a pot of water until just soft. Drain, holding the beet with a fork, use a sharp knife to peel off the skin. Cut off the root end, slice and serve, or use in your favorite recipe. Try to leave the beet whole to cook, this will help to keep the color in the beet.

Carrots - These are available year round and are the most liked vegetable by many. There are numerous varieties, ranging in shape from short, long and thin to thick. All are shaped like a finger, with a green leafy top. This top should be cut off before storing, it could cause the vegetable to rot or take nutrients from the carrot. Carrots that are picked while still young are called baby carrots, which are sweet in flavor, but crisp in texture. Most of the packaged "baby" or "mini" carrots are actually carrots that are misshapened and are mechanically pared down to resemble small carrots. If the carrots are left in the ground too long the center of the carrot will become "woody" or tough and fibrous. Carrots can be eaten raw or cooked. Whenever possible, peel and wash carrots before cooking. Organophosphate pesticides are extremely toxic, and can be used on carrots while they grow. The old tale of eating carrots to improve eyesight is somewhat true. Carrots are vital for cancer prevention, excellent for eyesight, circulation and the heart. They are helpful for skin and liver function. It is best to eat older cooked carrots, new baby carrots are tasty but lack most of the important carotenoids. The mature carrot contains enough beta carotene for your body to convert to a daily requirement of vitamin A. Carrots help the mucous membranes to protect the lungs and performance of the entire respiratory system. Night vision is improved with vitamin A. Beta carotene is absorbed better by the body from cooked carrots and has numerous important functions, especially as a cancer protector. Research shows carrots as an antiaging food, they help to protect against ultraviolet radiation, which protects the skin from wrinkles and damage. The antioxidant vitamins E and C are helpful for those with arterial disease, it can improve the flow of blood in the coronary arteries of the heart. Carrots are great additions to salads, soups or as a side dish with main meals. You can also use carrots in baking, like carrot cake or muffins.

Florence Fennel - There are numerous varieties of fennel which have been cultivated for over two thousand years. The bulb has a delicate flavor, similar to anise, that blends well with fish. Medicinally, the seeds have been used for centuries. The oils, anisic acid, anethole, fenchone and limonine give the unequal flavor and medicinal properties. Fennel bulbs are low in calories, but have few vitamins or minerals. To use, trim off the root end and cut off the stem. Slice lengthwise, wash and it is ready to be used. Slice or chop and add raw in salads, grill, broil, braise or boil and add to main dishes or as a side dish.

Jerusalem Artichoke - Also known as Sun Chokes, the name Jerusalem artichoke can be confusing. It is not related to the artichoke in any way. It's name is derived from the Italian word for sunflower, girasole, and the flavor resembles that of an artichoke. It is a native of North America and grows from six to twelve feet high. The tubers grow underground and are oblong or elongated, in one piece or in branches, and weigh about four ounces. The skin is very thin, it's color beige to yellow and sometimes with brown, red or purple tinges. The flesh is white with a sweet flavor. These tubers look like a small nubby potato. The taste is nutty sweet and the texture crisp. When you purchase Jerusalem artichokes they should be firm and have an unmarked, glossy tan to matte brown skin, with no green tint or signs of mold. Instead of starch, a chemical called inulin is in the artichoke. Since it does not get broken down through digestion, it is fermented by bacteria in the colon, and therefore, may cause gas. Jerusalem artichokes can be eaten raw or cooked, but they are best when used in stews and soups.

Jicama - Pronounced "hik-a-ma", this is a white fleshed tuber that can vary in size from barely one pound to more than five pounds. It is also known as Mexican yam bean. This turnip shaped tuber grows underground from a plant in the legume family. It can be eaten both cooked and raw. Originating in Mexico, it has traveled to the Philippines and was adapted by Chinese cooks. The flesh is light in color and the skin is thin and brown in color. The flesh is crisp and juicy, but with a nondescript flavor, often said to be a cross between an apple and a potato. The outer skin must be peeled before eating. When purchasing, the jicama should be blemish free since it's freshness can deteriate quickly. Sliced or julienned raw in salads or boiled, stirfried or baked like a potato, the jicama is gaining popularity across North America.

B. A. Smit

Parsnip - This vegetable deserves better recognition. These are similar in shape and size as carrots, but the color is a pale yellow. The flavor is very unique. Parsnips have a delicate, different flavor and are tastiest after the first frost of winter. They are helpful for constipation and fatigue. Parsnips are also an ample source of folic acid, potassium, fiber, trace minerals and vitamins E and B. This vegetable is a great addition to stews, mashed with potatoes, or cut the same as, then boiled with carrots.

Radishes - Originating in Southern Asia, radishes are now cultivated throughout North America, Britain, Europe, Japan and China. They are small, often the size of cherry tomatoes. The flesh is white with a pink blush from the red skin. The texture is crisp and tastes hot, akin to pepper. Some radish varieties are elongated, and specialty radishes can be round like the common variety, but with other colors, striped, purple or orange. Radish are a part of the Cruciferae Family, and like others in it's family, contains glucosilinates and other sulphurous compounds which are important for those at risk for cancer. For the small size, radish have many nutrients, including potassium, sulphur, calcium, vitamin C, selenium and folic acid. The radish helps chest, liver and gall bladder ailments, helps to prevent cancer and aids digestion. The juice of the radish stimulates the discharge of bile from the gall bladder. Too much of this hot, peppery vegetable can irritate the liver, gall bladder and kidneys. The radish is best eaten raw. The most common use for the radish is raw in salads, either sliced or left whole. As a rule, they are not cooked before eating. Another variety, Daikon, are in size and shape like a carrot, but with a white flesh. This variety can be cooked and is a much milder flavor than the common radish.

Salsify - This is also known as the oyster plant. White salsify has an appearance that is like the parsnip. Black salsify is long, shaped like a stick, with a matte black skin. Both types of salsify can be served as a side dish. The flavor is earthy, similar to foods like asparagus, artichoke hearts and even oysters.

Taro - A plant grown in the tropics, taro is cultivated for it's large underground tubers. They are rich in starch and are easy to digest. When young, the leaves are known as elephant ears and are eaten as greens. The tubers can be baked, boiled, fried or used in soup. They are not tasty when raw. Poi, a staple food of the tropics, is made from taro root.

Turnips and Rutabagas - These are often thought of as the same vegetable, but are two different, but similar, vegetables. Turnip are round, a little larger than a beet, with a purple tone at the stem end. The flesh is white to tan in color. The flavor is close to the rutabaga, which is larger, often coated in wax, with a yellow flesh. Both of these vegetables are great with winter comfort foods, such as stews, soups and casseroles. To prepare these vegetables, slice off the root end, cut the vegetable into one inch slices, cut the outer skin off then cut the piece into small chunks and use as desired.

Turnips - These are another member of the Cruciferae Family and are sometimes confused with rutabagas. As with all vegetables within this family, the turnip is very healthy. Beneficial for arthritis, chest infections and gout, the turnip is also a good cancer protector. Turnip can be eaten raw in salads, boiled or added to stews and soups. Combining the turnip with carrots creates a tasty dinner vegetable. Turnips are a favorable source of vitamin C, fiber, potassium, phosphorus, calcium and some B vitamins. It is thought that the turnip was the genetic origin of the Chinese cabbage. It traveled to Siberia, then into Europe, so turnip have been cultivated for over four thousand years. The green leafy top of the plant is a delicate, tasty spring vegetable. For centuries, they have been used as treatment for arthritis and gout, since they help to eliminate uric acid from the body.

Rutabagas - A large and healthful member of the Cruciferae Family, rutabagas are good for skin problems and a cancer protector. They are best boiled or in stews, soups or casseroles. Rutabaga and potato, cooked then mashed together, create a flavorful change from plain mashed potatoes. The other good combination is carrots and rutabaga. The rutabaga has a light, delicate flavor with the most anticancer properties than other plants in it's family. There are notable amounts of vitamins C and A, trace amounts of minerals and fiber, plus a little sodium. Rutabaga, like other Cruciferae, contain goitrogens and those with thyroid problems or long term thyroxine treatment, should eat them in moderation. Even though you would need to consume large amounts daily to be at risk, the goitrogenic factor interferes with the ability of the thyroid gland to absorb iodine.

Potatoes
Introducton

Potatoes are versatile, nutritious and can be cooked in many ways. There are many varieties of potato. Though called potatoes, sweet potatoes and yams are similar, but not related to the potato. Sweet potatoes are members of the Genus Dioscorea, yams of the Genus Impomoea and potatoes belong to the nightshade family, Solanum. All varieties aid digestive problems, help constipation, chronic fatigue syndrome and anemia. They are best eaten baked in their skin, boiled in a small amount of water or steamed. The potato originated in South America, then traveled worldwide, with popularity found in both England and Ireland. Potatoes contain B complex vitamins, minerals, fiber and vitamin C. Baked potatoes are nutritionally best with many important nutrients, including potassium, found in the skin. Potatoes are not fattening alone, but what you top them with and how you cook them adds to the calories. Potatoes that have sprouted, turned green or are damaged may contain a toxic chemical, solanine. The amount of solanine will increase as the potato is exposed to light. Small amounts of this chemical may make you feel unwell, large amounts may be fatal. Potatoes are a part of the nightshade family Solanaceae. Within this family are eggplants, tomatoes, bell peppers and chilies. This family of food can irritate rheumatoid arthritis, causing pain and inflammation. If you are affected by this ailment, you may want to limit the amount of food that you eat from this family. No matter which variety you choose, all potatoes should be kept in a cool, dry, dark area to retain their quality. To give you some choices for potatoes, I have included some of the more common in this section.

Bliss - These potatoes are the same as red potatoes, but much smaller, less than one and a half inches in size. They are excellent steamed or oven roasted.

Chef's - This potato is round, firm, with a white skin that has a hint of brown. These potatoes are available year round, in a variety of sizes from small to fist sized. The younger the potato, the more moist the flesh, making this potato a bad choice to use for baked potatoes. Chef's potatoes are popular in salads, soups, pan fried, puréed or used as a side dish.

Heirloom - This variety is becoming more popular. There are many varieties included in this category. Caribe potatoes are a deep purple skinned type with a blue tinged flesh. Banana or fingerling potatoes are elongated in shape with a light brown skin and creamy colored flesh. Other varieties include Ruby Cresent, Russian Banana and Peruvian Blue. Most of the heirloom varieties have different starch contents, so it is best to experiment with cooking techniques.

Idaho or Russet - Known by both names, these potatoes are more oblong than round. The skin is brown. This variety is probably the most common of all potatoes and is often peeled, boiled then mashed. They can also be fried and are excellent baked.

Irish - This variety is often oddly shaped and is best boiled.

Red - Often small, round and firm, they have a smooth pink to dark red skin. The flesh is white. Available year round, the younger potatoes are the moistest. Red potatoes are excellent boiled then added to salads, pan fried or oven roasted. They are usually smaller than russet or baking potatoes.

Salt - Only about one inch in size, these are popular for steaming or boiling whole.

Sweet - These have an orange tinged tan skin. The flesh is a deep yellow color, moist, with a sweeter flavor than regular potatoes. Sweet potatoes are more tapered than round. Generally, sweet potatoes are roasted, but can also be peeled then boiled, pan fried or added to soups, stews or casseroles. They can also be peeled, cut into strips and fried. Known as sweet potato fries, they are becoming very popular.

Yams - These are often confused with sweet potatoes, but they are a different vegetable. Yams are a more tan to brown in color. The flesh is more orange than the yellow flesh of the sweet potato. Yams can be used the same as the sweet potato, but the flavor of the yam is more mild than the sweet potato.

Yellow or New - These potatoes are very similar to the red variety, but with a very pale yellow to tan colored skin. They can be cooked the same as the red potato.

Yukon Gold - Also known as Yellow Fin potatoes, the skin can vary in color from brown to tan to red. The flesh is a pale golden color. These potatoes are a good variety for baking, boiling then adding to salads, or mashing and serving as a side dish. They can also be pan fried.

B. A. Smit

Soft Vegetables

Avocado - First cultivated in Peru almost nine thousand years ago, this vegetable is oval in shape with bumpy, almost black leather like skin. The flesh is green near the skin and fades to yellow near the center where there is a large stone. The avocado has a very smooth, light flavor. Like apples, when sliced, the cut surface should be rubbed with lemon or lime to prevent browning. Haas avocados are more pear shaped with a dark rough skin. The avocados grown in Florida, U.S.A. seem to have a smoother skin and a brighter green color. When ripe, the avocado will be just slightly soft. If you purchase one that is not ripe, leave at room temperature to ripen. Always serve avocado at room temperature which allows the flavor to be enhanced. Best known as the main ingredient in guacamole, avocado is also popular in salads and Mexican style dishes. Avocados are good for the circulation and heart. Also, they are exceptional for the skin, relief of P.M.S. and are a cancer protector. They are tastiest when eaten ripe and raw. The natives of Guatemala use the entire plant, fruit, rind, seeds, leaves and bark for medicinal practices. Avocados are a good source of potassium, vitamin E and the B vitamins, including B6, which helps stabilize mood swings in women who suffer from P.M.S. They are high in nutrients, including monounsaturated fats and aleic acid, which makes avocado a strong antioxidant food. This is vital to fight cancer, strokes and heart disease. There are chemicals within the skin and flesh of the avocado that encourage the production of collagen, which is useful to decrease wrinkles, giving a fresh, youthful appearance to the skin. This makes avocado popular as a skin treatment. The fats in avocados are easy to digest and contain antibacterial and antifungal chemicals which makes it an ideal food for sick children, convalescents and invalids.

Corn - Named maize by the Native Indians, corn is cultivated for several food type purposes. Corn on the cob is a variety cultivated specifically for eating, not converting into flour or cornmeal as other varieties are. This type of corn is slightly sweet and delicious boiled on the cob. Corn is good for vegetarians, providing fiber and energy. Corn is a good source of fiber, protein, vitamins E and A, folic acid and some of the B vitamins. Corn is available fresh, frozen or canned. The canned corn may contain up to five times as much natural sugar as fresh corn, and a large amount of salt. Corn also is made into starch, meal, flour and oil. It is also made into pasta, a good choice for gluten free diets. For more information on corn, look in other sections of this book including Grains and Flours.

Water

Introduction

Water has provided internal and external therapy for many centuries. We bathe in it, play in it, exercise in it and relax in it. We can quench our thirst, cook with it, brew tea, coffee and other beverages with it, and douse flames with it. It is a vital part of our life. Over the entire planet there is only about one percent of the water fit for human consumption. The rest of the water is made up of ice fields, glaciers and salt water. So it is equally vital that we are careful with how we use water.

Water can be found in vegetables and fruit. Lettuce, watermelon and bananas are the most common. These foods can contain between seventy five and ninety five percent water. Chicken and bread can also contain water, chicken can have over fifty percent and bread over twenty five percent.

Water is vital for our body to remain healthy. It replenishes and nourishes our entire system. Water is used to help waste move through our bowels. It keeps our body heat regulated. When exercising, you must drink fluids to replenish those lost through sweat. It is ideal to drink at least eight glasses per day. It does not have to be water, though it is the best fluid. Pure fruit juices and low fat milk can be considered in your eight glasses, but caffine and alcohol act as diuretics, making the kidneys create more urine than a normal average.

B. A. Smit

Bottled Water Check List

- Signs of tampering. Some Third World countries refill empty bottles with whatever water is nearest. Also, tampered bottles may have something added to it.
- The expiry date. Some waters will go flat, loose their nutrients with time, or bacteria may develop.
- The mineral content. A high sodium amount is not recommended for people with high blood pressure, heart disease, liver or kidney problems.
- Low sodium and low mineral. These waters are best for young children and babies.

Tips

- If you drink a lot of bottled water, try buying one large container instead of numerous smaller bottles. It will be more economical.
- Have bottled water handy, in lunches, for car outings, this can encourage the whole family to use.
- Don't buy a few months worth at one time. The trace amounts of bacteria that could be in the water can begin to multiply if the water is not used by the "best before" date.
- After opening a bottle of water, store in the fridge and use within five to seven days.
- Especially when there is more than yourself in the household, never drink from the bottle. Your mouth could contain germs that will contaminate the water.
- Practise boiling all water, including tap water, to be consumed by babies and toddlers.
- If you are buying bottled water only because you don't like the taste of your tap water, perhaps a chlorine taste, buy a filter system for your tap water. The cost will be minimal compared to buying bottled water.
- Chlorine can evaporate. Let your tap water sit in a jug in the fridge over night to improve the flavor.
- Mineral water has become very popular, but when ordering one in a restaurant, ensure that it is opened in front of you. This will prove to you of the original content, not a refill of water from the tap or other sources.

Mineral Water

This water must come from a single, underground source. It must not contain bacteria or chemicals. The water must always have the same mineral content. Mineral water can be exposed to ultraviolet light and filtering, but other forms of disinfecting or sterilizing are not allowed. When water comes out of the ground it may be gassy. The addition of carbon dioxide may increase the fizz or mechanical methods may decrease the fizz. Mineral water must be bottled near it's source. Labels must include the mineral content. There are strict conditions governing the terms used. Those terms include low mineral content, rich in mineral salts and suitable for low sodium diets. Bottled mineral water or sparkling mineral water is water that has minerals added. The most common minerals are potassium, sulphate, magnesium and calcium. Read labels carefully. Too much mineral content can be unsuitable for young children. Some waters with high sodium levels are not healthy for those who suffer from high blood pressure.

Spring and Table Water

Bottling companies can use water from a spring or a tap. The water must be the same standard as tap water. The companies don't have to name the source of water. They can mix different waters, filter then disinfect it, and bottle it. They do not have to put much information on the label.

Distilled Water

This type of water is processed to eliminate impurities from the water.

Filtered Water

This water can be an economical source if used properly. Activated charcoal is within the filter and chemicals stick to it as the tap water passes through it. The Brita brand filter system is a common type of home filtration system. If the filter is changed at regular intervals you will benefit, but if you neglect to change the filter, harmful bacteria may begin to grow and will contaminate your water. This can put your health at risk.

B. A. Smit

Chlorination

This is used in most water supplies to help eliminate bacteria organisms. Chloroform is a cancer causing substance that can be created by organic matter in the water, but this is very rare as treatment of water supplies have greatly improved. The process of chlorination kills the bacteria within the water supply, therefore, dramatically decreasing the chance of chloroform being created.

Hard and Soft Waters

Areas with large amounts of limestone or chalk have hard water, defined by calcium salts that can make the water somewhat alkaline.

Areas with granite have soft water that is quite acidic. Copper, cadmium and lead can seep into the water supply, causing a corrosive effect on the metal of pipes used to carry the water. This is why lead pipes are no longer used in the homes built since the mid 1970's.

Tap Water

Tap water comes from either surface or underground sources. Surface includes rivers, lakes and reservoirs, which is the most common source for major cities. Underground is the most common in rural areas. The water comes from underground caves that have collected water or from underground springs. These sources should be tested regularly for contaminates, about once a year. A chlorine unit is advised as well. Most of today's water is filtered and purified, leaving less risk of contamination. Tap water has always been taken for granted and thought to be safe. Today, there is valid concern of pollutants seeping into the water supply. This is why so many people have turned to bottled water. Knowing more about where your tap water originates is advised, but you should not stop your daily intake of water.

Two Week Meal Plan

Introduction

Two Week Meal Plan

Introduction

People eat food for two main reasons. One is the fact that they are hungry, the second is for the taste and flavor. When your diet is restricted, eating food because you are hungry is usually the only reason. This book will put the taste and flavor back into your diet.

As I have stated earlier, there are several reasons that I wrote this book. When you have a restricted diet, due to allergy or illness, you must keep your body as healthy as possible. This book gives you the basic knowledge so you, and your doctor, can make informed decisions on your diet. Take the knowledge from this book to help you create a new diet that is healthy for you.

Along with the meal plan, I am including a group of recipes to try during the two weeks. I am sure if you begin with the meal plan and recipes, you will start to feel better and you will be on your way to **A New Kind of Normal.** Again, go over this plan with your doctor, and remember, these recipes are given as a guide to help you discover foods that you can eat and enjoy. Take the knowledge from this meal plan to help you create a new diet that is healthy for you. You can use the meal plan as a guide, choose foods within the same food group that you like and can tolerate. If you would like beef instead of bison or yogurt instead of milk, it is your choice.

The recipes that I have created are easy to adapt to your diet. When the recipe calls for milk, use your substitute, or if you can use garlic or onion, add those to your recipe. These recipes are a guide, a format that can still taste good when substitutes are used.

The menu I have created is for fourteen days, two weeks. It should give you a chance to test out how to eat your foods based on the daily food guide. I am sure that, after two weeks, you will be able to continue eating a balanced, but not boring diet, and you will actually begin to enjoy **A New Kind of Normal** lifestyle.

A note on beginning this meal plan. Some people who begin this plan may feel worse for the first few days to a week, this is normal, it is your body trying to eliminate the toxins and other build ups from not eating the foods that are compatable to your system. Please give this plan a chance to balance out your body's needs. I'm sure that in the long run, you will feel better.

B. A. Smit

Two Week Meal Plan

Day 1

Breakfast:

1 cup hot cereal with milk
1 slice toast with margarine and 1 tbsp nut butter

Snack:

1 fresh fruit - pear, banana or apple

Lunch:

1 cup salad with dressing
1 hard boiled egg
2 corn thins with margarine
1 glass milk

Snack:

1 muffin with margarine
1 glass V-8 type juice

Dinner:

1 cup rice
2 1/2 oz salmon, sole or cod, baked with herbs and lemon
1/2 cup each, carrots and spinach

Snack:

2 corn thins with margarine and 1/2 cup dried fruit
OR
2 pieces of cranberry square and 1/2 cup dried fruit

Day 2

Breakfast:

1 cup fruit salad
2 corn thins or rice cakes with margarine and 2 tbsp nut butter

Snack:

1 muffin with margarine
    OR
1 piece of cake or pie

Lunch:

1 cucumber and tomato sandwich with margarine and mayonnaise
1 fresh fruit - pear, banana or cantaloupe
1 glass milk or 1 cup custard

Snack:

1/2 cup fruitsauce with 2 cookies or 2 slices of fruit bread

Dinner:

1 boiled potato with margarine
1 chicken thigh or pork chop baked
1/2 cup each, peas and carrots
1 glass milk

Snack:

2 pieces of toffee nut square
     OR
2 corn thins with margarine

B. A. Smit

Day 3

Breakfast:

2 boiled eggs
1 slice toast with margarine
1 glass of fruit juice

Snack:

1 fresh fruit with 2 corn thins with margarine

Lunch:

Rice salad with fruit and vegetables
1 glass milk

Snack:

1 muffin with margarine

Dinner:

1 cup pasta with 1/2 cup tomato sauce that 1/2 cup peas and 4 oz ground, pan fried
beef, bison or lamb has been added
1 cup custard with fruit

Snack:

1/2 cup fruitsauce

Day 4

    Breakfast:

3/4 cup cold cereal with milk and dried fruit
1 slice toast with margarine

    Snack:

2 cookies
  OR
1 piece of cake
1 glass fruit juice

    Lunch:

1/2 cup tuna salad on lettuce
2 corn thins or rice cakes with margarine
1 fresh fruit - pear, apple or banana

    Snack:

2 slices fruitbread

    Dinner:

1 boiled potato with margarine
2 slices (4 oz) turkey meatloaf
1/2 cup each, grean beans and corn

    Snack:

1 fruit smoothie
1 muffin with margarine

B. A. Smit

Day 5

Breakfast:

2 pancakes with margarine and syrup
2 slices turkey bacon
1 fresh fruit - orange, pear or apple

Snack:

2 corn thins with margarine
1 glass fruit juice

Lunch:

1 bowl vegetable soup
1 slice toast with margarine
1 glass milk

Snack:

1/2 cup dried fruit

Dinner:

1 cup rice
4 oz chicken or beef, stirfried with 1/2 cup each, broccoli and carrots
1 cup custard

Snack:

1 muffin with margarine
    OR
2 cups popcorn

Day 6

Breakfast:

1 muffin with fresh fruit - pear, banana or apple

Snack:

2 slices fruitbread

Lunch:

1 cup bean salad on 1/2 cup fresh spinach
2 corn thins with margarine
1 glass milk

Snack:

1/2 cup fruitsauce with 2 cookies

Dinner:

4 oz steak, bison, beef or lamb made into stew with 1/2 cup each, turnip and carrot
1 cup mashed potato with margarine
1 cup fresh fruit

Snack:

1 smoothie with 1 piece of cake

B. A. Smit

Day 7

Breakfast:

2 slices french toast with syrup
fresh fruit - orange, pear or banana

Snack:

1/2 cup raw vegetables

Lunch:

Chicken and lettuce sandwich
fruit smoothie

Snack:

2 corn thins or rice cakes with margarine
1 glass V-8 type juice

Dinner:

Shrimp noodle salad
1 dinner roll or 1 slice toast with margarine
1 cup custard or tapioca

Snack:

1/2 cup fruitsauce

Day 8

Breakfast:

1 cup fresh fruit salad
1 slice toast with margarine

Snack:

1 muffin
   OR
2 pieces of cranberry square

Lunch:

1 bowl bison and vegetable soup
2 corn thins with margarine

Snack:

1 fresh fruit - pear, peach or apple

Dinner:

4 oz turkey stirfried with 1/2 cup each, celery and carrot
1 cup rice noodles
1 glass V-8 type juice

Snack:

Fruit smoothie with 2 cookies

B. A. Smit

Day 9

Breakfast:

1 cup hot porridge with dried fruit and milk
1 slice toast with margarine

Snack:

1 glass V-8 type juice
2 corn thins or rice cakes with margarine

Lunch:

1 cup macaroni and cheese
1/2 cup diced cucumber and tomato

Snack:

1 muffin
  OR
1 piece of cake

Dinner:

4 oz bison or beef with beans in tomato sauce over 1 cup mashed potato OR
1 pork chop with potato on the side
3/4 cup stirfried zucchini, corn and carrot

Snack:

1 fresh fruit - apple, banana or peach

Day 10

Breakfast:

2 slices turkey bacon with 1 poached egg
1 slice toast with margarine
1 fresh fruit - orange, pear or apple

Snack:

1/2 cup fruitsauce
1 piece of pie

Lunch:

2 cups rice salad with fruit and vegetables
1 muffin with margarine
1 glass milk or yogurt

Snack:

2 corn thins or rice cakes with margarine

Dinner:

1 boiled potato
2 slices salmon loaf
1/2 cup each, green beans and carrots
1 cup tapioca

Snack:

1 fresh fruit - banana, pear or apple

B. A. Smit

Day 11

Breakfast:

2 waffles with margarine and syrup
1 fruit smoothie

Snack:

2 corn thins with margarine and 2 tbsp nut butter

Lunch:

Cheese and lettuce sandwich
1/2 cup raw vegetables
1 fresh fruit - apple, orange or pear

Snack:

1 muffin with margarine
   OR
2 cookies
1 glass V-8 type juice

Dinner:

1 chicken thigh, lamb chop or pork chop, baked
1/2 cup rice
1/2 cup each, turnip and broccoli

Snack:

1/2 cup fruitsauce

Day 12

Breakfast:

1 cup cold cereal with 1/2 cup fresh or frozen berries

Snack:

1 fruit smoothie
2 cookies
   OR
2 pieces of cranberry square

Lunch:

1 cup green salad with dressing and 1 1/2 oz cheese
1 slice toast with margarine

Snack:

1 glass V-8 type juice
1 muffin with margarine

Dinner:

Shepherd's Pie - with bison or beef
1 cup custard

Snack:

1 fresh fruit - orange, banana or pear

B. A. Smit

Day 13

Breakfast:

2 boiled eggs
2 corn thins or 2 rice cakes with margarine

Snack:

1 piece of cake
    OR
2 slices of fruitbread
1 glass fruit juice

Lunch:

Cheese, fruit and vegetable platter
1 slice toast and margarine

Snack:

2 cups popcorn

Dinner:

4 oz breaded turkey, pan fried
1/2 cup fruitsauce for dipping
1/2 cup each, cauliflower and cabbage
1/2 cup rice
1 fresh fruit - peach, apple or pear

Snack:

1 cup chocolate pudding
2 cookies

Day 14

Breakfast:

1 fruit smoothie
1 muffin with margarine

Snack:

1 fresh fruit - orange, banana or peach

Lunch:

1 hard boiled egg
1 cup raw vegetables
2 corn thins or rice cakes with margarine
1/2 cup fruitsauce

Snack:

1/2 cup dried fruit
tortilla chips

Dinner:

Shrimp stir fry with green beans, celery and carrots
1 cup rice noodles
1 cup tapioca

Snack:

1 muffin
   OR
2 pieces of toffee nut square

B. A. Smit

Recipes

Introduction

These recipes are designed as a basic formula. When you are using these recipes, you can substitute your ingredients based on your restrictions. The flour blend can be your types of flour; milk and margarine your types and the dried fruit and nuts can also be your choice. The sweetener is identified as dry or liquid. If you can't use the type of sweetener suggested, substitute your own. But remember the rule of wet for wet, dry for dry. If the recipe calls for a wet sweetener (like syrup) and you have only a dry variety, you can use your dry sweetener mixed with a liquid, like fruit juice, to keep the recipe balanced. So if the recipe calls for 1/2 cup maple syrup, you can use your dry sweetener mixed with juice to make the 1/2 cup amount.

Five Cup Blend

When baking, gluten helps to create the texture and flavor of your baked goodies. Without it, you must adjust your ingredients to help create the same quality of baked goodies. The five cup blend was designed to give the right amount of gluten free ingredients to create the balance needed to achieve the same quality of texture and flavor as with products containing gluten.

As I stated in the Baking and Cooking Gluten Free section, a blend of gluten free flours, starches and gum will produce a better quality of baked goods. Using a combination of these products in a five cup blend will make it easier to create a flavorful baked product. It will give you a much better texture each time you bake. You will find the Five Cup Blend recipe in the Baking and Cooking Gluten Free section. There are several recipes in this section that are made with this blend.

Breakfast:

Six Grain Hot Cereal
3/4 cup quinoa
1 cup cornmeal
3/4 cup buckwheat groats
1/4 cup ground flax seeds
1 cup rice cereal (cream of rice type)
1/3 cup buckwheat or quinoa flakes
1/2 cup quick cooking tapioca

Mix well and store in an airtight container. Use in the following recipe.

        To make one serving:
3/4 cup water
1/4 cup cereal mix
dash of salt
1/2 tsp cinnamon

Mix together in a small pot over medium heat. Stir until mixture begins to boil. Lower heat and simmer for ten minutes.

For a twist, add 1/4 cup diced, dried fruit to cereal and water then cook as directed. You can also use 1/4 cup fruit juice with 1/2 cup water instead of the 3/4 cup water.

Tips for Cold Cereal
    There are more and more choices available for gluten free cereals. Read labels to ensure that the ingredients are fine for your diet. I often add my own ingredients to plain puffed rice or corn cereal. I dice dried fruit, dates, apricots or cranberries along with chopped walnuts, pecans or slivered almonds then add to the cereal. I use 3/4 cup cold cereal, 1/3 cup dried fruit and 1 tablespoon of nuts with the cereal and then add the milk over it all. You can use any type of cold cereal with the fruits and nuts of your choice.

B. A. Smit

Pancakes

1 egg
1 1/4 - 1 1/2 cups milk or your substitute*
1 tsp vanilla
2 tbsp vegetable oil
1 1/4 cups five cup blend**
   OR (1 cup your flour with 3 tbsp corn or tapioca starch and 1 tsp xanthan or guar gum)
dash of salt
1 1/2 tsp baking powder

In a small bowl, mix the dry ingredients, set aside. In a medium bowl, mix the wet ingredients until well blended. Add the dry ingredients to the wet ingredients and mix until just blended. Heat a griddle or fry pan to medium high heat. Grease with about one teaspoon of margarine. Pour pancake batter onto pan, about one quarter of a cup per pancake. Cook until top appears dry and bubbles form. Flip and cook until evenly browned. Repeat until all the batter is used. Serve with syrup or your favorite topping. These freeze well. I take out what I need and microwave for thirty seconds then toast to thaw and reheat the pancakes.

* Depending on the type of flour used, the batter may be too thin or thick. Using a 1/4 cup measure, add more flour or milk until a thick, but pourable batter is achieved.
** The five cup blend can be found in the Baking and Cooking Gluten Free section of this book. It is a blend of flours, starches and gum that can be used as a premix for baking.

French Toast

2 slices gluten free bread, lightly toasted, you can use your choice of bread
2 eggs
1/4 cup milk or your substitute
1/2 tsp cinnamon
1 tsp vanilla
1 tbsp dry sweetener

Cut the toast into 1/2 inch sized cubes and set aside. I use gluten, yeast free rice flour bread. I cut the slice to half the thickness and toast. Then I cut the cubes. In a medium sized bowl, whisk the eggs until well beaten. Add the remaining ingredients except the toast. Mix well then add the toast cubes. Mix to coat the cubes. Place in the fridge for about thirty minutes. Heat a fry pan over medium heat and grease with one teaspoon margarine. Drop batter by the spoonful onto the pan then flatten to resemble a pancake. Cook for about two minutes or until the toast is lightly browned. Flip and cook until browned. Repeat until mixture is all cooked. Serve with fruitsauce, syrup or your favorite topping.

Lunch:

Rice Salad
1 cup cooked rice; wild rice blend, white or brown
1/4 cup each: diced celery
                   coarsely grated carrot
                   dried cranberries, raisins or chopped dried dates
                   diced red or green pepper
2 tbsp minced onion, optional
2 tbsp lemon juice
2 tbsp oil
2 tbsp apple or orange juice
1/2 tsp each: basil, oregano and thyme

In a medium sized bowl, combine the fruit and vegetables with the juices, oil and herbs. Mix until well blended. Add the rice and mix well. Place in the fridge for at least two hours before serving.

Mac n Cheese
In a medium sized pot, fill 2/3 full of water with one tablespoon oil. Over medium high heat bring to a boil. Add 1 1/2 cup macaroni, any type, elbow, rotini or bowtie. You can use rice, corn or vegetable pasta. Return to a boil and keep near boiling until the macaroni is cooked. Drain.

Sauce
2 tbsp margarine, can be lactose free
2 tbsp rice flour, or your choice
1/2 tsp each, salt and pepper
1 cup cheese, grated, your choice

In a medium sized pot over medium heat, melt the margarine. Add the flour, stirring constantly. Slowly add the milk, stirring constantly. Add the salt and pepper, continue to stir until the mixture begins to thicken and nears the boiling point. Add the cheese, lower the heat to simmer, stir until the cheese melts. Remove from heat.

Extras:
1/4 cup each: diced onion, green pepper and tomato
1 tbsp margarine

In a small fry pan over medium high heat, melt the margarine. Add the onion and green pepper and sauté 2-3 minutes to soften. You can omit any of these if you want.

Mix the macaroni into the sauce, add the onion mixture and the tomatoes. Mix until well blended and serve.

         B. A. Smit

Tuna Salad
1 can (170 g) tuna, drained
1 cup fine rice noodles, cooked then chopped
1/4 cup diced celery
1/4 cup coarsely grated carrot
1/4 cup mayonnaise, your choice
dash each, salt and pepper
1/2 tsp poultry seasoning
1/4 cup chopped nuts, your choice
1/4 cup dried cranberries

Combine all ingredients in a medium sized bowl. Mix until well blended. Cover and place in the fridge for one hour. Serve on a bed of torn lettuce.

Garden Salad with Raspberry Dressing
2 cups lettuce, torn into bite size pieces
2 cups spinach, washed and torn
1 cup fresh bean sprouts
1/2 cup grated cheese, your choice
1/2 cup chopped dried fruit, dates, apricots or cranberries, your choice
1/2 cup chopped nuts, your choice
2 hard boiled eggs, peeled and coarsely chopped
1 carrot, peeled and coarsely grated
2 celery stalks, diced
or your choice of vegetables; tomato, cucumber, etc.

In a large bowl, toss all the ingredients until well blended. To serve, divide salad evenly onto plates and drizzle with the dressing.

Raspberry Dressing
1/2 cup fresh or frozen raspberries
2/3 cup apple juice
1 tbsp lemon juice
1/4 tsp each, salt and pepper
1 1/2 tsp dry mustard
1/3 cup oil
1 tbsp dry sweetener, your choice
1/2 tsp tarragon
1/2 tsp fennel seeds
1 tsp oregano
about 1/3 cup water

Place all ingredients into a blender except the water. Blend until mixed, adding the water one tablespoon at a time until desired consistency is reached. Drizzle over salad and store remaining dressing in the fridge. It will keep for up to one week.

Bean Salad

1/2 cup each: canned chic peas, drained
canned green beans, drained
canned yellow beans, drained
1/4 cup sliced onion, optional
1/3 cup sliced or diced red pepper
1 tbsp fennel seeds
1/2 tsp chili powder
1/2 tsp dry mustard
1/4 cup oil
2 tbsp orange juice

In a large bowl, mix all ingredients together. When well blended, cover and place in the fridge for at least one hour before serving.

B. A. Smit

Dinner:

Turkey Meatloaf
1 lb ground turkey
1 tbsp sage
1 tbsp basil
dash each, salt and pepper
1/3 cup cooked rice; white, brown or wild rice blend
1/4 cup diced celery
1 egg

Preheat oven to 350°.
Mix all ingredients together in a medium sized bowl. Place in a lightly greased loaf pan or an 8" x 8" pan. Shape into a loaf. Bake in a preheated oven at 350° for about 35 to 45 minutes. Slice and serve.

Shrimp Noodle Salad
2 - 3 cups thin, transparent type rice noodles
1 carrot peeled and coarsely grated
1 cup snow peas cut in half lengthwise
1/2 each, red and green pepper thinly sliced
2 cups cooked fresh shrimp
1 1/2 cups fresh bean sprouts

Prep vegetables. In a medium sized pot fill 2/3 full with water and a dash of salt. Over medium high heat, bring to a boil. Add the noodles and cook for about five minutes until almost cooked. Add the carrots and snow peas. Remove from heat and let stand covered for five minutes. Reserve about 1/3 cup of the liquid and drain the remaining liquid from the pot. Set aside.

Dressing
1/4 cup lemon juice
3 tbsp oil
3 tbsp maple syrup or your choice of sweetener
2 tbsp minced fresh ginger
3 tbsp orange juice
dash each, salt and pepper
1/3 cup reserved liquid

In a small bowl, whisk the ingredients together and set aside.

In a large bowl, combine the noodle mixture, remaining vegetables, shrimp and dressing. Mix well. Place in the fridge for one hour before serving.

Salmon Loaf

2 (170 g) cans salmon, drained, remove bones and skin, optional
1 cup mashed potato or cooked rice
2 eggs
1/2 cup coarsely grated zucchini or diced celery
1/4 cup milk, your choice
dash each, salt and pepper
1 tsp sage
1 tsp tarragon

Preheat oven to 325º.
In a medium sized bowl, mash the salmon and add the remaining ingredients. Mix until well blended. Place in a lightly greased loaf pan. Place the pan in a slightly larger pan filled with about one inch of water. Check during baking and add more water if needed. Bake in the oven for about thirty minutes. Test with a toothpick, place into center of loaf, if it comes out clean, and the loaf is lightly browned, the loaf is done. Slice and serve.

You can use lightly greased muffin cups but reduce the cooking time to about twenty minutes.

Shepherd's Pie

1 lb ground bison or beef
1/2 cup frozen peas
1 carrot, peeled and coarsely grated or diced
1 can (12 - 14 oz) diced tomatoes, include the liquid
dash each, salt and pepper
1/2 tsp chili powder
2 cups mashed potatoes
1 egg
2 tbsp margarine, melted

Preheat oven to 350º.
In a medium sized fry pan over medium high heat, fry the meat. Add the peas, carrots and tomatoes. Lower heat to medium low and simmer for about ten minutes. Add the seasonings and place in a lightly greased 9" x 13" baking dish. In a small bowl, mix the potatoes and egg until well blended. Spoon onto the casserole and spread gently to cover the mixture. Drizzle with the margarine and bake in a 350º oven for about 30 minutes or the casserole begins to bubble. Let sit for ten minutes before serving.

Snacks:

Fruitbread
1 1/2 cups five cup blend
  OR (1 1/4 cup your flour with 1 tsp xanthan or guar gum and 1/4 cup cornstarch)
1/2 cup cold cooked white rice
3/4 cup dry sweetener
3 tsp baking powder
1/4 tsp salt
1/2 tsp cloves
1 1/2 tsp cinnamon
1 tsp ginger
1/3 cup oil
1 cup milk, your choice
1/2 cup drained canned pineapple, crushed or tidbit
1/4 cup each, dried dates and apricots, chopped
1/4 cup chopped walnuts, almonds or pecans
1/4 cup dried cranberries
1 egg

Preheat oven to 350º.
In a small bowl, mix 1/2 cup of the flour blend with the dried fruits. Blend well to coat the fruit and set aside. In a medium sized bowl, mix together all the dry ingredients except the nuts. In a large sized bowl, mix together all the wet ingredients except the pineapple. Pour the dry ingredients into the wet ingredients. Mix until well blended. Add the drained pineapple and the dried fruits mixture. Blend well and mix in the nuts last, gently mixing until well blended. Pour into greased mini loaf or muffin pan. Bake in a 350º oven for about twenty minutes. The loaf or muffin will be springy when touched lightly. Cool in pan for about ten minutes then remove to a rack to finish cooling.

You can use your own choice of fruits in this recipe.

Carob Chip Cookies

1/2 cup margarine
1/2 cup dry sweetener
2 eggs
1 tsp vanilla
1 3/4 cups five cup blend
  OR (1 1/2 cups your flour with 1 tsp xanthan or guar gum and 1/4 cup cornstarch)
1 tsp cinnamon
1/2 tsp baking soda
1/4 tsp salt
1/3 cup chopped nuts, walnuts, pecans or almonds
1/2 cup carob chips or chocolate chips

Preheat oven to 350º.

In a medium sized bowl, cream margarine and sweetener until light and fluffy. Add the eggs one at a time and mix well. Stir in the vanilla. Set aside. In a small bowl, blend together the five cup blend, cinnamon, baking soda and salt. Add one third of this mixture into the creamed mixture and mix well. Add one third more, mix well and then the remaining mixture and mix until well blended. Stir in nuts and carob chips. Mix only until they are evenly distributed throughout the dough. On a parchment paper lined cookie sheet, drop one tablespoon of dough, flatten slightly with a fork. Bake for 8 - 12 minutes to test dough. The cookie should be a golden brown. If the cookie flattens too much, add 1/4 cup of the five cup blend to the dough. Test one more cookie, continue to add more five cup blend, 1/4 cup at a time until you are happy with the test cookie. Then bake a whole cookie sheet at a time. Store in an airtight container or freeze the cookies.

B. A. Smit

Chocolate Cake - This is a dairy and egg free cake.

1 1/2 cups five cup blend
  OR (1 1/4 cups your flour with 1 tsp xanthan or guar gum and 1/4 cup cornstarch)
3/4 cup dry sweetener
1 tsp baking soda
1/2 tsp salt
1/3 cup vegetable oil
1 tbsp lemon juice
1 tsp vanilla
1/2 cup cocoa
2/3 cup cold water
1/3 cup cold coffee

Preheat oven to 350º.
In a medium sized bowl, mix the five cup blend, sweetener, baking soda and salt. Mix well. Add the cocoa and mix until well blended. Make three holes in the mixture. In the first hole, add the vanilla, the second hole the lemon juice and the third hole the oil. Pour the water and coffee over the whole mixture. Mix until well blended. Pour into an 8" x 8" nonstick pan. Bake in preheated oven for about twenty to twenty five minutes. A toothpick inserted into the center should come out clean. The cake should be springy when lightly touched in the center. Let cool on a rack for ten minutes then remove from pan and return to rack to cool completely.

Toffee Nut Squares

Crust:

1/2 cup margarine

1 cup five cup blend

  OR (2/3 cup your flour with 1 tsp xanthan or guar gum and 1/3 cup cornstarch)

1/3 cup dry sweetener

In a medium sized bowl, beat the margarine until fluffy. Add the remaining ingredients and mix until it forms a dough. Press into a parchment paper lined 8" x 8" pan and set aside to make filling.

Filling:

2/3 cup maple or corn syrup

1/2 cup dry sweetener

2 eggs

2 tbsp margarine

dash of salt

1 tsp vanilla

1 cup chopped nuts, walnuts, almonds or pecans

Preheat oven to 400°.

In a large bowl, mix together the syrup, sweetener and eggs. Beat until well blended. Add the margarine, salt and vanilla. Mix until well blended. Stir in the nuts. Pour into prepared pan and bake in a 400° oven for 10 minutes. Lower heat to 350° and bake until set, about twenty to twenty five minutes. Cool for at least thirty minutes before cutting into squares.

B. A. Smit

Nutty Chocolate Pie
Crust:
Follow the same recipe as the Toffee Nut Squares crust and press into the bottom and sides of a pie plate. Set aside.

Filling:
3 squares unsweetened chocolate
1/4 cup margarine
3/4 cup maple or corn syrup
1/2 cup dry sweetener
3 eggs
dash of salt
1 tsp vanilla
1 1/3 cup chopped nuts

Preheat oven to 375°.
Over medium heat in a medium sized pot, melt the chocolate squares with the margarine. Remove from the heat and add the syrup and sweetener. Mix well. Mix in the eggs, salt and vanilla. Beat until well blended. Add the nuts and mix well. Pour into prepared pie plate. Bake until set, about forty minutes. A toothpick inserted into the center should come out clean. Cool for thirty minutes before cutting.

Cranberry Squares
Crust:
Preheat oven to 325°.
Use the crust recipe from the Toffee Nut Squares. Press into an 8" x 8" parchment paper lined pan. Bake in a 325° oven for about 5 - 8 minutes. This is not to bake the crust, but to start the process so the crust will not become soggy when baked with the filling.

Filling:
3 eggs
2/3 cup maple or corn syrup
1 tsp baking powder
3 tbsp cornstarch
1/2 tsp cinnamon
1/4 tsp salt
1 cup dried cranberries, coarsely chopped
3/4 cup chopped nuts, walnuts, almonds or pecans
1/2 cup applesauce

Preheat oven to 325°.
In a medium sized bowl, beat the eggs and sweetener. Set aside. In a small bowl, mix together the baking powder, cornstarch and salt. Stir into egg mixture. Add the cinnamon, cranberries, nuts and applesauce. Mix until well blended. Pour into prepared pan. Bake at 325° for about thirty to thirty five minutes until almost firm. A toothpick inserted into the center should come out clean. Cool in pan for thirty minutes before cutting.

Reference Guide

Women's Day Encyclopedia of Cookery
1979 Edition for Women's Day
Dist. by Funk and Wagnall's
Copyright 1966, 1973, 1979 by CBS Publications
a division of Consumer Publishing Division of CBS Inc.

The New Vegetarian Cookbook - Gary Null
MacMillan Publishing Co. Inc.
866 Third Ave. New York, N.Y. 10022
Collier MacMillan Canada Ltd.
Copyright 1980

The All Natural Allergy Cookbook - Jeanne Marie Martin
Published by Harbour Publishing
P.O. Box 219
Madeira Park, B.C. Canada V0N 2H0
Copyright 1991

Betty Crocker International Cookbook
Published in Canada by Random House of Canada Limited
Toronto, Ontario, Canada
Copyright 1980 by General Mills Inc.
Minneapolis, Minnesota, U.S.A.

Canadian Cookbook - Nellie Lyle Pattinson
Ryerson Press
McGraw - Hill Company of Canada Ltd.
Toronto, Ontario, Canada
Copyright 1923, 1953, 1961
The Ryerson Press 1969

The Professional Chef
The C.I.A. Permission Dept.
John Wiley and Sons Inc.
605 Third Ave.
New York, N.Y. U.S.A.
10158 - 0012

The Versatile Grain and the Elegant Bean
Sheryl and Mel London
Simon and Shuster
Simon and Shuster Building
Rockefeller Centre
1230 Avenue of the Americas
New York, N.Y. 10020
Copyright 1992 by Symbiosis Inc.

The Bean Bible - Aliza Green
Running Press Publishers
125 South Twenty Second Street
Philadelphia, Pennsylvania U.S.A. 19103 - 4399

Healing Foods
Micheal Van Straten (1997)
Key Porter Books
70 The Esplanade, Toronto, Ontario, Canada M5E 1R2

Against the Grain - Jax Peters Lowell
Published in Canada by:
Fitzhenry and Whiteside Ltd.
195 Allstate Parkway, Markham, Ontario, Canada L3R 4T8

Reader's Digest - Eating for Good Health
Editor in Chief
U.S. General Books
260 Madison Ave.
New York, N.Y. U.S.A. 10016

Index

A

Acids:
  conditionally essential 16
  essential amino 16, 177
Additives, Gluten Free:
  acetic acid 36
  adipic acid 36
  benzoic acid 36
  BHA and BHT 36
  calcium disodium EDTA 36
  carboxymethyl cellulose 36, 79
  fumaric acid 36
  lactic acid 36
  malic acid 36
  polysorbate 60;80 36
  propylene glycol 36
  sodium benzoate 36
  sodium metabisulphite 36
  sodium nitrate 36
  sodium sulphite 36
  stearic acid 36
  tartaric acid 36, 79
  tartrazine 36
  titanium dioxide 36
agar agar 79
amaranth 69, 135
antioxidants 22
arrowroot flour 66, 69
atta 131

B

bacteria 3-4, 88, 249-51
bakeware 61
baking powder 33, 78
baking soda 78
barley 30, 33, 131, 179-80
beta carotene 18, 36, 216-18, 226-8
Beverages:
  containing gluten 85
  other gluten free 87
  rice 85, 87
  soy 85-7

bloating/gas 28
bran 30, 133
buckwheat 66-7, 69, 135 *see also* kasha
bulgar 30, 131
buttermilk 84, 92

C

calories 8-10, 15-16
caramel color 36, 78
carbohydrates 9-11
carrageen gum 78
celiac disease 20, 28
cereal binding 30
Cheese 32, 89-91
  blue or bleu 89, 91
  brie 89-90
  bucheron 90
  camembert 89-90
  cheddar 84, 89-90
  chèvre 90
  feta 90
  fontina 90
  gjetost 90
  marchego 90
  montrachet 90
  mozzarella 84, 89-90
  ricotta salata 90
  romano 89-90
  roquefort 89, 91
cholesterol 13-16, 93, 202-4
chronic fatigue 28, 121-2, 125
Cooking Terms:
  al dente 54
  au gratin 54
  au jus 54
  bake 54
  barbecue 54
  baste 54
  batter 54
  beat 54
  bechamel 54
  blanch 54

B. A. Smit

B. A. Smit

Soybeans:
  black soy sauce   180
  Chinese pastes   179
  fermented black beans   179
  lecithin   36, 79, 179
  miso   179-80
  shoyu   180
  soy flour   66-7, 70, 180
  soy milk   180
  soy sauce   180
  soybean sprouts   180
  tamari   180
tempah   181
tips on legumes   162
Tofu (Japanese):
  kinu, silken   181
  momen or regular   181
  yakidotu   181
Unusual:
  goober peas   164
  winged beans   164
  yam beans   164, 240
Lipoproteins:
  high density (HDL)   15
  low density (LDL)   15
liquor   103

M

macrominerals   19
malt   30, 104, 131
malt extract   30
malt flavoring   30
malt syrup   30
maltodextrin   36, 79
matzoh meal   132
Measurements   49-51
  abbreviations   50
  converting   49-51
  oven temperatures and terms   51
  weights   50

Meats:
  Beef   190-1
    brisket   191
    chuck   191
    flank   191
    loin   191
    ribs   191
    round   191
    shank   191
  Chicken   196
    roasting guide   196
  ducks   199
  Game Birds   200
    . pheasant   200
    quail   200
    snipe   200
    wild duck   200
  geese   199
  kosher   189
  lamb   194
  pork   193
  Poultry   195
    free range   195
    natural   195
    organic   195
  Turkey   197
    roasting guide   197-8
  veal   192
mesquite flour   139
microminerals   19
migraines   24-5
Millet   70, 139-40
  flour   70, 140
  meal   140
  puffed   140
  wholegrain   140
minerals   18-19, 182, 240-3
modified food starch   30-1
monounsaturated fats   13-15
montina flour   139
mouth ulcers   28, 119, 228
mutual supplementation   16

B. A. Smit

soy flour 66-7, 70, 180
spelt 30, 132, 145
starch 30-1, 66-9, 81
Starches:
  arrowroot 66-7, 81
  cornstarch 66, 81, 136
  potato 66, 81
  sago 81
  sassafras 81
  tapioca 67, 81
Sweeteners 33, 36, 84, 136-7, 206-11
  fruit concentrate 209
  fruit juice 209
  Gluten Free:
    aspartame 36
    brown sugar 36, 207
    corn syrup/solids 36, 136-7, 210
    dextrose 36
    fructose 36, 207
    glucose 36, 210
    invert sugar 36
    lactose 36, 84
    mannitol 36
    molasses 36, 211
    sorbitol 36
    sucralose 36, 209
    sucrose 36, 208
    white sugar 36, 207
    xylitol 36
  saccharin 209
  Splenda 209
  stevia 209
  Sugars:
    beet 207
    brown 36, 207
    cane 207
    coarse white 207
    confectioner 207
    date 207
    demerara 207
    fructose 36, 207
    granulated white 36, 207
    muscovado 207
    raw 208

sucrose 36, 208
superfine 208
turbinado 208
Syrups:
  agave 210
  corn 36, 136-7, 210
  glucose 36, 210
  high fructose corn syrup (HFCS)
   210
  honey 210
  maple 210
  molasses 36, 211
  rice 144, 211
  sorghum 211

T

tapioca flour 67, 70, 81, 145
taro 145, 241
teff 70, 145
trans fats 13, 25, 203
triticale 30, 37, 132
two week meal plan 255-68

U

utensils 61-2

V

Vegetables 215-45
  Brassicas:
    bok choy 216
    broccoli 216
    broccoli rabe 216
    Brussel sprouts 38, 216-17
    cauliflower 217
    kale 217, 219
    kohlrabi 217
    okra 217
    pakchoi 217
    spinach 218
  Cabbage:
    green 218

B. A. Smit